MW00636399

The Wrestler's Dissertation

Dr. Antonio Graceffo

Shanghai University of Sport PhD in *Wushu*,
Chinese and Western Wrestling

Mary Labita Press

Copyright Page

The Wrestler's Dissertation by Antonio Graceffo, Published by Mary Labita Press, Long Island, New York

© 2017 Antonio Graceffo

antonio_graceffo@hotmail.com

ISBN: 978-0-9998305-0-5

About this book

In 2013, I was awarded a scholarship by the Chinese government to pursue a PhD in Wushu at Shanghai University of Sport, where I was the only foreign candidate in my class. The entire course was taught in Chinese, and I had to write and defend my PhD dissertation in Mandarin. Over a period of three years, I practiced various types of wrestling, including Chinese style wrestling (shuai jiao), sanda, Greco Roman, freestyle, MMA, and a limited amount of judo, catch, sambo, and jujitsu. Most of this training took place at Shanghai University of Sport, but I also trained sanda at the Shaolin Temple, Song Shan Mountain, Henan Province, and Chinese style wrestling in Beijing with Meng Shifu of the lineage of Grand Master Wang Wenyong. Additionally, I spent several months each year training in other countries, freestyle wrestling in Cambodia, sanda in Vietnam, MMA in Malaysia, judo and grappling in Thailand, judo, jujitsu, and sambo in New York, and catch wrestling in Singapore.

In addition to the physical training, I was conducting academic research leading towards my dissertation "A Cross Cultural Comparison of Chinese and Western Wrestlin,." Under the direction of my PhD advisor, Professor Dai Guobing, the Dean of the Wu Shu Institute of Shanghai University of Sport. The unique thing about the sports university was that not only was my advisor a professor, and well respected academic in the field of martial arts, but he was also a master of his family's styles of tai chi and wushu.

By the time I sat down to write my actual dissertation, I had carefully read and annotated roughly 2,000 sources, both in English and Chinese. Reading the Chinese texts was a painstaking activity, sometimes requiring an entire day to read a single page. After my first draft was done, it went through several stages of revision, rejections and approvals, by Professor Dai Guobing, my study brothers and sisters, as well as the Wu Shu Institute of the university. Before tackling a PhD I had already published 7 books, which all had some relation to martial arts, so I thought I knew how to write. The problem was, however, that a PhD dissertation, as an academic text, was a whole new experience for me. And little by little, after the recommended revisions, I saw most of the interesting parts of my dissertation being rejected, until all that remained was a boring, stuffy, academic work, which no one outside of a university would ever want to read.

I passed my defense and graduated my PhD having fulfilled my publishing requirements by publishing articles, but had no intention of publishing my dissertation because I felt that not only was it boring, but that after so many revisions and alterations, it did not reflect my experience or research interests at the sports university.

The next year and a half, after graduation, was spent teaching at universities in China while I was pursuing a second PhD in economics. Now, moving in international academic circles, I was often asked if I had published my dissertation. Each time I said that I had not, I felt as if I had not only wasted three years of grueling research but also that there was so much good information in my first draft which could add to the body of martial arts knowledge in the world.

In 2017, I was on holiday in Bali, practicing Balinese traditional wrestling called Mepantigan, in a jungle camp, up in the hills. The atmosphere was wonderful. The environment was lush and beautiful. The Mepantigan family became my close friends and suddenly, I had an epiphany. There were people in the world who had never been the only American PhD candidate in the wushu department of a Chinese sports university and who had never spent three years reading 2,000 texts about wrestling. Perhaps they could benefit from reading that first draft of my dissertation.

So, I returned to China, resigned from my position as program director at the university, and headed back to Bali to train in martial arts while I wrote this book. The first step was to find the first draft of my dissertation and translate it into English. Next, I went back through the thousands of pages of notes and added back everything I thought was interesting but which had been cut from the academic text. Next, I found the interviews I had done with martial arts masters and wrestlers, and added their stories to the book.

Working on The Wrestler's Dissertation has been one of the most pleasant experiences I have had in some time. Each new chapter was both an incidence of discovery and a trip down memory lane, leading me to remember why I started my martial arts journey 38 years ago.

In writing the second to last chapter "Chapter 12: Chinese Wrestlers," I was listening to all of the interviews I conducted just before leaving Shanghai University of Sport, including one with my PhD advisor, Professor Dai Guobing, who asked me "Will you engage in martial arts or economics? You just told me your job is economics, but your career, your energy, you interests, and your development are all in the martial arts. If you go to Shanghai University or go to Fudan University to teach economics, becoming a professor and becoming a Chinese or internationally renowned professor is not likely. But if you Become a Chinese wushu culture communicator (author and professor), it is possible for you to gain international recognition, because you understand Chinese culture and western cultural and because you are also very powerful. So, take a look at what to do. Take a look at yourself. If you teach economics in Shanghai University, what do you want to do in the future? What will your title be? Will they give you any title? A foreign teacher without a title just receives a lecturer's wage. But a foreign teacher who also has a professional title. He should be called Professor. And he should get professor money. Associate professor should get associate professor money, lecturer gets lecturer Money…Which one do you want? Which one will you bet?"

It took me a year and a half to understand, but I think I am beginning to believe he was giving me some very intelligent advice. And this book is a first step in my journey of serving as a bridge, and helping to share knowledge of Chinese and Western martial arts.

Antonio Graceffo, PhD, China-MBA,
Headed to India for kushti wrestling training.

Acknowledgements

Completing this book, just like learning martial arts, has been a long journey and a gradual process which was only possible because of the wonderful people who assisted me along the way. Consequently, I would like to thank several of the people who helped me through the writing of my PhD dissertation and this book: My PhD advisor, from Shanghai University of Sport Wu Shu Institute, Professor Dai Guobing and my study brothers and sisters, particularly Han Hongyu and Duan Limei. I would also like to thank my martial arts instructors, Liuxing (sanda), Hong Fangyuan (wrestling), Lukai (judo), Jiang Laoshi (sanda ge dou), and Jap Leun (Cambodian wrestling). An additional and massive THANK YOU goes to my training brother Yang Wenbin, and my younger brothers, Luo Yuanzhou, Liuxing, Zhengtong, and Jiang Huaying, who kept me sane during my years of studies. I would also like to thank my research assistant at Shanghai University of Sport (SUS) Song Kelong, my research assistant and translator at Shanghai University (SHU) Xu Laixi "West", as well as my proofreaders Ben Allen, Richard Crasta and Ame Proietti.

Table of Contents

Chapter 1: Intro to Chinese Wrestling

Chinese style wrestling, most commonly referred to as *Shuai jiao* (摔角), is a distinct wrestling style unique to China. As such, many similarities and differences can be drawn with other forms of wrestling.

Although athletes in both judo and Chinese traditional wrestling wear a similar uniform, with long trousers, a martial arts style belt, and a wrestling jacket, the two arts are very different. Chinese style wrestling, unlike modern judo, allows wrestlers to use their hands to attack their opponent's legs. Under current judo competition rules, techniques such as single and double leg takedowns are illegal; however, they are permitted in *Shuai jiao*. Both judo and Chinese wrestling allow foot sweeps, but the Chinese style trips and sweeps are very different from those executed in judo.[1] Both arts allow the competitors to grab clothing, but *Shuai jiao* allows the gripping of the inside of the sleeve and collar.

Chinese traditional wrestling also shares some similarities with Western wrestling. Both Western wrestling and Chinese style wrestling allow body locks, in which the upper body is grabbed, such as in a bear hug. One of the big differences, however, is that Western wrestling relies more on strength as opposed to Chinese wrestling, which relies more on technique. In contrast, it was the early traditions of Western wrestling, dating back to ancient Greece, that celebrated not only the technique, but the power of the wrestlers, as well as the aesthetics of their physiques.[2]

The Chinese consider *Shuai jiao* "a scientific endeavor." In addition to clean and accurate technique (as opposed to power), balance and leverage are also important. *Shuai jiao* throws rely more on utilizing the natural structure of the body for leverage.

Consequently, academic research into Chinese wrestling focuses more on biomechanics than on physiological or biochemical research related to muscle development and function.[3]

The rules and goals in the two sports are also very different. Chinese wrestling does not allow the ground fighting that exists in judo or Western wrestling. As such, the techniques, and training of Chinese wrestling differ extensively from Western wrestling partly because of the requirements for a win. Both judo and Western matches can be won on the ground by submission in judo, or by a pin in wrestling. In Chinese wrestling, however, matches are won by accumulating points earned by throwing the opponent to the ground. A fall is assessed once any part of a wrestler's body, excluding the soles of the feet, touches the ground. This means that sacrifice throws and other techniques where both wrestlers hit the mat are vigorously discouraged, regardless of which competitor lands on top. In addition, throws such as these are seen as clumsy by the traditional Chinese masters of *Shuai jiao*. A beautifully executed throw, relying on perfectly applied technique, is held in higher regard than a sloppy win, where strength overcomes.

Physics plays a large role in *Shuai jiao*. The angle of attack, center of gravity, distance, weight, force and direction are all elements of a wrestling attack. In Chinese style wrestling, the level of the hands is very important. Unlike Western style wrestling, in Chinese style wrestling, the opponents wear jackets. Therefore, the hands are held relatively high, and competitors are trained to shoot out and grasp the opponent's jacket or belt. By pulling on the clothing, a wrestler can control the height and center of gravity of his opponent. The exact moment when an opponent is off balance is very short. So any attack must come quickly, taking advantage of this brief opening by tripping or throwing the opponent.[4] Hence, one of the many names Chinese wrestling has been given over the centuries is *kuai jiao* (快角) or fast wrestling.

Traditionally, *Shuai jiao* matches were held outdoors in a dirt circle, whereas modern *Shuai jiao* matches are often held on

Olympic style wrestling mats. At the beginning of a match, the two wrestlers walk several times around the outside of the circle, until the referee calls them to the center. They give the Chinese salute *xingli* (行礼), with left hand over right fist, to the judges, and then to each other. The referee then gives the signal for the match to begin. Generally, the two wrestlers instantly secure a grip on their opponent's uniform, but they may wait a while before actually attacking. Similar to circling in boxing or Western wrestling, the two will go around in circles, tugging on each other's lapels, sleeves, collar, or belt as a "feeling out" process, before committing to an attack. The tempo can change very rapidly, with attacks suddenly coming with animal quickness, justifying the name fast wrestling.[5] This unique pacing serves two purposes: First, it helps to expose an opponent's weaknesses, and second, it allows a wrestler to establish his own position of advantage from which to launch an attack.

These aspects of Chinese wrestling do not differ greatly from Western wrestling. In any form of combat, the opponents must estimate one another, and anticipate their movements. Over the course of a Chinese wrestling match, however, the pace changes frequently. Opponents move in and out, adjusting the distance. When they see an opening in their opponent's stance, they attack. The difference between *Shuai jiao* and Western wrestling is the suddenness of the attack. Other than the constant hold they maintain on each other's clothing, *Shuai jiao* wrestlers almost never lock up, body, to body, in an epic struggle of strength. Western wrestlers sometimes look like two mighty mountain bucks locking antlers and struggling, muscle against muscle, till one emerges victorious. The *Shuai jiao* wrestler behaves more like the crocodile, which bides its time, and then suddenly leaps out of the river, like lightning, striking at the throat of the unsuspecting prey.

The absence of ground fighting means that a *Shuai jiao* match represents complete engagement from start to finish. Consequently, some Chinese traditionalists see aspects of judo or Western wrestling as boring, as they interpret the ground fighting as stalling. This is one reason why *Shuai jiao* has no ground fighting. The other reason is because *Shuai jiao* matches used to be held in fields at fairs and festival before huge, standing crowds. If the wrestlers went to the ground, no one would be able to see the action. And of course, rolling around on the dusty ground can be uncomfortable for the wrestlers.[6]

The history of *Shuai jiao* varies greatly from the history of Western wrestling due to its lack of influence from non-Chinese arts. Whereas Western wrestling is composed of the history of many countries, the history of Chinese wrestling involves only the ancient Chinese kingdoms. During the Qin and Han dynasties, six kingdoms were unified all of the way to the Central Plains, bordering on the northern outskirts of the Hun nation, where horse riding and wrestling were considered manly pursuits.[7] It is presumed that *shuai jiao* was influenced not so much from abroad as from the various ethnic styles of wrestling within the borders of what eventually became China.

Across China, historical artifacts have been found bearing images of wrestlers and wrestling. Wrestling images have been uncovered dating all the way back to the Han Dynasty (206 BC–220 AD), but the greatest ancient wrestling discovery occurred in 1997, in the Qinling Mountains in Jiangling, Hubei Province. Here, a tomb was unearthed, dating back to the Qin Dynasty (221 to 206 BC). The sides of the tomb depicted images of Chinese wrestlers, with no shirts, wearing triangular loin cloths and a long belt around their waist. The wrestlers are surrounded by a crowd and are separated by a single figure, with his arms outstretched, and a curtain draped over his shoulders. The image is believed to be proof that wrestling matches, complete with audience and referee, were held more than 2,000 years ago in China.[8]

Much of the historical evidence of Chinese style wrestling demonstrates that apart from being a sport, it fulfilled several roles in ancient Chinese society, as a self-defense and military martial art. From the Zhou Dynasty (1046-256 BC), through the Han, Tang, and finally Song dynasty (960- 1279 AD), wrestling developed from a form of military training to a folk sport and performance activity.[9] During the Song Dynasty, national wrestling competitions were held and an early set of rules established, including a referee. It is interesting to note that at that time, these competitions were called *Xiāng pū* (相扑) which is also the Chinese name for Sumo. The images depict the shirtless wrestlers wearing a kind of thong-shaped loin cloth, similar to what modern Japanese sumo wrestlers wear. In public fairs and festivals, "sumo" or wrestling became the most popular spectator event. Competitions were held in Kaifeng, the capital of the Northern Song Dynasty, but it was Taishan Temple, in Shandong Province, that was the site of the largest tournament in the country. Early wrestling books, dating back to the Song Dynasty, have been found, and these books name the famous wrestlers of the day, such as two wrestlers from Lin'an City, with the apropos names of: Hit the Mountain Down (撞山倒 Zhuàng shān dǎo, and Week Black Big (周黑大 zhōu hēi dà).[10]

Chinese style wrestling also served to protect the Emperor, as it was taught to royal guards, palace guards, and bodyguards. The era of the Qing Dynasty (1644–1912) is considered to be the heyday of Chinese wrestling, when the Royal Guards in the capital conducted training and developed exceptional skills. Chinese historical records attribute this flourishing of wrestling to the influence of the Manchurian wrestlers, which is consistent with the theory that the various regional or ethnic styles of wrestling influenced *Shuai jiao*.[11] A book from the era describes wrestling as an effective form of unarmed combat, and defines wrestling' as "to seize the neck of the opponent and make him fall to the ground, this is a pure wrestling action."[12]

During the late Qing Dynasty, opium addiction had become a serious problem in China, making the people weak and sick. Wrestling was promoted as a means of fitness and sport, to counteract the drug culture. Chinese style wrestling was a sport that required very little money or equipment and which could be practiced anywhere. It could be practiced outdoors in fields, in villages, or in the cities. It could also be promoted to all regions of China as well as exported to foreign countries. As wrestling could be practiced by both poor and rich alike, it was referred to as the sport of "court and prairie."[13]

Over a period of thousands of years, Chinese traditional wrestling went through many stages of development. The names, rules, and techniques of Chinese style wrestling changed over the years. Even with the birth of the new Chinese republic, in 1912, wrestling remained an important feature of the culture.[14]

Wrestling remained an important part of Chinese culture until the end of the Second World War. However, after the founding of the People's Republic of China in 1949, the government established Soviet style sports schools to train national athletes. Traditional sports, however, were not a priority. In fact, during the Cultural Revolution, Chinese traditional wrestling was one of the activities specifically banned by the government.[15] After the economic liberalizations of 1978, the government began dedicating more money to training for modern sports, but the general populace was more focused on recovering from poverty than on training in traditional sports. Consequently, wrestling continued to decline.

The rise of awareness of the Olympics in China, since Beijing 2008, shifted the focus even further away from Chinese martial arts and more towards modern international sports, including Olympic wrestling, at the expense of traditional sports, including Chinese wrestling. Currently, because karate was included in the 2016 Olympics and will be included in the 2020 Olympics, there are more resources being devoted to this foreign art than to Chinese traditional wrestling. This is particularly ironic, given the enmity most Chinese hold for Japan.

Meanwhile, other voices in Chinese society and government have suggested that traditional sport is closely related with the dignity of a region or of a nation, and that to preserve the country's honor and traditions, traditional wrestling has to overcome the attractions of the modern world and be preserved.[16]

In 2000, Chinese wrestling was added back to the university curriculum. The Ministry of Education and the State Sports General Administration jointly issued a document permitting 74 colleges and universities across the country to operate a separate Chinese sports unit. Several sports universities have also added Chinese wrestling to their curriculum, including Shanghai University of Sport, Tianjin Institute of Physical Education, and Wuhan Institute of Physical Education. *Shuai jiao* has also been given official recognition as a school sport for inclusion in school physical education programs, and as a course at sports schools.[17] A national student's championship, at both university and junior level, has also been established.[18] At the elementary and secondary school level, proponents feel that the benefits of *Shuai jiao*, in addition to the obvious increase in physical fitness, include learning "sportsmanlike" behavior and fair play. It is also argued that it will increase students' appreciation of the sport and by starting early, will cultivate the teachers of tomorrow.[19]

Since 2002, there has been a slow increase in the number of *Shuai jiao* athletes, teams and competitions, but there are still many problems with development. For example, there are far more men than women practicing the art, and qualified coaches are hard to find. A fifty-year drought in wrestling development has left the country with a shortage of trainers and experienced practitioners. In poorer regions of China, local people don't have money to support wrestling training and competitions, and coaching salaries are often small, so coaches have to find other sources of income.[20] As a result, the people teaching Chinese wrestling at universities are generally not masters. Frequently, they are modern Olympic wrestlers with some cross-training in Chinese wrestling. As Chinese wrestling is a non-Olympic sport, it has been a low priority for the government. To date, no one has found a way to turn *Shuai jiao* into a commercial sport, like basketball or football, so there is no way for the sport to earn its own money. *Shuai jiao* continues to depend on government grants and donations from private companies and individuals to survive.

However, *shuai jiao* has grown in popularity outside of China, with schools and competitions being held in 20 countries around the world. In France alone, there are 25 registered clubs which compete each year in the Chinese wrestling Paris Mayor's Cup International Invitational Tournament. Chinese wrestling is also said to be a favorite of former French President Jacques Chirac.[21] While this increased international exposure is a positive sign, international competitions have been extremely small, non-commercial events with minimal press coverage. Consequently, winning an international championship in Chinese wrestling does not garner a country a great deal of prestige. This, once again, makes Chinese wrestling a low priority for the Chinese government.[22]

Some of the leading masters in China fear that promoting *Shuai jiao* as an international sport will expose the art to absorbing culture and techniques from outside of China. A dissertation published in 2004 in the Journal of Anhui Sports Science, analyzing the development of Chinese traditional wrestling in Huaibei Sports School, found that "the beautiful wrestling was gone."[23] In other words, the wrestlers were still wrestling, but they had lost much of the original Chinese character of the art. The old-style masters feel that a significant difference between Chinese wrestling and modern Western wrestling is that Chinese wrestling includes not only the physical pursuit, but also a philosophical and spiritual component.[24] They worry that if *Shuai jiao* becomes mixed with other forms of wrestling, this spiritual component would be lost.

Other proponents of *Shuai jiao* believe that inclusion in the Olympics would guarantee the art's survival, but that inclusion seems unlikely. Unlike Western wrestling, which now belongs to the world, Chinese style wrestling still belongs to China. A disadvantage for the promotion of Chinese wrestling as an Olympic sport is that the name "Chinese style wrestling" contains the word "Chinese." This detracts from the international recognition of a sport. The Olympic committee prefers to approve sports whose name does not contain the name of a specific country. For example, judo is not officially called Japanese Judo, and taekwondo is not called "Korean Foot Fighting."[25]

Even in China, although *Shuai jiao* was added to the curriculum of some schools and universities, research by Jilin Institute of Physical Education found that the *Shuai jiao* programs in colleges were weak. Students were more interested in learning foreign sports than in learning *Shuai jiao*. They found that the programs suffered from a lack of trained teachers, and that students did not understand the cultural importance of the art. Critically, students reported that they didn't believe university administrations put much emphasis on the promotion of Chinese traditional wrestling. As a result, the students' motivation to learn Chinese traditional wrestling was low. The same research discovered that 0 percent of Chinese style wrestling teachers in universities held a PhD.[26] This is in sharp contrast to Western style wrestling teachers: coaches for Greco-Roman and freestyle wrestling across China are generally fully trained and hold a bachelor's degree, a master's degree, or even a PhD in wrestling from a sports university.

Whereas Western style wrestling is an inclusive activity, taught in thousands of high schools and universities across the US, in China, *Shuai jiao* is only taught at any significant level to professional sports majors at a handful of specialized sports schools and sport universities.[27] The Jilin research suggested increasing the teaching of the history and significance of *Shuai jiao* and promoting it as a national traditional sport.[28]

Promoting *Shuai jiao* as part of the national identity has been problematic, because Chinese style wrestling is not featured in enough films and TV shows, even in China. In other countries, national sports receive a lot of media attention, with write ups in newspapers and reports on television news. *Shuai jiao* receives very little coverage, while basketball, football and even Chinese *sanda* (散打) (kick boxing) are widely reported on.[29]

One way of promoting the development of Chinese style wrestling has been to incorporate *Shuai jiao* into police training programs. The Hebei Province police academy conducted a feasibility study to see if *Shuai jiao* was suitable for police training. They determined that *Shuai jiao* could not only improve physical and mental health, but also improve the officers' combat effectiveness. As an officer with *Shuai jiao* training could take an opponent down without injuring them, *Shuai jiao* as a hand-to-hand combat system seems appropriate for police who want to mitigate rather than escalate a situation.[30]

While the police may be more receptive to a nationalist agenda, Chinese young people are not. The current generation of Chinese students were born after 1990, which means that they are largely "only children" (the result of the one-child policy) who have grown up in an affluent China, with 12 years of English at school. They have been exposed to the internet their entire lives, and they enjoy foreign movies and TV shows. They also love modern sports, particularly basketball. Traditional Chinese wrestling, a sport associated with their grandparents' generation, holds little appeal for them.

Boredom is another factor that modern university and school students identified as a deterrent in the study and practice of Chinese traditional wrestling. Chinese traditional wrestling training is based on a set of 19 exercises called *jiben gong* (basic movements) (基本功), which have to be executed with perfect form thousands of times per day. Modern students often lack the patience necessary to undergo this type of traditional training. The Jilin research suggested creating a new syllabus that would be more appealing to today's young people.[31] A similar issue is that there is a lack of resources for the teaching of traditional Chinese wrestling.. Western wrestling, in contrast, is taught through a seemingly endless supply of videos and books around the world.

Another problem is the lack of facilities. Unlike in the US, most high schools and universities in China, apart from sports schools, do not have wrestling mats. Therefore, Chinese wrestling is taught outdoors. This means that in bad weather or on rainy days, training has to be cancelled.

Although Chinese style wrestling is struggling, it is making a slow comeback. In Huaibei City, for example, a few years ago, there were only ten teams. Today, there are 48.[32] In some cities, *Shuai jiao* associations have been established: Beijing, Tianjin, Hebei, Shanxi, Inner Mongolia, Shandong, Anhui and others. These cities also organize tournaments and performances to help develop the art.

The other glimmer of hope for the continued existence of *Shuai jiao* is the close association between Chinese wrestling and *sanda*. *Sanda* is a Chinese kick boxing art which enjoys tremendous status as both an amateur and professional sport in China. *Sanda* allows kicking, punching and *Shuai jiao* style takedowns. A report by Beijing Sport University determined that the average *sanda* fighter used *Shuai jiao* take downs between 12.5 percent and 43.5 percent of the time.[33] Kicks are the long-range weapons of *sanda*. Punches are for medium range, but in close, most *sanda* fighters will go for a *Shuai jiao* takedown. Historically, throws were a significant source of scoring points for *sanda* fighters, and matches could be won on throws, as well as knockouts or points.[34] Apart from their effectiveness, *sanda* fighters use *Shuai jiao* throws because they are easy for the judges to score, and the audience finds the throws exciting. *Sanda* fighters who have good *Shuai jiao* skills are often crowd favorites, garnering higher purses.

Government support, the addition of *Shuai jiao* to school physical education programs, commercialization, inclusion in the Olympics, association with foreign wrestling, or incorporation with *sanda* may all become factors contributing to the preservation of *sanda*, but as a traditional martial art, *Shuai jiao* is still at risk of losing its cultural identity. Whichever route *Shuai jiao* takes, it seems important to increase the cultural association between *Shuai jiao* and the 5000 years of recorded Chinese history.[35]

Meanwhile, Western wrestling is already very developed and accepted as an international sport. The number of people training in Western wrestling around the world is tremendous compared to the number of people practicing Chinese style wrestling. In the US alone there are more than a quarter of a million scholastic and collegiate wrestlers. Additionally, Western wrestling has been studied and researched by top academics in multiple countries for the better part of a century. The training techniques and systems are based on the most advanced science and technology, and are continuously developing. Most importantly, because of the lack of a specific cultural identity, Western wrestling can be improved, rather than diluted, by absorbing techniques from the various countries where it is practiced.

Chinese and Western wrestling are two forms of grappling which share some similarities of technique, but which differ dramatically in their cultural perception and their place in the modern world.

Chapter 2: Western Wrestling Time Line

In contrast to Chinese wrestling, whose history is primarily centered on China and the various regions and ethnic minorities incorporated in China, the development of Western wrestling follows a path similar to the development of Western civilization.

Western wrestling began in the Middle East, where the oldest known image of wrestlers dates back to 3000 BC in Sumeria. Western wrestling developed alongside the ancient Olympics, the Pankration in Greece, the gladiatorial games of Rome, Greco-Roman wrestling, catch wrestling, and then to the United States for modern Olympic wrestling, professional wrestling, and finally modern-day MMA. The following is a timeline of this development.

3000 BC

The earliest images of Western wrestling are depicted in Sumeria.[36]

2600 BC

A bronze figurine of two wrestlers is sculpted in Khafaji, Iraq.[37]

2300 BC

Images of wrestlers are drawn in an Egyptian burial tomb.[38]

2000 BC

The Epic of Gilgamesh is written, giving one of the first literary references to wrestling, when Gilgamesh wrestles against Enkidu.[39]

708 BC

Ancient Greek Wrestling is added to the Olympic Games. Wins are allowed not only by pin, but also by submission.[40]

646 BC

Greek Pankration, a fighting art which combined wrestling, boxing, submissions, and kicks, and was a popular spectator sport at the time, is added to the Olympics, alongside wrestling and boxing. All three are contested as separate sports.[41]

<u>540 BC</u>

Milo of Croton becomes wrestling's first superstar. A six-time Olympic champion, once in the boy's division and five times in the men's division (between 536 and 520 BC), his competitive wrestling career spans 24 years. He eats 20 pounds of meat and 20 pounds of bread, and drinks eighteen pints of wine daily. Legends say that his training routine includes carrying a baby calf around for years. This anecdote has been called the first documented example of progressive weight training. As the calf grew, so did Milo's strength.[42]

<u>480 BC</u>

Theogenes of Thasos – considered to be one of the greatest athletes in Ancient Greece, is – active. He wins at the Olympic Games twice, once in boxing and once in Pankration. He also wins as many as 1,300 boxing and Pankration championships, in other Greek games, spanning a career of decades.[43] A famous statue, erected in 330 B.C, called The Boxer of Quirinal, or the Terme Boxer, has been discussed in a short story called, "The Pugilist at Rest," published in *The New Yorker* in 1991. In that story the author, Thom Jones, stated that he believed the famous statue commemorated the life of Theogenes of Thasos.[44]

<u>264 BC</u>

The first recorded Gladiatorial Games are held in the Forum in Rome.[45]During the Roman era, Pankration mutates into the gladiatorial games. Due to the superior military planning and strategy of the Roman legions, the power of the individual soldier diminished. Wrestling remained a beloved sport in both the Olympics and in military training.

<u>1848 AD</u>

Greco-Roman wrestling is born in France. The Greco-Roman style is unique in that it forbids attacks to the legs. As such, wrestlers require powerful upper bodies and must have the ability to lift and throw their opponents.[46]

<u>1865 – 1922 AD</u>

Professional catch wrestling becomes one of the most popular spectator sports in the US.[47]

<u>1870s AD</u>

Catch-as-catch-can, or Lancashire wrestling, or just "Catch wrestling" is invented in Lancashire, England. Catch wrestling matches can be won by pin or submission. They have no time limit. A title fight once lasts for over 11 hours.[48]

<u>1896 AD</u>

The first modern Olympic Games are held, with Greco-Roman wrestling included. Subsequently, it will be included in every summer Olympics held since 1920.[49]

<u>1904 AD</u>

The St. Louis Olympics is held, with Catch wrestling included. The US wins in all medal categories, due to the participants being solely US citizens. Catch wrestling is also included in the 1908 London Games and the 1920 Antwerp Games.[50]

<u>1908 AD</u>

Catch wrestler Frank Alvin Gotch defeats George Hackenschmidt to become the first American professional wrestler to win the world heavyweight title. He holds the title between 1908 and 1913.[51]

<u>1920 AD</u>

Earl Caddock, "The Man of a Thousand Holds," defeats Joe Stecher in Madison Square Garden, to regain the heavyweight champion title. Caddock had been forced to give up this title gained in 1917, due to his service during WWI. The match was filmed and is, to date, the oldest known wrestling film.[52]

<u>1920s AD</u>

Professional wrestling becomes scripted. Because catch wrestling matches could last for hours, end in a draw, and have long periods of one or the other competitor stuck in a hold, "fake professional wrestling" is seen as a more exciting form of entertainment.

<u>1922 AD</u>

The last "real" catch wrestling title fight is held between Ed "Strangler" Lewis and Earl Caddock. Although Caddock loses the match, he is considered to be the last legitimate champion.[53]

<u>1922 AD</u>

Catch wrestling is dropped from both the Olympics and the Amateur Athletic Union (AAU) in favor of freestyle and Greco-Roman wrestling. Both freestyle and Greco-Roman remain in the Olympics today.[54]

<u>1939-1950s AD</u>

Gorgeous George Wagner changes the face of pro wrestling forever, by creating his own costumes and character. He intentionally makes himself the most hated and the best paid man in professional wrestling. He also became the first TV wrestler.[55]

<u>1970s AD</u>

Andre the Giant becomes the first international star of professional wrestling. He becomes the first closed circuit TV star, and the highest paid wrestler in history to date.[56]

<u>1980s AD</u>

Hulk Hogan becomes the first pay-per-view wrestling star. His period of super-stardom, dubbed Hulkamania, is like nothing that has been seen before or since. Hulk Hogan appears on Saturday morning cartoons, movies, action figures, vitamins, exercise equipment, board games and thousands of other products. He is credited with elevating the World Wrestling Federation (WWF) to a billion dollar industry.[57]

<u>1993 AD</u>

First Ultimate Fighting Championships (UFC) is held in the US. The sport of Mixed Martial Arts (MMA) is born. Although all martial arts are permissible in MMA, the main arts which the fighters study are: wrestling, Brazilian Jujitsu, Muay Thai, and boxing. Fights are won by choke, submission, KO, TKO, referee stoppage, or judge's decision.[58]

16

<u>1993 AD onward</u>

Wrestlers see MMA as a way of earning money, and the UFC becomes dominated by former high school and collegiate wrestlers. In the 2000s, approximately 80 percent of UFC champions are former wrestlers.

<u>Late 1990s – 2000s AD</u>

There is a resurgence of interest in many classical forms of wrestling, most notably catch wrestling and Pankration, partially due to the popularity of MMA. Grappling tournaments become extremely popular, with practitioners studying and combining a variety of arts from wrestling and Brazilian Jujitsu, judo, sambo, catch wrestling, and Chinese *Shuai jiao*.

<u>2014 AD onwards</u>

The most famous catch wrestler in the world today is probably former UFC Heavyweight Champion, Josh Barnett. He is a former King of Pancrase and Metamoris Brazilian Jujitsu Heavyweight Champion. His official MMA record, as of October 2017 is 35 wins and 8 losses.[59]

Chapter 3: Ancient Wrestling

Those other wrestlers are men of skill; but I, as befits the sons of Sparta, prevail by strength. –Ancient Wrestler from Sparta.[60]

The general consensus among experts seems to be that whilst wrestling is not only one of the oldest sports, it in fact dates all of the way back to prehistoric man. "There, on the rock walls of their dwelling, the men of forty centuries ago immortalized their scenes of the hunt and the dance. It was at this time that, along with play, love, hunting and war, man learned to wrestle."[61] It is even argued that wrestling and boxing are older than armed combat, as man was already fighting, long before he learned to make weapons.

The history of wrestling spans across millenniums. Wrestling is depicted in European cave drawings dating back to between 15,000 and 20,000 years ago.[62] One of the oldest archeological records of wrestling dates back to 5,000 years ago, during he Sumerian era.[63] However, wrestling is most likely much older than records indicate. Wrestling may be one of the first physical activities that prehistoric man engaged in, along with mating and hunting, as wrestling was most likely a key survival skill. Beginning with instinctual, animalistic combat, with time, early men probably developed fighting techniques to secure food and to protect their family.[64]

"The most popular athletic contest in the classical world was wrestling."[65] Centuries before the era of the Greeks, the Egyptians and Nubians were already wrestling. Given the prominence of wrestling in Ancient Egyptian art, it was clearly widespread. "Wrestling scenes first appear in the Old Kingdom tomb of Ptahhotep (2300 BC)"[66] And an ancient Egyptian drawing was found in the tombs of Beni-Hassan (2000-1085 BC) depicting 400 pairs of wrestlers.[67] Interestingly, many of the ancient techniques displayed in this drawing are still in use today: ankle pick, single-leg, collar and elbow lockup, wrist tie-up, underhook, bear hug, and arm drag.[68] Other wrestling images also depict foreign wrestlers, most notably Nubians.

Wrestling between Nubians and Egyptians seems to have been common place. A painting on the wall of the tomb of Tyanen, an Egyptian officer (d. 1410 B.C), depicts the earliest images of Nubian wrestlers from northern Sudan and southern Egypt.[69] Even the tomb of Ramses III (1217 BC−1155 BC) displays the image of an Egyptian/Nubian wrestling match. *Aithiopica*, an ancient Greek novel portraying the history of Ethiopia, written by Heliodorus of Emesa, seems to confirm an ancient African tradition of wrestling that persisted until the late Roman Empire. According to legend, the Nubian people began wrestling by imitating a species of young monkeys they saw wrestling with each other. Like the monkeys, the Nubian wrestlers would rub their hands on the ground, stamp their feet, and roar like bulls.[70]

Traces of wrestling can also be found in literature. The earliest writing which depicts wrestling is the epic of Gilgamesh (approximately 3000 BC), which was inscribed with cuneiform characters on a stone tablet.[71] Scholars believe that it originated from a series of Sumerian legends.[72] The epic goes that Gilgamesh, who was one-third man and two-thirds god, travelled the world hunting monsters. He was similar to the Greek heroes Hercules and Ulysses, who have also been depicted wrestling animals.[73] In the epic, Gilgamesh angered the gods, so in response they created a Wildman, Enkidu, who lived among the animals, yet was as strong as the hero, Gilgamesh.[74] Their wrestling fight lasted all night, at the end of which Gilgamesh and Enkidu became friends.[75] They travelled the world together, having many adventures and fighting and defeating countless enemies. In their final fight together, they killed the Bull of Heaven sent by the goddess Ishtar. However, the gods frowned upon this killing, and it eventually lead to the demise of the two friends.[76] Images of Gilgamesh wrestling the bull, or Gilgamesh wrestling the hair-covered Enkidu, have reoccurred in works of art frequently over the centuries.

From the beginning of the Greek era, wrestling was a key feature of their literature. As far back as the 13th century BC, when the Greeks besieged Troy, there were stories of wrestling matches.[77] Wrestling even features in the works of Ancient Greece's most famous writer, Homer, who wrote *The Iliad* and *The Odyssey*, depicting semi-mythical events that happened between 1200 BC and 800 BC"[78]

Homer describes two wrestling matches, one of which is between the Greek heroes Ajax and Odysseus at the funeral of Achilles. When Odysseus fought Ajax, he twice used a leg sweep and a leg-hook technique to throw Ajax.[79] These throws are still used in modern wrestling, but are extremely prominent in Chinese *Shuai jiao* wrestling and other forms of traditional wrestling where points can be scored by forcing your opponent's knee to touch the ground. The other match described by Homer was between Peleus and Atlanta, also occurring during a funeral.[80]

Greek mythology was full of stories of gods and goddesses wrestling among themselves. In fact, the Greek author Philostratos claimed that Palaistra, the daughter of Hermes, invented wrestling, and that the entire world rejoiced at the discovery because the "iron weapons of war would be cast aside and the stadia would gain sweeter glory than the military camps."[81] According to Philostratos, the Greek military enjoyed tremendous success in combat because of their wrestling training. "The Spartans at Thermopylae employed their bare hands after losing their spears and swords."[82]

Other Greek legends attribute the invention of wrestling to the god Apollo. "Hermes, the great god of the gymnasium, presided personally over wrestling exercises, and his protégé Autolycus taught the art to Hercules."[83] Hercules defeated Antaeus in a wrestling match by lifting him up over his head.[84] Zeus, the king of the gods, had to beat his father Cronus in a wrestling match before becoming ruler of the Earth.[85] "The poet Pindar describes how the gods Zeus and Cronus wrestled for possession of the universe along the river Alpheus at Olympia. Zeus was victorious, and Olympic festivals dating from the Eighth Century BC commemorated his triumph."[86]

The Old Testament of the Bible also contains a story about wrestling in Genesis 32:22-32 and Hosea, chapter 12. In the story, Jacob wrestles with an angel. The fight lasts all night, and when it is over, Jacob has not lost, but his hip has been put out of joint. In recognition of his bravery, the angel gives Jacob the new name of "Israel" which means, "He who struggles with God."[87]

Wrestling imagery also existed in the Greek colony of Pamphylia, which produced coins bearing the images of wrestlers during the period 450 BC–325 BC.[88] Wrestling was also the subject of the oldest instructional sports manual ever found, a wrestling text book that was discovered in Egypt in the late 19th Century. Written in Greek language, on an 18-inch wide fragment of papyrus, the document is thought to date back to between 100 AD and 200 AD. Techniques described in the book include the headlock, the underhook, the clinch, and foot sweeps.[89]

The book is currently on display at the Rare Book and Manuscript Library at Columbia University. According to the Wrestling Hall of Fame, the document was originally discovered by a group of Oxford University students. "In 1907, the artifact was among fragments of papyrus shipped to Columbia, which at that time was among the schools pioneering college wrestling in the USA."[90] Wrestling Hall of Fame historian Don Sayenga published a report stating: "This document helps wrestling as a sport if more people recognize that wrestling is the oldest sport. Not only is wrestling the oldest sport, but it has indisputable artifacts."[91]

"Throughout history, wrestling has always existed...But it was the Greeks who made wrestling into a competitive spectator sport."[92] Nearly 3,000 years ago, the Greek ruler, Athenian Prince Theseus, created the first set of formalized wrestling rules which were similar to modern catch wrestling, which allows attacks to the legs, and wins by submission, pin or choke. "No doubt arm and other joint submissions were used primarily as a way of forcing the opponent to turn over onto his back. However, if he refused to move he would have to submit, and thus the threat of forcing submission lies behind the use of these locks."[93] In modern Greco-Roman wrestling, submissions are not allowed as a way of winning, as they are in mixed martial arts (MMA). However, in MMA, just as in ancient Greece, certain painful holds which may be applied to force an opponent to turn over on his back are permitted.

According to Homer, wrestlers wore belts and/or loincloths.[94] Later, the rules of Greek wrestling changed, and the wrestlers wrestled naked. Today, Chinese *Shuai jiao* wrestling, as well as many forms of traditional wrestling, wear some type of belt or garment which can be grabbed. In contrast, modern Western wrestling, although not nude, does not allow the grabbing of clothing.

The ancient Greek version of the sport also required the wrestlers to coat themselves with oil.[95] Pinning wasn't limited to placing the opponent's two shoulder blades on the canvas, as it is today. "The competitor who first threw his opponent or first brought him down – either on his back, hips, chest, knees or elbows – was proclaimed winner."[96] This type of victory is similar to the rules of Chinese and other traditional wrestling arts, where a fall is assessed when any part of the body, apart from the feet, touch the ground.

An ancient historian, Pausanias, wrote about Theseus, who is believed to have refined ancient Greek wrestling. "Only size and might mattered until Theseus introduced the qualities needed by a good wrestler: strength and a great build."[97] An early Sicilian wrestler, Orikadmos, was said to have established the early rules: Striking, grabbing the groin, and biting were not allowed. "If the wrestlers went out of bounds, the referee halted the contest and returned them to the center of the pit, where they resumed with the same hold."[98]

Two forms of wrestling were practiced in Ancient Greece. The first was orthia pale (upright wrestling), which could be won simply by throwing the opponent to the ground three times. The second form of wrestling was called kato pale (ground wrestling), which could be won through pinning or joint submission. The fight normally went on until one athlete admitted defeat and voluntarily gave up (submitted). The rules were similar to Pankration, except that Pankration also allowed striking.[99] Early traditional forms of wrestling around the world tended to be won by throwing the opponent to the ground. Pinning and submissions appeared to be more advanced rules which were added to the art later in its development. In early Olympic wrestling (776 BC – 393 AD) wins could also be garnered on points. This seems to be the highest evolution of sport, because to assess on points would require a strict set of rules, with point allocations, as well as judges and the ability record and compare scores. Wrestling was the only sport of the ancient Olympics that could be won by points.[100]

The complexity of wrestling can be seen by drawing comparisons with other sports. Two of the other earliest sports are believed to be running and throwing, the scoring of which requires a measurement of distance, or a visual comparison of who throws further or crosses the finish line sooner. Thus, the scoring system of wrestling demonstrates the advanced nature of Greek wrestling.

Wrestling was also the only sport that could be won by the opponent voluntarily admitting defeat. The rules of Greek wrestling called for the best of three falls (throws), but also allowed choking and submissions. In this case, the opponent would resist as long as he could. When he could no longer endure the pain, or recognized that defeat and bodily harm were inevitable, he would signal his own defeat, thus ending the wrestling match. Interestingly, Greek wrestling allowed chokes and submissions, but did not allow the intentional breaking of fingers. Such a rule can also be found in modern MMA, where although competitors are permitted to break each other's arms, they are prohibited from intentionally breaking an opponent's fingers.

The Rules of Ancient Greek Wrestling[101]

1) No intentional hitting or kicking is permitted.
2) No gouging the eyes or biting is permitted, since even the Pankration does not allow this.

3) It is the discretion of the holders of the games to decide whether or not twisting the fingers with the intention of forcing the opponent to concede defeat is permitted.

4) Grasping the genitals is not permitted.

5) All other holds intended to persuade the opponent to concede defeat through pain or fear are permitted, and are an integral part of the contest.

6) Infractions shall be punished by immediate whipping by the referee until the undesirable behavior is stopped.

7) Three points must be scored to win the wrestling match.

8) A point can be scored in any of three ways:

a) Pinning the opponent's back touching the ground.

b) By verbal admission or by tapping on the ground.

c) By the opponent making contact with ground outside the allocated wrestling-match ground with any part of his/her body.

9) After scoring a point, the opponent must be given time to rise onto his/her feet, and a few moments more before the wrestling may continue.

10) The wrestling match both starts and ends at the signal of the referee.

11) The referee can at any time stop the wrestling match if she/he believes a point has been scored.

12) The referee or other officials in charge of the contest shall resolve any dispute the contestants have about scoring, and their decision shall be final.

13) The wrestling-ground shall be a large square, 28.5 Meters by 28.5 Meters, or any other size determined by the holders of the games. The wrestling ground should be made of sand or earth.

14) The contestants shall begin the wrestling match at the center of the wrestling-ground outside of each other's touching-range, the precise distance being at the discretion of the referee.

15) All other more specific details are at the discretion of the officials presiding over the games.[102]

Works of art, supported by literature, suggest that the wrestlers often began the stand-up wrestling in a locked-up or "ram" position (collar and wrist). They would grab the back of their opponent's neck and wrist, then press against each other, head-to-head.[103]There were no weight divisions in the early Greek Olympics, but there were separate categories for boys, 17-20 years old, and men. The Games lasted five days, with boys' wrestling on the third, and men's wrestling on the fourth day. Day Five was the awards ceremony.[104] Such a prominent position in the schedule highlights the importance of wrestling for the Greek's.

"The most highly respected Ancient Greek sports were individual, not team events…wrestling… was the most popular of the combat sports in which to participate, even if its brutal cousins were more popular for watching."[105]The term "brutal cousins" refers to Pankration and boxing, the two more violent of the three Greek combat sports: wrestling, Pankration, and boxing.

During the ancient Olympic Games, beginning in 708 BC, wrestling was the final event of the Pentathlon; after the discus, the javelin, the long jump, and the foot race.[106] "Lists of Olympic wrestling winners have been recorded since 708 BC"[107]

Most of the training of the ancient Greek wrestlers consisted of training with a cooperative partner, to practice techniques.[108] Even today, this is still common practice, with wrestlers working most of the time against a compliant partner to learn and perfect techniques. Only a small part of training consists of live sparring against an unwilling opponent so as to minimize the risk of injury. Greek wrestlers also used a variety of strength and conditioning exercises. Breathing exercises were deemed essential. Ancient Greek theories of breathing stemmed from the work of Aristotle, who wrote: "The soul is air. Air moves and is cognizant. Air that we breathe gives us the soul, life and consciousness.' The athletes, inspired by Aristotle, concluded that air was the pneuma (spirit), or vital force of all life."[109]

A List of Ancient Exercises from
Galen's De Sanitate Tuenda[110]

Philosotratus mentions that jumping weights are to be used by all athletes for strengthening the shoulders and hands, and round ones for strengthening the fingers as well[29]. The round ones are harder to grip and thus afford better exercise for the fingers. Galen divides his exercises into three categories, which we may term 'strong', 'rapid' and 'violent', which is a combination of the preceding two: kicking of the legs for Pankration, rope-climbing for wrestling, holding the arms up for boxing.

Strong exercises:

1) Digging
2) Picking up something heavy
3) Picking up something heavy and walking with it
4) Walking uphill
5) Climbing a rope using hands and feet: commonly done to train boys in the wrestling schools
6) Hanging-onto a rope or beam for as long as possible
7) Holding the arms straight out in front with fists closed
8) Holding the arms straight up with fists closed
9) Holding out the arms while a partner pulls them down
10) The preceding three exercises but while holding something heavy such as jumping-weights
11) Breaking loose from a wrestling waist-lock
12) Holding onto a person trying to escape from the waist-lock
13) Picking up a man who is bending over at the hips and lifting him up and swinging him around
14) Doing the same but bending oneself at the hips also when picking him up
15) Pushing chest to chest trying to force the opponent backwards
16) Hanging from another's neck, attempting to drag him down

Exercises requiring a wrestling-pit:

a) Entwine your partner with both your legs around one of his and try to apply a choke or force his head backwards
b) The same but using only one leg to entwine the opponent's leg closest to yours
c) The same but using both legs to entwine both of the opponent's legs

Rapid[111]
1) Running
2) Shadow-boxing
3) Boxing
4) Hitting punching bags
5) Throwing and catching a small ball while running
6) Running back and forth, reducing the length each time by a little until finished
7) Stand on the balls of the feet, put the arms up in the air and rapidly and alternately bringing them forward and back; stand near a wall if afraid of losing one's balance
8) Rolling on the wrestling-ground rapidly by oneself or with others
9) Rapidly changing places with people next to one in a tightly packed group
10) Jumping up and kicking both legs together backwards
11) Kicking the legs forward alternately
12) Move the arms up and down rapidly with open or closed fist, increasing in speed

Violent:
1) Digging rapidly
2) Casting the discus
3) Jumping repeatedly with no rest
4) Throwing heavy spears and moving fast while wearing heavy armour

5) Any of the 'strong' exercises executed rapidly: presumably running uphill, swinging jumping-weights forward and back, and lifting them up and down, chin-ups and so on

Other exercises:[112]

1) Walking

2) Bending up and down repeatedly at the hips

3) Lifting a weight up from the ground

4) Holding up an object for a long time

5) Full and loud breathing

6) Placing two weights on the ground approximately six feet from each other, picking up the one on the left with the right hand and then the one on the right with the left hand, then in turn placing them back where they came from on the ground and doing this many times while keeping the feet stationary.[113]

From this list of exercises, it can be surmised that the Greeks understood which muscles were more important for wrestling. Furthermore, they knew how to isolate and work the specific muscles. For wrestling, the Greeks clearly thought that the back, shoulders, and legs, were extremely important. However, there is no mention of stomach exercises. That being said, with the inclusion of a few additions exercises, such as bicep curls and bench press, the ancient Greek routine is surprisingly similar to that of modern wrestlers.

The popularity and importance of wrestling in ancient Greece gave rise to sporting celebrities. The most famous Greek wrestler was Milo of Kroton, a six-time Olympic champion (from 540 to 516 BC).[114] Milo was born in a southern Italian colony of Greece, and won the Olympic wrestling in the boys' division at the 60th Olympiad, 540 BC. Following his progression to the men's division, he was five-time wrestling champion, from the 62nd to 66th Olympiad, 532 to 516 BCE.[115] Milo was not only a champion wrestler, but famous for his feats of incredible strength.

"His size and physique were intimidating, and his strength and technique perfect – and many people accordingly believed that he was the son of Zeus." He was said to eat more than eight kilograms of meat every day. Some say that he even once carried an adult bull on his shoulders, all the way to the Olympic stadium, where he slaughtered and devoured it.[116] Milo has been called "the father of progressive resistance training." According to legend, Milo carried a baby calf around with him, and as the calf grew, so did Milo's strength.[117]

Theagenes of Thasos

Theagenes is considered to be one of the greatest athletes and wrestlers of the ancient world. He won the Olympic boxing tournament in the seventy-fifth Olympiad of 480 BC; and in the next Olympics, he won the title in Pankration.[118]

"He's believed to have won 1400 events in his 25-year career, or in other words, "one event every single week." "He was so dominant in boxing that he didn't lose a single fight in 22 years!"[119]A famous statue, from 330 B.C, called Quirinal Boxer, or the Terme Boxer, was discussed in a short story called, *The Pugilist at Rest*. In that story, the author, Thom Jones, stated that he believed the famous statue commemorated the life of Theogenes of Thasos.[120]

Today, wrestling entertainment is "fake" wrestling, or one in which the outcome of the wrestling match is predetermined. Apparently, even this concept of "fixed" or "worked" matches dates back to ancient Greece. Researchers have uncovered a document from 267 AD, which was a contract to "fix" a wrestling match, between two wrestlers named Nicantinous and Demetrius, competing in the Great Antinoeia Games, in Antinopolis, Egypt. The contract stipulates that the father of Nicantinous will pay Demetrius 3,800 drachma if he allows Nicantinous to win. Historians believe that the games were so financially lucrative that bribery became more and more common.[121]

The Greek era eventually gave rise to the Roman era, with Romans adopting much of Greek culture, including wrestling. "Wrestling was the favourite sport of young aristocrats, soldiers and shepherds. According to Classius Dion, the palestra was at the origin of the military success of the Romans."[122] Apart from the military, wrestling also served as entertainment, played out in circus shows, with the winners becoming celebrities. The Romans eliminated the more violent holds of Greek wrestling, and introduced their own methods, which were more attuned to the early Greek, pre-Pankration tradition. As a result, Greco-Roman wrestling was born, in which holds below the waist are not permitted. This naturally favored more broad-shouldered, top-heavy competitors.[123] During this time, the wrestling and Pankration of the Greeks slowly mutated into armed combat and the gladiatorial games.

When the Roman Empire converted to Christianity, the days of professional fighting spectacles ended. The last gladiator school was closed in the 4th Century AD.[124] In 393, Emperor Theodosius I prohibited all pagan games and outlawed the Olympic Games.[125] Thus, the Olympics and wrestling disappeared for more than a millennium.

Defending the single-leg
takedown in sanda.

Sanda throws can look like judo.

A universal hip-throw
in sanda.

Traditional Chinese shuai jiao
trip used in sanda.

Greco-Roman throw from the knees, without touching the opponent's legs.

Body-lock throw used in sanda.

Sanda inside leg-hook throw.

Leg-hook used in sanda competition.

Sanda utilizes single and double leg takedowns like freestyle wrestling.

Greco-Roman takedown without the use of leg tripping.

Greco-Roman wrestlers have the greatest physical strength.

Catch wrestling utilizes wrestling style ground fighting from the knees.

Greco-Roman pin

Suplex, one of the most
devastating Greco-Roman
throws

Catch wrestling utilizes many
of the same submissions as judo
and jujitsu.

Many throws ae identical across
various codes of wrestling.

Chapter 4: Pankration

Pankration, often called the original mixed martial art, was an ancient Greek sport which combined wrestling with boxing. In addition to bare-knuckle boxing punches, Pankration permitted joint locks, throws, and chokes. The only techniques prohibited were biting and eye-gouging.[126] Pankration represented the culmination of the physical, the mental, and the spiritual, in the toughest form of no-holds-barred fighting which has ever been sanctioned at a national or pan- national level.[127] The Greeks considered Pankration the ultimate test of strength and courage.

It is important to note that ancient Greek wrestling permitted joint locks and submissions, as well as attacks to the legs with the hands or legs, therefore it was not that different from the rules of Pankration. Compared to Chinese martial arts, most of the throws of Pankration would be permitted in *Shuai jiao* wrestling, and Pankration joint locks were similar to Chinese *chin na* techniques. In addition, ancient images of Pankration show kick catching and throwing techniques identical to Chinese *sanda*. One could also draw a parallel with modern judo, as both arts allow throws, strangleholds, and joint locks. A similarity with modern Greco-Roman wrestling would be that most classical wrestlers controlled the opponent's upper body and used that control to complete a throw.[128]

In the evolution of wrestling, another similarity between Chinese wrestling and Western wrestling is that while Chinese traditional wrestling became part of modern *sanda*, ancient Western wrestling and boxing became Pankration. From this, it is Pankration that is the ancestor of modern mixed martial arts (MMA).[129]

Pankration History: Greek Era

The recorded history of Pankration spans more than 3,000 years. The oldest written evidence of Pankration can be found in the 586th lyric of Orfica in the ancient poem "Argonautica ", which researchers believe dates as far back as the 12th Millennium BC.[130]

Much of the history and legends of Pankration were depicted on Greek and Roman pottery. One famous vase depicts the mythical origin of Pankration by Hercules. According to legend, Hercules invented Pankration in order to win wrestling tournaments. The Greek author Pausanias wrote that Hercules won both wrestling and Pankration competitions in Olympus on the same day. Hercules also won a Pankration competition organized by the Argonauts.[131]

In other legends, the heroes Heracles and Theseus are said to have invented Pankration as a result of using both wrestling and boxing in their confrontations with opponents. Plutarch wrote that Theseus invented Pankration to defeat the Minotaur in the Labyrinth.[132] Another legendary inventor of Pankration was Heracles, who is often portrayed in ancient artwork using Pankration to subdue the Nemean lion.

In 648 BC, Pankration was added to the 33rd Olympic games as a sport separate from wrestling or boxing. At that time, only adult males were permitted to compete. In 200 BC, a youth male Pankration event was added to the Youth Olympic Games. Conducted over a period of three consecutive days, the Pankration tournament soon became extremely popular and continued as an ancient Olympic Sport up to 393 AD.[133]

The Pankrationists competed in the nude, their bodies coated with sand to create friction for a better grip. Matches were held in a dirt pit called a *skamma* not dissimilar to the ones used to practice Chinese traditional wrestling.[134] A referee controlled the fight pit, using a heavy rod to enforce the rules. Once the match began, the men were free to strike or grapple as they wished. There were no rounds and no time limits. Matches ended when one contestant was unable to continue fighting. Modern MMA fighters tap the mat to signal defeat. Ancient Pankrationists would raise one finger to concede. Competition was so ferocious that matches often ended in death.[135]

Because of the lack of weight divisions, and the large sums of prize money available, Pankration was generally dominated by heavyweights.[136] Although there were no weight divisions, there were age divisions, and the Boys' Pankration event became extremely popular after it was added in the 2nd Century BC.[137]

A similar ruleset to the Pankration was used in the first major televised MMA fight, the Ultimate Fighting Competition (UFC), held in 1993. In this, the only forbidden techniques were biting and eye-gouging. There were no weight limits, and no time limits. Another similarity was the tournament format. Pankrationists fought in a series of regional tournaments, leading up to the Olympics, which could have as many as four levels of eliminators and as many as 16 fighters.[138] This tournament style format was used in the early days of MMA, where most fight events included a 16-man tournament. In modern freestyle wrestling, a tournament format is often used in championship events where there may be more than two teams, each putting up a wrestler in a given weight category. An elimination tournament would be held to determine the overall winner.

It seems that Pankration has many more similarities with modern Western martial arts than with Chinese traditional wrestling. Both ancient Greek wrestling and Pankration allowed joint locks, which are not allowed in *Shuai jiao* wrestling. Additionally, both Pankration and ancient Greek wrestling allowed fighting on the ground. In ancient Greek wrestling, competitors could gain points by pinning their opponent. In this way, both of these ancient Greek arts share more similarities with modern freestyle wrestling or MMA than with *shuai jiao,* which prohibits joint locks and ground fighting.

Historians maintain that while Pankration included both wrestling and boxing, wrestling was the more important component, as most fights ended on the ground. The fighter with better wrestling or submission skills generally won.[139] This is very similar to modern MMA, where the majority of champions and contenders tend to come from the discipline of wrestling, rather than from other martial arts. In Chinese martial arts history, wrestling was also recognized as being the dominant fighting art. An old Chinese saying proclaims, "A man who studies *Wushu* for ten years will lose to a man who studied wrestling for one."[140]

Pankration Training

Pankration training was held in a gymnasium called a "Palaestra," which always contained a statue of Hermes. Training consisted of "Pyrrhics," similar to judo training, with a compliant opponent. The movements were repeated, over and over, until they were perfected. Various forms of wrestling comprised the training regime, as did Greek boxing, called Pigmachia. Body hardening techniques were used, as in martial arts, where various parts of the body were repeatedly beaten until the nerves died and the Pankrationist could withstand the pain of a fight. Strength and speed training were part of the training, as were discus and javelin throwing. Training of one to ten months was a prerequisite before competing.[141]

Evidence exists that Pankrationists were trained in spinning and jumping kicks, but it is believed that they were not used in actual competition, because slippery mud and fatigue prevented such techniques from being effective.[142] This is very similar to Chinese martial arts in the sense that *Wushu* training, which is generally a precursor to *sanda* training, includes high jumps and spinning kicks. Whilst these techniques look very impressive and require tremendous dexterity and athleticism, they are almost never used in *sanda* fighting. Even Chinese *Shuai jiao* wrestlers include high kicks as part of their training, although the kicks are not used in actual matches.

The palaestra was effectively a wrestling school, where the Pankrationists were allocated a separate room, called a Korykeion, for their training. The Korykeion was equipped with punching and kicking balls called korykos, which hung from the ceiling beams.[143] Just as in Chinese martial arts, the training went step by step, with the fighter only advancing to the next phase of training after demonstrating mastery of the previous step. Once a fighter reached a certain level of training, he was permitted to start sparring. This step by step approach is also used in Chinese *Shuai jiao* wrestling, where wrestlers train in a series of movements, called *ji ben gong*, and only begin sparring once they have mastered the basic techniques. xxx

Novices began their training wearing padded gloves and ear protection when sparring. Stretching and shadow boxing were part of the training. Medicine ball type training was done by striking a bag and then letting the bag hit the fighter in the stomach to tighten the abdominal muscles.[144]

To maintain their general health, the athletes were given frequent massages, enemas, and hot baths. Their diet consisted of very little bread, but copious quantities of meat, dry fruits, fresh cheese, and wheat. Legend has it that the famed wrestler, Milon of Kroton, once killed an ox with his bare hands and consumed the entire animal.[145]

Military Application

Historians believe that the Olympic sport Pankration was derived from the military version of Pankration. Pankration was developed by the military as a way of training and keeping soldiers occupied and entertained while waiting for the next war. "To fill the time during years of peace, Greeks had sporting contests, mostly based around preparing Greek men for war."[146]

Just as Chinese traditional wrestling was once taught to soldiers and palace guards, both Western wrestling and Pankration "formed the basis for all combat training for the ancient Greek soldiers – including the famous Spartan warriors and the soldiers of Alexander's Macedonian Phalanxes."[147] Alexander and his men invaded India in 326 BC, taking Pankration with them, practicing the art in a collapsible tent while they were on the move.[148] Many martial arts enthusiasts like to believe that Alexander carried Pankration to Asia and India, and that it was the predecessor to Asian martial arts such as kung fu, karate, and Japanese jiu-jitsu.[149] Others believe that the influence went the other way and that, because of Alexander's travels,

Pankration was able to absorb elements of Asian and Indian martial arts and incorporate them into Pankration."[150]

Pankration eventually became the basis for hand-to-hand combat for the Greek hoplites. In combat, hoplites would use their wrestling skills to stay balanced. If they were knocked down, the wrestling training helped them spring back to their feet more quickly than their opponent, which was often the difference between life and death.[151] During the Classical and Hellenistic periods (500-150 BC), Pankration was considered a complement to the spear and shield training which the infantry received, and was of particular importance as a close quarters fighting system. It is thought that the Spartans even used Pankration at the famous battle of Thermopylae, once their spears and shields were destroyed or lost.[152]

Pankration Techniques

Many of the techniques of Pankration overlap with modern freestyle wrestling. "A Pankratiast would sometimes throw himself on his back to accomplish a throw, known today as Sacrifice Throws."[153] Sacrifice throws are very common in modern Olympic freestyle wrestling and MMA, but are not allowed in Chinese traditional wrestling or *san da*. In both Chinese traditional wrestling and *sanda*, the opponent who hits the ground first loses points. So, a sacrifice throw would also penalize the thrower.

A Pankration training manual describes a throw called "the Stomach Throw," where a "Pankratiast would grab his opponent by the shoulders or arms and throw himself backwards, planting his foot in his opponent's stomach, pulling him over his head."[154] This technique would not be useful in Chinese traditional wrestling or *sanda*, because the wrestler must not allow himself to fall on the ground landing on his back. It is, however, used in modern freestyle and Greco-Roman wrestling, and also in Judo, where it is called *Tomoe nage*.

As Pankration contained such a wide variety of techniques, with kicking, punching, wrestling and ground fighting, different fighters and different regions specialized in different techniques. "The

40

Spartans, for instance, who practiced Pankration as part of their training but did not compete in it…, preferred hard foot sweeps to bring an opponent to the ground."[155] Hard foot sweeps are very common in Chinese traditional wrestling and *sanda*, but less common in modern freestyle wrestling.

As *sanda* and Pankration both include kicks, they both require kick catching and throwing. The throws used, once the kick is caught, are variations of the single-leg and double leg takedown which are used in both Chinese *Shuai jiao* and modern freestyle wrestling.

The straight kick with the bottom of the foot to the abdomen was a common technique used in Pankration. Similar kicks are used in modern *sanda* and MMA, and countered in much the same way. The athlete being kicked steps to the outside of the kick, simultaneously scooping the inside of the kicking leg and grasping it behind the knee. They then pull the kicker's leg forward and up, unbalancing their opponent. If the kicker does not fall straight away, the catcher can advance, with punches to the face, or can complete the throw by grabbing the back of the kicker's shoulder, pulling them to the ground. Another option is for the catcher to grab the kicker's base leg and take him down in a form of double-leg takedown familiar to both Chinese and Western wrestlers.

The Pankration reverse waist-lock is a position common to modern wrestling, frequently used in MMA, and not unknown to Chinese traditional wrestling. Vietnamese-American *sanda* legend and collegiate wrestling champion Cung Le won many of his *sanda* fights using this position. From the reverse waist lock, the throw is completed by employing the suplex, where the thrower sets his own hips against the opponent's hips, lifts them straight up in the air, rotates slightly, and then drives them head first into the ground. As one of the rules of Chinese traditional wrestling is to not injure the opponent, the opponent would generally be dumped on his chest, rather than on his head. In Pankration, modern wrestling, or MMA, because there are no rules preventing the thrower from touching the ground or from hitting the ground first, a reverse waist lock throw can be completed by utilizing a sit-through technique, where the thrower hits the ground first, taking the opponent over his head, rolling, and landing in a pin or a control position.

Pankration in the Roman Era

Greek culture held athleticism and bravery in combat in high esteem. In the Mycenaean-Greek world (1600-1100 BC), success in battle depended on a king having the best trained warriors. Therefore, individual fitness and combat skills were crucial. The most heroic warriors were glorified and deified across their homeland. Ancient literature, such as the *Iliad* and the *Odyssey*, are excellent examples of this admiration. The importance placed on the early Olympics further added to this worship of the perceived perfect human form. Athletes, boxers, wrestlers, and Pankrationists all competed in the nude, with winners being transformed into statues and paintings suggesting that these warriors occupied an aesthetic, cultural, and even spiritual place in Greek society.[156]

Eventually, however, around 750 BC, the Greek era gave way to the Roman era.[157] The Romans were fantastic military strategists, with success in battle dependent on intelligent generals creating massive battle plans, carried out with mathematical precision. Under the Romans, the power or skill of the individual soldier became less important, moving toward the importance of the "unit." This marked the beginning of the decline of Pankration.

The Romans worshipped Jupiter (Zeus in Greece), and honored him by continuing the Olympic Games.[158] The Romans continued to practice both boxing and wrestling as distinct sports. Pankration remained a part of the Olympics, and was still taught to the infantry, but the heyday of Pankration ended with the Greek era. Under the Romans, Pankration no longer existed as a professional form of sports entertainment. Instead, Pankration became incorporated into the gladiatorial games.[159]

Chapter 5: The Gladiators

As a pair of gladiators enter the area, prepared to fight to the death, they are greeted by elated Romans. "In ancient Rome, death had become a form of entertainment."[160] Before fighting, gladiators had to swear the following oath: "I will endure to be burned, to be bound, to be beaten, and to be killed by the sword."[161]

During the Greek era sport, particularly combat sports such as boxing, Pankration, and wrestling, were essential elements of the Hellenistic culture. Aside from the Olympics, the Greeks held other sporting events over a period of more than 1,000 years, with sport offering a path to wealth and glory.[162] Ancient Greek pottery and mosaics have been found depicting hundreds of images of sports games. Archeologists have uncovered the sites of early Olympic games, including training areas and weightlifting equipment.[163] Such archeological evidence signifies the prominence of sport in Greek culture.

Following the Roman conquest of Greece in 146 BC[164], the Romans adopted many elements of Greek culture, including sports. Both wrestling and Pankration were absorbed into Roman culture. Under the rules of Greek wrestling and Pankration, eye gouging, biting, and disemboweling, were all prohibited. But in Rome, the most violent sports became the most popular with spectators.[165] For this reason, Greek Pankration and wrestling evolved into the gladiatorial games. These games were professional spectacles which represented huge financial interest. As combat sport became driven by profit, it also became more violent.[166] Unlike the Greek games, Roman gladiatorial contests more often ended in death.

The Romans had been exposed to Greek culture long before they conquered Greece, and there was some hesitancy about absorbing Greek culture. Polite Roman society thought the gymnasia, where men practiced wrestling and boxing in the nude, were both effeminate and immoral. Whilst the Romans enjoyed watching chariot races, gladiator fights, or boxing matches, the wealthy and the well-bred would not participate in the games. Consequently, most of the participants were slaves.[167] Campus Martius, a large playing field near the center of Rome, was one of the most popular places where the Roman youth participated in boxing and wrestling as a form of exercise and personal entertainment, but they would not compete in the games as a public spectacle.[168]

However, after 146 BC, Roman attitudes toward the legacy of ancient Greece began to change, as even wealthy Romans adorned their gardens with statues of Greek athletes. Public games began making their way into the culture as part of religious observance. The Etruscans of Northern Italy were the first to hold gladiator battles and chariot races as a sacrifice to the gods.[169]

After the death of Julius Caesar in 44 BC, the succeeding emperors sponsored gladiatorial games with state money, as a way of appeasing the masses and averting a revolt. Gladiatorial games became a political tool to keep the public occupied and distract them from scrutinizing the actions of the Senate.[170] Games were held ten to twelve times per year, making people forget widespread unemployment and poverty.[171]

Certain emperors, such as Augustus, Nero, and Domitian, were known to admire Greek culture and were influential in promoting Greek sports. The first Greek games in Rome were held in AD 86 by Domitian. A circuit of Greek sports already existed in the empire; but now, Rome would become a prominent host of the Greek-style games.[172]

As the games grew in popularity and size, they became increasingly more elaborate. Coliseums and small amphitheaters began to appear throughout the empire. The popularity of the games reached its zenith in the first and second centuries AD.[173] Under Augustus Caesar, "the games achieved a variety and splendor never before seen."[174] Augustus Caesar claimed that in the eight gladiatorial games he had held, a total of 10,000 men fought to the death.[175]

While much of the culture of Rome came originally from the Greeks, the Romans then exported this Romanized Greek culture to other parts of the globe. Rome was a vast empire, having conquered otherwise independent lands and kingdoms and brought them under a single rule and imposed Roman culture on them. Two of the most common features of Romanized cities were the amphitheater, where gladiatorial games were held, and baths, the ruins of which can be found in many of the former Roman cities.[176] Archeologists have recently discovered evidence of Roman gladiatorial games being held in the Roman province of Smyrna, located in modern Turkey.[177] Gladiatorial games were also exported back to the Roman provinces in Greece. According to ancient Greek author Philostratos (VA 4.22), Roman games, which ended in death, were held beneath the Acropolis in Athens.[178]

Emperor Nero Claudius Caesar, who ruled Rome from 54-68 AD, was the first Roman emperor to build a public gymnasium.[179] Although the Roman gymnasia promoted the Greek sports tradition, they were not as important to the Romans as the amphitheaters and colossal stadia (stadiums).[180] Circuses, as well as running races for men and horses, were all held in these stadia, as were wrestling and boxing matches. The stadia were even built to house the wrestling training camps.[181] Sports gambling was another activity enjoyed by the Romans at the stadia. By far, however, the most popular events were the gladiatorial games.[182]

In 177 AD, Lucius Aurelius Commodus ascended to the throne of Rome. Commodus was known for being mentally weak but physically strong. He excelled in martial sports such as riding, hunting and fighting, and was a builder of public gymnasia. He became infamous for participating in the games, racing chariots, fighting animals, executing rivals and even fighting as a gladiator.[183] "When all the statistics of the races won, the animals killed, and the gladiators bested are computed, many historians have acknowledged Commodus as the greatest athlete who ever lived."[184]

The Coliseum of Rome

Among the many stadiums built, the Coliseum of Rome (also known as the Flavian Amphitheatre) was by far the largest and most famous gladiatorial arena of all the Roman Empire. It is the largest amphitheater in the world, 12 stories tall, with seating for an estimated 50,000 to 80,000 spectators. Construction of the Coliseum began under Emperor Vespasian in 70 AD, and was completed in 80 AD under Emperor Titus. Further work was done during the reign of Domitian (81–96 AD).[185] It was like nothing the world had seen before, and was "watertight and could be flooded to hold naval battles."[186]

To celebrate the inauguration of the Coliseum, one hundred days of games were held, with 3,000 men fighting in a single day and 9,000 animals killed on another.[187] The games became a huge business, with vast sums of money being earned from ticket sales and gambling. Even the gladiators were well paid, providing they survived.

Successful gladiators became wealthy and famous, and were the celebrities of their day.[188] Famous Gladiators were lauded by the Romans and regarded as sex symbols. Gladiator-related graffiti, painted on city walls, still survives to this day, giving some insight into how popular these professional warriors were. Archeologists have uncovered graffiti which reads "Crescens, the net fighter, holds the hearts of all the girls" and "Caladus, the Thracian, makes all the girls sigh."[189] Games were advertised on billboards, and top gladiators attracted a fan base because of their courage, skill, and in some cases, even their good looks.[190] Successful gladiators had legions of fans and female admirers, although it was illegal for gladiators to pursue a relationship with a citizen. The games were promoted through advertising campaigns, and gladiators endorsed products just as athletes do today. Brochures were handed out, giving details about the various fighters. Before the games, the gladiators were paraded through the streets, and a banquet was held in their honor.[191]

Although most gladiators were slaves, even freedmen sometimes chose the life of a gladiator because of the allure of the money and fame that awaited a great champion.[192] The winner of a single high-profile bout could receive the entire annual salary of a Roman soldier.[193]

These games, however, have far smaller and far more lethal roots.

Humble Beginnings

Initially, gladiatorial battles weren't the incredibly ornate public spectacles that they became. Historians believe that the first instance of gladiatorial games ever being held was at the funeral of Junius Brutus Pera in 264 BC, where slaves were made to fight to honor his death.[194] Early gladiatorial battles were private affairs funded by noble families.[195] These had evolved out of an ancient Etruscan funeral ritual, whereby warriors would make a blood sacrifice by fighting to the death, to honor the spirit of a fallen chieftain.[196] The fights were intended to demonstrate Roman virtues of strength, courage, and determination.[197]

Later, by the 2nd century BC, the religious significance had been removed from the games, and they became a public spectacle. Emperors used the games to control the public, and politicians used them to sway voters at election time and to celebrate Roman military victories.[198]

The Rules of Gladiatorial Combat

As the games grew in size and popularity, they became more sophisticated and more regulated. Historians know that the gladiatorial battles had a strict set of rules and a referee, but sadly, the exact ruleset has been lost.[199]

Contrary to popular belief, the men did not always fight to the death. Historians believe that only about ten percent of gladiators died in the arena.[200] Although the fight was clearly over when one man died, if a man was wounded or did not wish to continue, he could gesture a conceding hand motion. At that point, the crowd of spectators would determine whether he lived or died.[201] If a gladiator were knocked down, knocked unconscious, or disarmed, the winning gladiator would look to the editor controlling the event to be told if he should kill his opponent.[202] As gladiatorial games became more lucrative, the gladiators themselves became very valuable. As a result, the promoters did not want to see them killed very often.[203] If a gladiator was killed in the arena, his owner had to be paid for his replacement.[204] One could argue that the gladiators were an extension of the wrestlers of ancient Greece, in that they fought for pride, fame, and money, and were only occasionally killed.

Gladiatorial fights were held in amphitheaters alongside other bloodthirsty attractions, such as *venationes* (animal hunts, or contests between beasts or between beasts and men), and public executions (*noxii*).[205] Other non-gladiatorial spectacles involved forcing large groups of criminals into the arena and then releasing wild animals from across the empire, such as leopards or lions, to kill them.[206] Animals, including lions, bears, rhinos, tigers, elephants, and giraffes were often made to fight against each other.[207] Other possibilities were matches between a gladiator and an animal, or multiple gladiators and animals.[208] Occasionally, however, animals were set upon a victim tied to a stake.[209]

Gladiatorial matches came in all shapes and sizes. Sometimes a match consisted of a single pair of gladiators. At other times, whole battles were staged. A famous event once held by Emperor Trajan consisted of 5,000 pairs of gladiators, and lasted for 117 days.[210]

Brutality and Civilization

The history of the Romans is full of contradictions. On the one hand, the Romans are seen as having civilized the Western world. On the other hand, they enjoyed watching gladiators die as a form of entertainment.[211] However, the love of blood sport is not unique to the Romans. Blood Sports, defined as "any sport that involves the killing or shedding of blood of an animal,"[212] have always been a part of human society. Bull fighting in Spain and Mexico, cock

48

fighting in Cambodia, horse fighting in China, dog fighting in the US, and bear baiting in Pakistan would all be examples of blood sports in various cultures.[213] Even in the contemporary US, Senator John McCain referred to mixed martial arts (MMA) as "human cockfighting," and moved to have the sport banned.[214] Blood sports seem to be present in some form in nearly every culture, although the form and degree of acceptance of the sports varies widely from country to country.[215]

The Romans are generally held up as an example of a highly evolved society with advanced knowledge in the fields of science, literature, medicine, mathematics, military, and politics. But many critics have wondered: If the Romans were so advanced, why did they so vehemently embrace the gladiatorial games? Is it not the most brutal form of entertainment that has ever existed?

Experts have two theories to explain this apparent contradiction. The first is that "humans have a need to discharge their natural aggression, which can be accomplished in war, or in a substitute for war like violent sports."[216] The other theory is "violence in sports merely reflects the aggressive tendencies of society."[217] And, "the more warlike a society is the more likely warlike sports will be."[218]

Regardless of which theory one subscribes to, it is historically true that even in Ancient Greece, the combat sports – boxing, Pankration, and wrestling – were the most popular. The gladiatorial games in Rome can be seen as the next step to this, an increase in the violence of combat sport. Wrestling is thought to be the oldest of the combat sports. It is also the least violent, in that it only allowed submissions and chokes. Pankration was the next step, adding kicking and punching. The gladiatorial games were the next evolution, with the addition of weapons.[219] In modern society, weapons have been removed from sport, and MMA can be seen as the modern evolution of Pankration.

In general, the games became increasingly more violent throughout the Roman era. The gladiatorial fights to the death, public executions, and animal fights were less about achieving the

Greek ideal of physical perfection and strength and bravery, and were more about brutalizing one's opponent.[220]

According to the Greek interpretation of violence, the Greeks felt the most violent sport of the ancient world was boxing, which they conducted without gloves. Wrestling was considered the least violent of combat sports as, although chokes and joint lock submissions were allowed, a fighter could concede before being seriously injured. The Greeks even considered Pankration less violent than boxing, because the art was largely dominated by wrestling rather than boxing techniques.[221]

Critics of the Games

The Greek ideal of the athlete seems to have become distorted during Roman times.[222] Can Roman gladiators even be considered athletes? One does not usually think of athletes as killing people. But on the other hand, even in gladiatorial battles both men usually survived. Still, there was a clear difference between the Greek athletes, who competed to achieve an ideal of physical perfection, and the Roman gladiators who competed to satisfy the blood lust of spectators.[223] Consequently, just as MMA draws criticism today, even in ancient times, the games had critics. Both pagans and Christians opposed the games, not necessarily because of the violence involved, but because of the loss of control among the shouting audience.[224] It seems that even in ancient Rome, educated people disliked the drunken, shouting chaos of sports fans.

The ancient writer, Epictetus, seems to have supported athletes but despised both boxers and Pancrationists, seeing them in the same light as gladiators. "Hail incredible man!" but not those foul boxers and pancratiasts, nor those like them – the gladiators."[225] Other criticisms of the games protested along ethnic lines. They saw pure sport as being Greek, and gladiatorial games as being Roman. Some scholars take an idealistic view of the Greek games, seeing them as a romantic highpoint of Greek philosophy. They hold that the Greeks would have been too cultured to enjoy the savagery of the Roman games.[226]

The Romans saw the gladiators as representing Roman virtues. But this again is a contradiction. On the one hand, they were proud, powerful warriors, representing all that was good in Rome. On the other hand, they were mostly slaves, representing the lowest rung of society.[227]

The Christian Apostle Paul, a Roman citizen, represented himself as a wrestler, boxer, and gladiator, suggesting that he saw all of these combat sport athletes as equal. In First Corinthians 9:24–27, Paul talks about boxing and self-discipline. In Ephesians 6:12, he refers to wrestling, and in First Corinthians 4:9; 15:32, many believe he is referring to the gladiatorial contests as he mentions athletes who are condemned to death.[228] Paul evoked the image of wrestlers and gladiators as representing Roman virtue, a comparison he thought "the Corinthian audience could hear and accept as honorable, despite appearances."[229]

Violence exists in all societies, but is more prominent in one which was so heavily militarized as Rome. Consequently, the gladiatorial games were a means of keeping peace by commemorating war and violence. The games also represented a contact between the elite and the mob.[230] The empire was built on war and conquest, and conquest helped to support the games, which in turn, held the empire together. From the time of the Roman defeat of Carthage in 201 BC, the Empire continued to expand until two hundred years later, when it controlled 50-60 million people across the Mediterranean and most of northwestern Europe. The taxes which the provinces paid to Rome supported the army, and prisoners were often used in gladiatorial contests or animal fights in the Coliseum. Gladiatorial contests and public executions served the dual purpose of entertainment and confirming the power of the empire.[231] Politically, the gladiators brought a heroic image of combat to the Roman people, thus justifying support for the wars that waged hundreds of miles away.

Why did Men Agree to Fight as Gladiators?

The Olympic athletes of Greece were proud citizens, many of whom were of high birth. This is in stark contrast to the Roman gladiators, who were generally not citizens, but often slaves or prisoners, and certainly not of noble birth. The Greeks competed before an audience which shared their philosophical belief in the athletic ideal. The gladiators, however, competed before a paying crowd which longed for blood.[232] Whereas Greek athletes fought for the winner's laurels, Roman prisoners and slaves were destined to fight until they were killed or granted freedom.[233] Some criminals were even sent into the arena unarmed as a form of punishment.[234]

Although they came from the lowest rungs of society, being a winning gladiator had its advantages, much like becoming glamour figures and cult heroes.[235] Winning gladiators built large followings, with thousands of fans turning out to watch their battles. They were often given gifts, money, and sometimes even freedom by their fans and owners.[236]

Young women expressed their love for favored gladiators in graffiti written on the walls of the gladiator schools. Noble women, even the wives of emperors, were rumored to have had affairs with gladiators.[237] These affairs had to be kept secret, as they were illegal. One theory of why women of privilege would choose to have an affair with a gladiator was that there was some strange allure to the fact that gladiators lived in close proximity to death.[238]

Gladiators often took heroic fight names, many of which were from mythology: Achilles, Ajax, Alkeides, Patroclus, or Polynices, others used Latin transliterations of heroic qualities, such as Victor, Martialis, Species, or Pinna.[239] This was particularly common for Greek gladiators, as by choosing names from Greek mythology they were able to maintain their ethnic identity and racial pride.[240]

While the potential for money, pride, fame, and beautiful women was an allure for gladiators, the life-span of a gladiator was short and unpleasant. Their lives were very difficult, usually ending badly. Like Russian Roulette, gladiatorial games were a numbers game. Each win brought the gladiator closer to death.[241] Most gladiators fought two to three times per year and died between the ages of 20 and 30. They generally had a career spanning 5-34 fights.[242] "One gladiator, Asteropaeus, notched 107 victories, and exceptional gladiators fought on into their 40s and 50s, sometimes retiring as free men. But these were the exceptions."[243]

As for those gladiators who survived to be granted their freedom, their prospects were not good. Other than death or being crippled, the best that most gladiators could hope for after a career in the arena was to work as bodyguards for the wealthy. Most, however, wound up hanging around the gladiator schools, working menial jobs, or even begging for alms.[244] The remains of gladiators recovered from cemeteries in England and Turkey showed signs of early death, gnarled bones, and blunt-force trauma, bespeaking of the harshness of their lives.[245]

The gladiators held a strange rank in society. On the one hand, they were admired and lusted after. On the other hand, they bore tattoos or brands to demonstrate their low status in society.[246] As a result, many noblemen saw attending the games as an activity that might damage their reputation. They were, according to the Christian author Tertullian, both loved and despised: "men give them their souls, women their bodies too'. Gladiators were 'both glorified and degraded."[247] Even in death, they remained outsiders. Because they lived their lives communing with death, gladiators were often precluded from being buried in public cemeteries.[248]

Gladiator Schools of Rome

Gladiators lived in barracks at training schools where they were fed, trained, and given the best medical attention available.[249] The doctors associated with the gladiatorial games were experts at treating cuts and external wounds. However, if a gladiator was stabbed, or injured in his internal organs, the doctors may have been helpless to save him.[250] Many gladiator schools flourished in and around Rome and the linistas – the agents or managers – bought and sold gladiators as soccer teams buy and sell players today. It was one of the most lucrative businesses in the Empire.[251] Given that the gladiators were so well fed and cared for, they were an expensive commodity.[252] As a result, their deaths weren't taken lightly.

Schools existed throughout the empire. And in Rome, the gladiator schools, or ludi, were concentrated close to the amphitheater. The largest of the four schools in Rome was called the Ludus Magnus, which was connected to the Coliseum. The gladiator school at Capua was famous because of its connection with the 73 BC slave rebellion, led by Spartacus. Gladiators generally only fought two or three times a year. If they saved enough money, they could buy their freedom.[253]

Although about a hundred ludi are thought to have existed in the Roman Empire, almost all have been destroyed.[254] The remains of a 1,800-year-old gladiator school were found at Carnuntum, the capital of Upper Pannonia in Roman times. It contained amphitheaters and Roman baths, individual cells for the gladiators, and a circular training arena.[255] Other gladiator schools existed in Augusta Traiana, in Tomis, and in Thasos, which offered gladiatorial games.[256]

Members of the gladiator barracks were constantly changing, as some were off on tours, and others were killed. Men of the same fighting style or weapon had the same trainer, and were housed together, often forming associations.[257] Spectators were invited to watch the gladiators practice so as to get the men used to performing in front of an audience.

Not all Gladiators were Slaves

Gladiators were usually chosen from criminals, slaves, prisoners of war, and people who had lost their Roman citizenship. However, some freeborn men and citizens, and even a few wealthy or powerful people, chose to fight in the gladiatorial games. Historians have found evidence that even some women actually volunteered to be gladiators. These people were willing to risk death for the possibility of fame and glory.[258]

New gladiators took an oath signifying that they were now the property of the lanist, the owner of the gladiator troupe. Upon taking the oath, they were given a large down payment. Afterwards, their life was no longer their own.[259] Becoming a gladiator meant trading Roman citizenship for membership in the troupe, which was called a familia. It also meant agreeing to being subjected to branding, chains, flogging, or death in the arena.[260] Those who became gladiators voluntarily, estimated at about 50 percent of the total, were called *auctorati*.[261] They sold their freedom for up to five years either to pay off debts, or to pursue fame in the arena.[262]

In 2007, mosaics and graffiti were uncovered documenting the life of a Roman citizen named Marcus Attilius, who sold himself to a gladiator school in order to pay off his debts.[263] In his first gladiatorial contest, Marcus Attilius defeated Nero's own gladiator, Hilarus, who had won his previous thirteen fights. Later, Attilius defeated Raecius Felix, who had won his previous twelve battles.[264]

Even emperors were not immune to the allures of the arena. Nero competed as a charioteer. Commodus fought under the name "Hercules the Hunter."[265] He went so far as to claim he was both Hercules and Romulus, the founder of Rome, and fought in the arena to prove to the Roman people that he was a god.[266] Consequently, historians have called Commodus a megalomaniac. He even dressed like Hercules, wearing lion skins and carrying a club.[267] In truth, he only fought in preliminary bouts in the arena, with blunted weapons. His opponents were gladiators armed only with wooden weapons, who knew that they were expected to lose. Consequently, Commodus easily won all of his fights.[268] Commodus also wounded animals and even captured and wounded Roman citizens, who he then killed in the arena.[269] He charged the Treasury sizeable sums for his participation in the games and fought so many times that he became a significant drain on the public coffers. Historians have estimated that the fee he charged for a single fight would have been enough to feed a thousand families for one year.[270]

Commodus met his end when he was assassinated in AD 192, and it is believed that his actions as a "gladiator" were the final straw, prompting his Inner Circle to go through with the regicide.[271] Numerous plots against his life were planned, but his death finally came at the hands of a wrestler named Narcissus. "The plot was orchestrated by his closest advisors, and apparently even included his mistress, Marcia."[272]

At least seven other Roman emperors and several senators fought as gladiators.[273] But none of them would be remembered in the same way as Commodus, who claimed to be a god, and then lived and died violently.

Famous Gladiators

Historians often gage the fame of a particular gladiator by the amount of graffiti about him they find. Recently, 1800-year-old graffiti was found in Oinoanda, a Roman city in southwest Turkey, showing that the Roman army used a champion gladiator named Lucius Septimius Flavillianus as a recruiter to take soldiers to Hierapolis, a town in Syria.[274]

Flavillianus was not only a champion gladiator, but also a champion of wrestling and Pankration. He was so successful, it was decreed that he would be made a "'cult figure in the band of heroes' after he died, with each tribe of the city erecting statues in his honor."[275]

Spiculus was a famous gladiator associated with Nero, in the First Century AD. After a successful career, Nero rewarded Spiculus with palaces, slaves, and wealth. When Nero was overthrown in AD 68, he ordered his servants to find Spiculus, because he wanted the famous gladiator to execute him. Unfortunately for Nero, Spiculus could not be found, and Nero died by his own hand.[276]

Carpophorus was a famous gladiator who fought animals. At the inauguration of the Flavian Amphitheatre, he defeated a bear, a lion, and a leopard at the same time.[277] He is said to have killed twenty wild animals in a single day, after which his fans and other gladiators compared him to Hercules.[278]

A gladiator named Flamma became famous for rejecting his freedom. He was awarded the rudis (a wooden sword signifying freedom) four times, but still chose to continue a fighting career as a gladiator. His gravestone, which stands in Sicily, includes the following information: "Flamma, secutor, lived 30 years, fought 34 times, won 21 times, fought to a draw 9 times, defeated 4 times."[279]

The highlight of the inaugural games at the opening of the Coliseum of Rome was a fight between Priscus and Verus. This fight was the only gladiatorial fight ever recorded in detail. Because both men had fought so valiantly, the Emperor Titus Flavius Caesar signaled that the fight should be stopped before either man was killed. Both were awarded a victory laurel and a rudis of freedom.[280]

The most famous gladiator of all time was, however, Spartacus, a Thracian, who led the largest slave revolt in the history of the Roman Empire. The exact origin of Spartacus is unclear. Some histories maintain that he was a Thracian soldier who had been captured and sold into slavery, and then sold to a gladiator school.[281] Other historians believe that he was a deserter from the Roman army who was sold to a gladiator school. In both versions of the story, he finds himself at the mercy of gladiator trainer Lentulus Batiatus, in Capua.[282] There, each gladiator was trained in a specific style of combat. In Spartacus's case, he was trained as a lightly armed gladiator.[283] That training, and perhaps a Roman soldier's background, were most likely instrumental in his success as the leader of a rebellion.

In 73 BC, Spartacus led the other gladiators in a revolt against Batiatus, the owner of the gladiator school. The uprising began with 200 gladiators, armed with kitchen implements and improvised weapons. Only about seventy-eight survived and escaped.[284] Almost immediately after their escape, Spartacus and his men attacked a cart which was carrying gladiator weapons, after which, they were able to arm themselves more properly.[285]

Spartacus and his troops made their way to Mount Vesuvius, fighting the Roman army as they went. Along the way, they raided for supplies and liberated slaves, recruiting them to join their growing army.[286] Soon, their ranks swelled to the tens of thousands.[287] The Spartacus revolt would become known as the Third Servile War, and would prove the most difficult rebellion the Empire ever saw as Spartacus's army of well-trained gladiators easily defeated the Roman legions that came against them.

They remained primarily in rural areas where there were few Roman soldiers and an abundance of slaves waiting to be liberated. Spartacus also insisted on splitting the winnings of their raids equally amongst all men. The promises of equality and freedom attracted a stream of new recruits to his army.[288] "Plutarch wrote, 'This success resulted in new recruits flocking to the force of Spartacus.'"[289] In time, he even succeeded in getting non-slaves to join his rebellion.[290] Shepherds and laborers, men with stout bodies accustomed to living hard, brutal lives exposed to the elements, joined the rebellion.

Spartacus's army had grown to 40,000 troops by the spring of 72 BC At this point, his army split. Some troops remained with his second-in-command Crixus, determined to stay in Italy, while Spartacus took his forces to the Alps to escape into Gaul. Crixus and his troops were eventually caught and killed by the Roman general Gellius.[291]

Later that year, Spartacus defeated three more Roman armies and reached Cisalpine Gaul.[292] Eventually, two Roman generals caught Spartacus in a pincer maneuver, trapping him between the forces of Gellius and Le Lentulus.

Despite this strong tactical position, Rome once again underestimated Spartacus. Whilst the first several forces they sent against him were small troops of unseasoned soldiers under young and inexperienced commanders, Rome had now sent two large armies to confront Spartacus. . However, they had failed to notice that Spartacus had developed his own formidable cavalry. Spartacus

58

was a Thracian, a group of people famous for being excellent horsemen.[293] Spartacus attacked and defeated Lentulus, stealing his supplies. Next, Spartacus's army made short work of the one last Roman army, commanded by Gaius Cassius Longinus, which stood between Spartacus and The Alps. He and his men were now free to climb to safety in Gaul. Despite freedom being within sight, for some unknown reason Spartacus and his men choose not to leave Italy. One theory is that the Gauls and Germans under Spartacus refused to leave Italy, instead wanting to remain in the country and pillage more.[294] No one is sure of the exact reason, but, Spartacus turned his army south and went back into Italy.

The Romans sent a commander named Glaber, who trapped the slave army at Mount Vesuvius, planning to starve them out. Spartacus ordered his men to cut vines, and make ropes, which they used to climb down the unprotected back side of the rock face. They took Glaber's men by surprise, defeating them. When the Romans were routed, Spartacus's men moved into the Roman camp and looted all of their weapons and supplies. As news of Spartacus's victory over Glaber spread, more slaves joined his army. With slaves from all corners of the empire, Spartacus divided the men into units according to their native language.[295]

The following year, "in 71BC the Roman commander Marcus Licinius Crassus forced Spartacus and his followers into the narrow peninsula of Rhegium (now Reggio di Calabria)."[296] Spartacus's luck and training helped him and his people escape through the Roman lines.

Spartacus and his army went on to defeat two more Roman armies before overrunning most of southern Italy, at which point their numbers had swelled to at least 90,000.[297] They fought their way to the Strait of Messina, hoping to hire boats to escape to Sicily. Spartacus made a deal with Sicilian pirates to ferry his people to safety, but the pirates cheated Spartacus, simply sailing away without him and his people.[298]

Around this time, his army split again as a group led by Castus and Gannicus broke away from Spartacus and set off on their own. Additionally, three separate Roman armies were on their way, led by Crassus, Marcus Terentius, Varro Lucullus, and Pompey. In the spring of 71 BC, the slave forces lead by Castus and Gannicus were defeated by Crassus.

At this point, historians believed Spartacus's force numbered 30,000. Rather than try and escape, Spartacus turned and attacked Crassus. During the battle, Spartacus personally tried, but failed, to kill Crassus. Spartacus is believed to have been killed in battle in 71 BC at the River Silarus.[299] Although Spartacus's body was never found, witnesses recognized his horse and saw that horse and rider had been killed.

After the battle, fleeing slaves were killed by the army of Roman General Pompey. As a warning against future slave rebellions, Crassus ordered 6,000 prisoners crucified along the Appian Way from Brundisium to Rome.[300]

The End of the Gladiators

As the Roman era took hold, Pankration experienced a steady decline, being overshadowed by the more violent and more commercial gladiatorial games. However, it was changes in the Roman religion that led to its ultimate demise.

In 393 AD, when Theodosius embraced the Christian religion, he banned all pagan festivals and holidays, including the Olympics. In 399 AD, the gladiator schools (ludi) were closed. Lastly, in 404 AD, Honorius officially cancelled all gladiatorial games. The gladiatorial games, just like Pankration, wrestling, and the Olympics, had all come to an end.[301] Thus, it would be more than 1,400 years until wrestling made its comeback in the first modern Olympics.

One could say that the gladiatorial games were the world's first major professional sporting event.[302] The Roman gladiators lived more than a millennium ago, and yet the concept of staging violent mock fights and betting on them is still alive today. While the gladiatorial games have been compared to modern MMA fights, because of the skill and violence involved, they are equally comparable to modern World Wrestling Entertainment (WWE) style "fake" wrestling. The gladiatorial fights had many of the same elements as WWE such as characters, costumes, fans and followers, sponsors, managers, and commercial interests. In terms of chronology, the gladiatorial fights came at the end of the early part of wrestling history, which was the last stage before wrestling went dormant until the first modern Olympics in 1896. But in a way, one could say that the gladiatorial fights were way ahead of their time, as they were closer to the pro wrestling and MMA of today than anything that had come before.

Chapter 6: Catch Wrestling

Today, the most popular form of wrestling entertainment is professional, World Wrestling Entertainment (WWE) style TV wrestling. These wrestling matches or shows feature comic-book like heroes in outlandish costumes with tremendously muscled bodies and theatrical personas fighting towards a predetermined outcome. Using a combination of flying leaps, precision acrobatics, and wrestling holds, they act out elaborate story lines where they hit each other with chairs and barbed wire, jump off of cages, and win by violating a set of nonexistent rules. Today's TV wrestling is often called "fake" because, first of all, the wrestlers don't intentionally hurt or kill each other. And second, the winners are predetermined, with the championship belt changing hands at the combined whim of the fans and the promoters. Alas, it was not always that way. Professional wrestling used to be real.

Wrestling competitions have been held in the USA since 1680, with famous historical figures taking part, including Presidents George Washington and Abraham Lincoln. "Lincoln typified early rural American wrestling in which an out of town challenger took on a local strongman."[303]

The US military also played its part in the evolution of the wrestling we see today. The US Civil War (1861-1865) attracted men from all over the world, some seeking adventure and some seeking US citizenship.[304] Angry young men from Ireland joined the US Civil War to gain training and experience that they could use in their own war against the British. British and Irish immigrants or soldiers of fortune, fighting in the Civil War, most likely brought British Empire wrestling styles, including Irish collar-and-elbow wrestling, Greco-Roman, Pehlwani Indian wrestling, and Lancashire catch wrestling to the US. Soldiers often engaged in wrestling matches to pass the time, or as part of training; and in this way, these styles were passed from man-to-man and country-to-country, with the most effective techniques being absorbed into what would become a new, American style of wrestling.

After the war ended, for those who remained in the US, jobs were difficult to find, especially in the Southern United States, where the economy and infrastructure were completely destroyed. As such, the carnival became an attractive option for young men. "Thousands of men used the combative skills they learned as youths and joined carnivals and traveling circuses as wrestlers and strongmen."[305] These travelling carnivals went to all parts of the US, which again helped spread European wrestling techniques to America, while absorbing regional wrestling styles from the US.

In the carnival wrestling system, a carnival would roll into town, offering cash rewards for the bravest and strongest men of the town to take on the wrestlers, called hookers or shooters, who represented the carnival.[306] The rules of these matches varied from place to place and time to time. Regardless of the specific rules, a joint lock submission was the most reliable way to win. Unsurprisingly, hookers and shooters who won all of their matches were paid better than those who lost, so it was generally in the best interest of the carnival wrestlers to keep improving and keep winning. Carnival wrestlers would take on multiple opponents each night, until the carnival moved on to the next town, where the process would start all over again. The sheer number and geographic scope of these matches resulted in the rapid development of American style wrestling.

By the 1880s, professional wrestling had become a big money sport.[307] Prior to World War I, wrestling was one of the most popular spectator sports of the Western world, on par with boxing, baseball, and horse racing. Wrestling combined strength and violence as contenders grappled to win two of three falls. Propelled by the rise of mass culture and mass communication, wrestling enjoyed a status unparalleled among other sports of the time. As a symbol of masculinity and nationalism, wrestling found a large audience in both North America and Europe.

The period of real professional wrestling runs from about the end of the American Civil War, 1865, to the mid 1920s. The biggest matches involving popular champions, such as Frank Gotch or George Hackenschmidt, drew massive crowds of spectators as well as attention from the international press. During wrestling's heyday, fans filled tremendous venues such as Madison Square Garden to watch wrestling matches which were true athletic contests, pitting two well-trained wrestlers against each other in one of two styles, Greco-Roman or catch wrestling. The wrestling contests held in Madison Square Garden were noble affairs, with high ticket prices.

Even when wrestling was real, wrestling always had a shady part it. During the pre-World War I era, the matches were often fixed for financial gain. However, they differ from modern "sports entertainment" in that early 20th century wrestlers were genuinely wrestlers. They were real men who had real skill in the sport of wrestling. After wrestling became "sports entertainment," the "wrestlers" doing the fake wrestling were more often bodybuilders, football players, and weightlifters.[308]

During the heyday of real professional wrestling, there were three primary styles, collar and elbow wrestling, Greco-Roman wrestling, and catch wrestling or "catch as catch can," which was also called Lancashire Wrestling.

Collar and elbow wrestling has its origins in Ireland. The name comes from the starting position. Opponents began the match gripping each other with one hand on the collar and one hand on the elbow. This same basic position is used in professional TV wrestling today, but not in Olympic-style wrestling.[309] In this way, it could be said that collar and elbow had a significant influence on modern professional wrestling.[310] The goal in collar and elbow wrestling is to throw your opponent on the ground and pin him for three seconds, the same as modern wrestling. However, with no system of points and no time limits, these matches could sometimes last for hours.[311]

Greco-Roman wrestling has similar victory conditions, of throwing the opponent to the ground and pinning him for three seconds. Thus, it requires tremendous upper body strength, because it is against the rules to attack the legs with either the hands or the legs. Although Greco-Roman remains an Olympic and collegiate sport today, it was Lancashire catch wrestling that for several decades was the most popular professional style, because fans felt the rules of Greco-Roman were too restrictive. Spectators were much more excited to watch the more violent catch wrestling, where matches could be won by throws, pins, or submissions. Consequently, it was catch that dominated the era of real professional wrestling.

The roots of catch wrestling can be traced to around the year 1490, in Lancashire, England, where catch-as-catch-can wrestling proved to be superior in matches against other wrestling styles.[312] "In the Queen's odd English, it was called catch or catch-as-catch-can wrestling, meaning, catch any opportunity you can to win."[313] Catch reached its peak during the 19th century, when Lancashire coal miners spent their free time wrestling and betting on wrestling. Blue collar men have always wrestled, but this style of Lancashire wrestling was one of the most brutal of all time.[314]

Catch contains a combination of traditional freestyle wrestling and Greco-Roman takedowns and pins, as well as joint locks and submissions.[315] In a submission, the attacker twists the joints of his opponent's arm, leg, or neck, until the opponent quits. In the old days of catch, an opponent could quit by saying the word "uncle." In an interview with grappling master 'Sambo Steve' Koepfer, he explained that "Saying 'uncle' was used to verbally give up. It comes from the Irish word 'anacol', meaning 'mercy', and was brought to America by Irish immigrants"

In the mid to late 19th century, catch met with a great deal of opposition due to the sheer violence involved. "With regard to Lancashire wrestling, there can be no question that it is the most barbarous of the English systems and more nearly approaches the French dog-fighting and tumbling than any other – – a fair stand up fight with the naked fists is the merest skim milk, in fact a perfect drawing room entertainment, in comparison."[316]

Catch is not the only submission art. Today, the most widely practiced submission grappling art is Brazilian jujitsu (BJJ), which evolved out of Japanese judo. While catch and BJJ are often compared, Jiu-jitsu translates to "the gentle art" and Judo translates to "the gentle way." Catch, on the other hand, is regarded throughout the world as "the violent art,"[317]

Where judo and jujitsu were designed so that a smaller man could defeat a bigger man, catch is wrestling, and wrestling requires the application of brute strength. For this reason, catch employs leverage and physics, but also domination and pain compliance.[318] Attacks on pressure points are used to keep the opponent on the defensive and set up finishing techniques.[319] Despite the nature of catch, catch wrestlers are not mere sadistic brutes. They must have a good understanding of body mechanics, and demonstrate flexibility and creative innovation in discovering applications of the finishing holds from all positions and in all situations.[320] Catch relies on a strategy of transitioning from one attempted submission to the next, until the wrestler succeeds in achieving the exact submission intended.

In the first modern Olympics, in 1896, Greco-Roman wrestling was chosen over catch. Whilst catch was more popular than Greco-Roman, it was deemed too violent for the Olympics. By the turn of the 20th Century, however, catch had become so popular that the Olympic committee was willing to ignore the violence and so, catch was added to the 1904 Olympic Games.[321]

The rules for professional catch wrestling were two-out-of-three falls, no time limit, and no-holds-barred. Falls could be assessed on either submissions or pins. Interestingly, the term "no holds barred" originally comes from catch wrestling, meaning that opponents would be allowed to use any techniques or any submission that they want in order to win. In order to adapt the sport for the 1904 Olympics, the AAU designed a new set of rules, using a single elimination tournament format with a six-minute time limit, plus a three-minute overtime. In the case that neither wrestler scored a submission victory, the judges would render a decision. There were seven weight classes. Moving away from the traditional "no-holds-barred tournament" format, certain painful catch wrestling techniques called "torture holds" were banned.[322]

As Americans were the only entrants in the wrestling category in the 1904 Olympic Games, the games also served as the American Amateur Athletic Union (AAU) championships.[323] A nice point of Olympic history trivia is that the US won 100 percent of the wrestling medals in 1904.

In the 1908 London Olympic games, both Greco-Roman and catch wrestling events were included. Catch made its next and final appearance in the Olympics in 1920. In 1922, both the Amateur Athletic Union (AAU) and the International Federation of Associated Wrestling (FILA) abandoned catch. Instead, freestyle and Greco-Roman wrestling would become the focus for American wrestlers.[324] While this marked the end of amateur catch wrestling, it still survived as a professional sport.[325]

In recent years, because of the popularity of mixed martial arts (MMA), there has been a resurgence of interest among fans in this dynamic and effective form of wrestling. They are generally shocked to learn that nearly a hundred years ago, catch used to be an Olympic sport.[326]

The Men Who Made Catch Wrestling Famous

Parallel to the development of catch in America, there was a wrestler called The Great Gama (1878 –1960). Known as "The Lion of the Punjab," The Great Gama is probably the best example of Indian Pehlwani wrestling, one of the many wrestling styles which influenced modern catch.

The Great Gama was born Ghulam Muhammad in 1880, in the Punjab, British India. At age 19, Gama stood 170 cm (5'5") tall and weighed 102 kg (225 lb.). Famously, he wrestled against India's reigning champion, Sultaniwala, who was 213 cm tall (6'10"), in a match which lasted eight hours and ended in a draw. After easily defeating all other Indian wrestlers, Gama went to Europe, where he extended a challenge to all comers, winning all of his matches.[327]

In the 1910 John Bull World Championship held in London, Gama wrestled Stanislaus Zbyszko, the Polish strongman who was the two-time world wrestling champion. Gama took Zbyszko down quickly. Finding no way to overcome Gama, Zbysko remained on his back for two and a half hours, fighting from a defensive position. At the three hour mark, the match was finally called a draw.[328] A rematch was scheduled, but Zbyszko didn't show up. So, Gama was awarded a purse of 250 pounds. He was also awarded the John Bull Belt, which meant that Gama could now claim to be the World Champion.[329] As great as Gama was, it is important to understand that in 1910, there was no unified world championship belt. While Gama had beaten every wrestler in India and England, he hadn't been to America or wrestled the American champions such as Frank Gotch. Allegedly, Gama extended challenges to the Americans, but they were never taken up.

Although Gama wasn't a world champion in the truest sense, his wrestling skill and his fight record were still incredible. "The Great Gama may be the only wrestler ever to remain undefeated throughout his professional career of over 5000 matches."[330]

As with any great fighter who accumulates a lengthy string of wins, The Great Gama was having trouble finding opponents. "After going for five years in the 1920s without being able to get an opponent, Gama finally got another crack at Stan Zbyszko, in 1928."[331] Gama won in less than one minute.[332]

Gama's strength was the stuff of legends. The Baroda Museum in Sayaji Baug displays a 2.5 feet cubical stone weighing 1200 kg (2,645 lb.), which Gama lifted in a public display on December 23, 1902.[333] Gama followed a Spartan training regimen which may be the reason for his impressive strength. He wrestled with as many as 40 training partners each day, and did 5000 Hindu squats and 3000 Hindu pushups. His strength training also consisted of traditional Indian exercise, such as lifting and manipulating heavily weighted mace balls and clubs. Today, a 95 kg (209.5 lb.) disc which Gama used for his workouts can be found at the National Institute of Sports Museum in Patiala, India.[334] This intense training regimen was accompanied by a specialized diet which consisted of 7.5 liters of milk daily, a great deal of fruit, and a pound and a half of crushed almonds blended with fruit juices.[335]

After 50 years of wrestling, Gama retired in 1952, completely undefeated. He was later commemorated as a character in the computer game, "Shadow Hearts: Covenant," and was the inspiration for the character "Darun Mister" in *Street Fighter EX*. Gama was one of the famous fighters who Bruce Lee researched and emulated, adopting many of Gama's strength training techniques.[336]

William Muldoon

"At the turn of the 19th century, William Muldoon was seen as the epitome of a professional wrestler."[337]

Although there was no unified title belt, and limited communication across the US in the 19th Century, the Greco-Roman wrestler William Muldoon (1852 – 1933) is considered to be America's first world wrestling champion. A policeman by profession, Muldoon was so popular as a wrestler that he actually is considered by many to have been the first professional athlete when, in 1881, he retired from the police force to become a fulltime wrestler and trainer.[338]

William Muldoon was born in upstate New York in 1852 to Irish immigrant parents. For some unknown reason, Muldoon claimed for years that his birth year was 1845, although it has been verified to be 1852. As a boy, he loved wrestling, and read extensively on the subject. At the age of 16, he signed up to fight in the American Civil War. Here, he wrestled soldiers he served with, and was so successful he was eventually called the champion of his regiment.[339]

Muldoon was just 20 years old when the war ended. Like many men of the era, he had trouble settling down. Eventually, he landed in New York City, where he worked as a bouncer. He heard about a nearby wrestling club and won his first professional match for $15. Muldoon developed a great reputation, due to the number of matches he won. He was hired to wrestle at Harry Hill's Club, a night club for the wealthy, which featured dinner, drinks, and boxing and wrestling shows.[340]

Muldoon joined the New York City police force in 1876, and was instrumental in founding the first Police Athletic League (PAL), a low cost or even free club designed to keep kids off the streets by offering them opportunities to train and compete in sports.[341]

A religious man, Muldoon neither drank alcohol nor smoked cigarettes. He was known, however, for having an explosive temper. Once, during his match against a Frenchman, the crowd began yelling "Break the Frenchie's' neck!" Muldoon actually stopped fighting long enough to criticize the crowd, telling them that their behavior showed bad sportsmanship.[342] Perhaps being dedicated to clean living and good morals was one of the reasons why he was so successful in the ring. In February of 1877, Muldoon defeated Andre Christol, winning the American heavyweight Greco-Roman wrestling championship. On January 19, 1880, he defeated Thiebaud Bauer, winning the world Greco-Roman championship title.[343]

Muldoon's fame grew and grew as a result of his excellence in the ring. Once, Muldoon was scheduled to wrestle a challenger from England named "Bibby," but the police chief wouldn't let him finish work early. As the Englishman was bragging that Muldoon was afraid, Muldoon got into the ring, wearing his police uniform. Muldoon won in less than one minute. Muldoon also won two more matches against famous wrestlers Sebastian Miller and John Gaffney. After these wins, Richard K. Fox, publisher of the Police Gazette, awarded William Muldoon with a gold pin, recognizing him as the first world champion in Greco-Roman.[344] At that time, the Police Gazette was the largest newspaper in America, and was also the first newspaper to carry regular sports coverage.[345]

Muldoon's famous rivalry with Clarence Whistler also contributed to his status among the American public. In 1881, Muldoon wrestled against Clarence Whistler in Greco-Roman wrestling. After 8 hours and 10 minutes, the match was declared a draw. A year later, they competed against each other again, in collar and elbow style wrestling. Once again, the match was a draw. In 1883, they wrestled a third and final time. At one point, Clarence Whistler threw Muldoon out of the ring. But Muldoon jumped back in, slamming Whistler so hard into the mat, that his collar bone was broken. Muldoon had finally won, and he returned to New York as a national hero.

Muldoon kept his world Greco-Roman wrestling title until he retired from the discipline in 1887, when he handed the championship to his student, Earnest Robert, from Brooklyn, New York.[346]

Following his retirement, Muldoon became a famous trainer, and in 1889, heavyweight bare-knuckle boxing champion, John L. Sullivan, hired Muldoon to train him for his final defense of the heavyweight title against the much younger and fitter Jack Kilrain. At the time, "Sullivan" was fifty pounds overweight. The ageing Sullivan was also wrecked from a combination of heavy drinking, old age, womanizing and partying. No sports writers believed Sullivan stood a chance. But with Muldoon as his trainer, John L. Sullivan won the match and remains the last heavyweight bare-knuckles boxing champion of the world.[347]

Muldoon continued to wrestle in competitions until 1892, when he finally retired, completely undefeated. He died in 1933 at the age of 81.[348]

Frank Gotch

Frank Gotch (1877-1917) is the man most often credited with popularizing professional wrestling in the US.[349] The first American heavyweight professional freestyle champion, he was World Heavyweight Wrestling Champion (from 1908 to 1913). Many Americans still consider Frank Gotch to be the best wrestler who has ever lived.[350]

Gotch was born in Humboldt, Iowa, the state most famous for wrestling in the USA. Many in Iowa today attribute Iowa's dominance in high school and collegiate wrestling to Frank Gotch. "We had people in this state of Iowa, before organized high school wrestling even existed, that were great wrestlers, world champions. And one of the most famous athletes of all time was Frank Gotch...I would compare the Frank Gotch legacy to that of Michael Jordan or Muhammad Ali."[351]

Gotch's parents were farmers, and he grew up working long hours on the farm. Professional baseball was only just beginning in the US. No one had heard of basketball, and so young boys grew up admiring the bare-knuckle prize fighters. Frank Gotch's hero was John L. Sullivan, and he hoped one day to be a world champion himself.[352]

Frank Gotch learned catch wrestling from an early age, and by the time he was 19, he was considered one of the best wrestlers in Humboldt. In 1899, Gotch entered his first professional wrestling match against Marshall Green. Green was seven years older than Gotch and considered to be the number one wrestler in Humboldt. The match was hotly contested, and Frank Gotch won by using a painful headlock. After that, Frank had a reputation, in his hometown, for being unbeatable. This reputation stood until a professional wrestler named Dan McLeod, who had been considered the American champion for a number of years, came to a nearby town to wrestle all comers. McLeod and Gotch wrestled for two hours on a cinder track before McLeod finally won. After the match, McLeod told Gotch he thought Gotch could become world champion with the right training.[353]

A month later, Gotch met "Farmer" Martin Burns, a man who has been called the greatest wrestling trainer of all time. Farmer Burns was sixteen years older than Gotch and also from Iowa. He began wrestling as a child and won his first important match while wearing his farmer clothes. Hence the nickname "farmer." In 1899, Burns wrestled Gotch twice. Gotch lost both bouts, but Burns was so impressed by Gotch's skill that he agreed to train Gotch and help him become the world champion.

Burns taught Gotch the toe hold, which became his signature finishing move. Gotch travelled to Alaska, where he won his first title, Champion of the Klondike.[354] He then returned to Iowa, winning the state wrestling championship and beating all the professional wrestlers in the Midwest. "Outside the ring, Frank Gotch was a very humble, easygoing individual, but he was a fierce competitor that had a tremendous mean streak. He was brutal."[355]

As humble as Gotch was outside the ring, inside he was tough and brutal. Whilst travelling the country, Gotch had a group of young wrestlers who trained with him and wrestled in shows for money. At one event, a foreign wrestler came to town and offered to fight all comers. He was very unforgiving, and he severely injured some of Frank's students, even breaking their bones. In response, Gotch disguised himself as a businessman and went to the theater and accepted the challenge to wrestle this foreigner. He changed into his wrestling clothes and he broke both shoulders of his foreign opponent. The foreigner never wrestled again.[356]

By today's standards, Frank was small for a heavyweight. He was only 180 cm (5' 9") and 95 kgkg (198.5 lLb.). Despite this, he is recognized by many experts as one of the greatest wrestlers who ever lived. In the book, *From Milo to Londos: The Story of Wrestling Through the Ages*, writer Nat Fleischer states "Gotch was…a superior wrestler, possessing tremendous strength, lightning quickness, genuine agility, cat-like reflexes, impeccable technique, superb ring generalship, a mastery of the use of leverage."[357] Fleischer goes on to credit Gotch with a vast knowledge of submission holds, and of always being in the best physical condition. "He was highly aggressive, but always remained calm. He had both the strength of the ancient wrestlers and the skill of the modern wrestlers. He was so competent in his wrestling skill that he could not be compared to any other wrestler."[358]

In 1900, Frank decided he was ready to compete for the American championship title. The current champion was an extremely tough steel worker from Cleveland, Ohio, named Tom Jenkins, an extremely powerful and rough individual. The first time they competed, Jenkins won by a small margin. In the 1904, rematch, although Frank Gotch was about 15 pounds lighter than Jenkins, he was in better shape, as he had had prepared diligently for the match. It was called the most brutal wrestling match of all time, and ended with Frank Gotch winning the title.[359]

Over the next several years, Gotch won and lost the American Heavyweight title several times, competing with Jenkins and a wrestler named Fred Beell. In 1908, Gotch got the opportunity to compete for the World Heavyweight Championship belt, held by Georg Hackenschmidt.

George Hackenschmidt was born in Estonia in the same year as Gotch. He grew up in Saint Petersburg, Russia where he became a champion weightlifter. Although he had set many records in weightlifting, he switched to wrestling, because he could make more money. Due to his incredible strength, he won dozens of wrestling titles. In 1903, he defeated a giant Turkish wrestler named Madrilly in London in less than a minute, with a powerful bear hug. With that win, Hackenschmidt acquired the nickname, "The Russian Lion." He became the most recognized heavyweight champion of the world and the most popular athlete in Europe. Eventually, the crowd called for a match between Gotch and Hackenschmidt.[360]

A crowd of approximately 8,000 turned out to watch the match on April 3rd, 1908, in Chicago. Many experts thought that Gotch, an Iowa farm boy, stood no chance against the ferocious Russian Lion. The match was extremely important to the development of wrestling, as it pitted the Greco-Roman wrestling style of Europe against the catch wrestling style of America.[361]

Gotch's friends from Humboldt believed he could win, and so did he. Using strategy learned from Farmer Burns, Gotch wore his opponent down. For just over two hours, Gotch pushed, moved, and frustrated Hackenschmidt, breaking Hackenschmidt mentally. Finally, The Russian Lion gave up the championship and Frank Gotch became the new champion of the world.[362]

After his world title win, Gotch also became one of the most popular athletes in America. Back in his hometown, there was a huge celebration. Frank's victory was so massive that high schools and colleges across the USA began adding wrestling teams. Gotch became a star, and even appeared in Broadway plays. President Teddy Roosevelt even invited Gotch to the White House and asked him to wrestle a Japanese jujitsu master, who had been giving lessons to the president. Gotch defeated the jujitsu master easily.[363]

Hackenschimdt returned to Europe and complained that Gotch had cheated. On September 4th, 1911, they had a rematch in front of a crowd of 30,000. During the three years between their two matches, Gotch had trained furiously, improving his skills. He won two of three falls in just 28 minutes.[364]

In his book, *100 Greatest Sports Heroes*, author Mac Davis wrote that Frank Gotch was loved by millions of people in the United States Canada and Mexico.[365] Davis credited Gotch with making wrestling a big sport. Davis went on to say that Gotch had babies, buildings, toys and even farm implements named in his honor. "The word Gotch was a synonym for quality and strength."[366]

In 1916, Gotch became extremely ill with kidney problems. He lost about 20 kg (44 lb.) of body weight and died on December 17, 1917, at the age of 39. On the day he died, stores and schools across Iowa closed. Thousands of people came to mourn his death.

Frank Gotch is responsible for wrestling becoming one of the most popular collegiate and scholastic sports across the country and embedding wrestling into the very fabric of his home state of Iowa. Iowa is the site of the nation's largest high school wrestling tournaments, and Iowa's success at collegiate level is impressive. Five of Iowa's universities have won national wrestling championships. University of Iowa and Iowa State University have won 25 National Collegiate Athletic Association (NCAA) championships, and University of Iowa has won 15 of the last 21. In addition, the city of Humboldt, Gotch's birthplace, hosts The Frank Gotch Youth Wrestling Tournament, which typically draws more than 300 participants. Amazing when one considers that Humboldt only has a population of about 4,400 people.[367]

The Gotch legacy has spawned other Iowa wrestling legends, such as Olympic gold medalist Dan Gable (who will be discussed at length later in this book), who wrestled 181 matches in high school and at Iowa State, with only one loss.

"Frank Gotch's legacy will live forever. Every time a wrestler takes to the mat anywhere in the state of Iowa or across the United States, the spirit of Frank Gotch is there."[368]

Earl Caddock

Earl Caddock (1888-1950), called "The Man of a Thousand Holds" (holds at that time were synonymous with submissions today), is seen by many as the best example of a champion from the era when professional wrestling was real.[369]

Earl Caddock was born in Huron, South Dakota on February 27, 1888. Caddock was sickly as a child, and after the family moved to Chicago, a doctor recommended he exercise at a local Young Men's Christian Association (YMCA), a low-cost gymnasium for young people across the world. After training in swimming, gymnastics, and wrestling, his health improved. He found his favorite sport was wrestling, and he read everything he could on the subject. He spent much of his free time perfecting the holds he learned from books, and even invented some of his own.[370]

In 1902, Caddock's father died and was sent to Iowa to work on his uncle's farm. In Iowa he continued to train and wrestle, winning numerous local championships. Caddock returned to Chicago to attend college at the Hebrew Institute, where he competed as a member of the wrestling team. Between 1909 and 1915 he won more amateur championships, at both middleweight and light heavyweight. He won the 1914 American Athletic Union (AAU) wrestling championship, in both light heavyweight and heavyweight. By the age of 27, Caddock "was viewed as the best amateur catch-as-catch-can wrestler in the world."[371] That's when he decided to become a professional wrestler.

His first professional match was a two-pin, one-hour time limit match in 1915, which he won. The same year, Caddock watched Joe Stecher, the Scissors King, win the World Title. Years earlier, Stecher had once beaten Caddock 2-falls-to-1, back in Iowa.[372] Since then, neither had had lost by pin. Over the next two years Caddock beat 23 opponents, with 46 consecutive pins. During all these matches, Caddock never lost a pin. Around this time, Caddock acquired a manager named Gene Malardy. It was Gene Malardy who gave Caddock the name "The Man of a Thousand Holds." Small for a heavyweight, at only 79 kg (174 lb.), Caddock's opponents often outweighed him by up to 20 kg (44 lb.). Caddock was able to win, however, because of his superior technique and use of holds.[373]

Caddock was famous for knowing a tremendous number of submission holds. If he couldn't win using one hold, he would try another, and another, until he won. One of his greatest strengths was his variety of techniques. Greco-Roman wrestling champion William Muldoon once said that it wasn't true that Caddock was "The Man of a Thousand Holds"; in Muldoon's opinion, Caddock knew "ten thousand holds."[374]

Malardy sent Caddock to learn professional wrestling from Martin "Farmer" Burns and Frank Gotch. Burns, a former American champion, was generally recognized as the best catch wrestling teacher in the world, and his student, Frank Gotch, was widely considered the greatest wrestler since Milos of Croton. In 1916, Caddock traveled with Burns and Gotch in the Sells-Floto circus, learning everything he could from them.[375]

Frank Gotch was originally scheduled to wrestle a man named Stecher. Sadly, Gotch broke his leg during training and died shortly after. This left Caddock as the next best choice to fight Stecher. Both men were completely undefeated. The men wrestled on April 9,

1917 in Omaha, Nebraska, in front of a crowd of almost 8,000 spectators. Most sports writers believed Caddock would lose. Unknown to them, however, he was very well trained, thanks to his coaching from Farmer Burns.[376]

An hour and twenty minutes into the match, Caddock fell out of the ring and hit his head. When he got back in the ring, he was quickly pinned by Stecher, who used his famous scissors lock, a submission hold where he wrapped his legs around Caddock's midsection. Unable to breathe, Caddock had no choice but to submit, for the first time in his career. The match resumed ten minutes later.[377]

Caddock won the second fall after one hour and forty minutes. The two men went back to their dressing room to rest and wait for the third fall. But Stecher was unable to continue, because he was simply too tired. He later told interviewers that when he was wrestling Caddock, he felt he was wrestling 5 men. Caddock was declared the new Heavyweight Champion of the World.

When the US declared war on Germany, entering World War One, Caddock volunteered for the army and wrestled in exhibition matches for the benefit of the Red Cross. When his unit was sent to the front, his wrestling career had to be interrupted.[378] In the war, Caddock experienced combat, endured harsh living conditions, and was subjected to poison gas attacks by the Germans. After the war, in 1920, Caddock returned to wrestling with a rematch against Joe Stretcher. Stretcher had been a sailor and Caddock a soldier, so the fight was billed as a battle between the armed services. The purse for this fight was $40,000. The match was held on January 30th, 1920 in New York City's Madison Square Garden. There were nearly 10,000 spectators and the ticket sales totaled nearly $100,000. Ringside seats cost $22. The match lasted almost two hours. Finally, Stecher won, and was declared the new heavyweight champion of the world.[379]

Caddock continued to wrestle and won most of his matches, except for his numerous attempts to regain the world heavyweight title. His final match was held on June 7, 1922, against heavyweight champion Ed Strangler Lewis. Caddock won one fall, but lost the match. Earl Caddock, "The Man of a Thousand Holds," died on August 25th, 1950, at age 62. To this day, he is considered the last legitimate professional wrestling champion of the world.[380]

After the Lewis vs. Caddock match, and through the 1920s, catch wrestling in America began to transition into the TV style wrestling entertainment which can be seen today in the World Wrestling Entertainment (WWE). But in Europe, real catch wrestling continued.

Billy Robinson

Billy Robinson, considered to be the best catch wrestler in England, was born in 1939. He had always dreamed of being a boxer, but a childhood injury damaged one of his eyes, and he was unable to pursue boxing. His uncle introduced him to wrestling, and he loved the sport.[381]

Billy Robinson had huge success with wrestling. In 1957, he won the British National Wrestling Championship, and in 1958 he became the European Open Wrestling Champion in the light heavyweight division. He was trained at the Snake Pit, the most famous gym for catch wrestling in the world, by Billy Riley. He became British Heavyweight Champion on January 18, 1967, and held that title for three years before voluntarily giving it up so that he could go to America and wrestle in the American Wrestling Association (AWA).[382] Transitioning to the AWA meant that Robinson was now wrestling in a TV wrestling association.

Robinson quickly became one of the best wrestlers in the AWA and won many titles. With the AWA, he traveled around the world, including Australia and Japan, where he wrestled against "Antonio Inoki," a famous Japanese wrestler who also wrestled against Muhammad Ali. In Japan, he was famous for fake wrestling as well as catch wrestling. At the Snake Pit Japan wrestling training academy, he helped coach the Japanese "shoot fighting" wrestlers. He also trained a number of famous MMA fighters such as Kazushi Sakuraba, Kiyoshi Tamura, and Josh Barnett. At the time of writing, 2017, he was still training new wrestlers and overseeing the training at Snake Pit USA.[383]

Karl Gotch

The Snake Pit became the premier catch wrestling academy, producing one of the most famous catch wrestlerd, Karl Gotch (1924–2007).[384] Karl Gotch is not to be confused with the great catch wrestler, Frank Gotch, who had been a world champion of legitimate catch wrestling half a century earlier. Karl Gotch was born in 1924, in Belgium, around the time that legitimate catch wrestling was in decline in America. Karl would go on to become famous as both a catch wrestler and a WWE style TV wrestler.

When Karl Gotch was 4 years old, his family moved to Hamburg, Germany. Aged nine, he discovered wrestling, and began training in wrestling clubs around Hamburg. Some of the details of his early life are obscured, but there are reports that he was interred in a concentration camp during World War II.[385]

In 1948, Gotch wrestled in the Olympics, using his birth name, Charles Istaz. Afterwards, he trained for 8 years at The Snake Pit in England. In 1959, he moved to America, where he changed his name to Karl Gotch, presumably in honor of the great catch wrestler Frank Gotch.[386]

Karl Gotch trained incessantly, and was known as a great technical wrestler. Karl Gotch did not lift weights, because he believed having too much muscle would cause him to lose flexibility and speed. Instead, he used a series of routines of calisthenics he learned from an Indian Pehlwani wrestler. In a1968 interview, Gotch said his exercise routine included 300 Hindu squats and 75 to 100 tiger-bend push-ups, followed by front and back bridges and abdominal exercises."[387]

In 1972, Karl Gotch went to Japan, where, for the next ten years, he taught wrestling to famous Japanese professional WWE style wrestlers, such as Antonio Inoki. In 1976, Inoki promoted a series of MMA style bouts against the champions of other martial arts, including Inoki's famous fight with the greatest boxer of all time, Muhammad Ali. From the 1920s to the 1950s, in the US, catch wrestling transitioned from real to fake WWE wrestling. However, in the 1990s, when MMA came to the US, it was 100 percent real, and is still real today. In contrast, in Japan, many of the MMA fights were fake, not dissimilar to American TV wrestling. Foreign and Japanese fighters in Japan were routinely paid to do a "worked match" or take a dive. MMA and Brazilian Jujitsu fighter, Renzo Gracie, was fighting in Japan at that time, and famously refused to fight in "worked matches."[388]

Questions about the authenticity of fights in Japan abound. Martial arts author, and legend, Donn F. Draeger, was quoted in *The Guardian* newspaper as saying, "Inoki's recent 'defeat' of Ruska was a farce. Ruska could kill him."[389] Draeger was referring to Inoki's fight against judo champion Willem "Wim" Ruska. The fight was billed as real, but many people, including Draeger, believed that it had to have been worked, because Willem Ruska was a legitimate champion who should have destroyed Inoki, a fake wrestler. Draeger went on to say that the Ali fight was a publicity gimmick. "If Inoki insists on it being real, the thing will never take place."[390] Real or not, these events were a chance for Inoki to demonstrate the techniques he learned from Karl Gotch. Despite the controversy, these events were incredibly popular in Japan.[391] They are also important milestones in the evolution of catch wrestling from real, to fake, and then back to real again, with MMA.

The Flying Frenchman

Part of the culture of wrestling in the US is the culture of immigration. Many of the wrestlers discussed in this chapter were born in foreign countries, but immigrated to America, bringing their specialized skills with them. They each added something to the development of wrestling in America, and this next section is about one such man.

The Flying Frenchman, Édouard Carpentier (1926 – 2010), was a European wrestler who brought gymnastics and acrobatics to American professional wrestling. Early fake wrestling of the 1950s was an extension of catch wrestling, and generally looked more or less like a catch wrestling match, with wrestlers taking holds and transitioning from one attempted submission to the other, until they had reached a predetermined conclusion. Toady, WWE wrestling contains a great deal of flying, leaping, and acrobatics. Much of this physical display can be traced to The Flying Frenchman.

The Flying Frenchman was born in 1926 in France to Russian parents. Originally called Edouard Ignacz Weiczorkiewicz, he later changed his name to The Flying Frenchman, Edouard Carpentier.[392] During WWII, while still a teenager, he joined the Resistance and fought against the Nazis. He was captured and incarcerated in a concentration camp. After the war, the French government awarded him a medal for bravery. He later competed in the Olympics, twice, on the French gymnastics team.[393]

By incorporating his gymnastic skills into his professional wrestling career, he changed the face of wrestling forever. In 1956, he was crowned wrestling champion of Europe. Having been victorious in Europe, he then travelled across the Atlantic to the United States. In 1957, he defeated Lou Thesz, in Chicago, to become the NWA Heavyweight Wrestling Champion.[394]

The Flying Frenchman wrestled in America through the 1970s, permanently cementing his place in wrestling history.

The Business of Wrestling

One of the main reasons why catch wrestling transitioned from real to fake was money.

The businessmen behind professional wrestling were the promoters. They organized the competitions and paid the wrestlers and bore expenses. The promoters also kept a large percentage of the money from ticket sales. Most of these fight events included both boxing and wrestling. They were often held in bars, where spectators paid money to watch. But in 1880, the sport had become so popular that the first stadium fight was held in Madison Square Garden Arena in New York City.[395]

The first professional wrestling association established in the USA was The National Wrestling Alliance (NWA). At first, the group tried to create a consistent set of rules and a unified championship. However, in time, the group held so much control over the business of wrestling that the US government intervened. They were found in violation of the Sherman Act, a law which prevented the formation of monopolies. In 1959, the US government forced the NWA to change its policies.[396]

In the first half of the 20th Century, wrestling became an international sport, largely controlled by the NWA.[397] The NWA sanctioned the first world champion of wrestling when Frank Gotch defeated Hackenschmidt, an event which took in $90,000 in ticket sales. Wrestling was big business, but the sport needed to be adapted to meet the audience's tastes. Initially, matches ran for hours, sometimes as long as 8 or even 11 hours. So, it was difficult for fans to watch an entire match. Another issue was that the rules were different from city to city and place to place. Thus, it was decided that wrestling needed time limits and a unified set of rules.[398]

Although unified rules and time limits were added, eventually, audiences grew bored of real catch wrestling matches. In the mid 1920s, professional catch wrestling gave way to fake professional WWE style wrestling, as see on TV today. The new "fake" wrestling was faster paced, and benefitted from outrageous characters and storylines. Fake wrestling made a lot of money from ticket sales and benefited from the ability to create ongoing feuds and storylines which could be repeated night after night in travelling shows, or sent out over the new medium of television to millions of viewers.

And so, real wrestling was in hibernation. Real catch died in the mid-1920s, giving way to fake wrestling, but it would reawaken in the 1990s, thanks to MMA.

After catching the kick, a sanda fighter lifts his opponent for a single-leg throw.

Driving through for a one-point takedown.

Catching the kick and going for a single-leg takedown.

Resisting the takedown.

Traditional wrestling team,
Beijing.

Shuaijiao competition

Two points.

Chinese traditional shuai jiao
competition.

A one-point throw.

Careful not to let the knee
touch the ground or the throw
will not count.

Shanghai University of Sport
traditional wrestling team, 2013

Deep single-leg takedown.

A universal throw utilized in Greco-Roman

Taking the opponent down from behind, without tripping his legs

Setup and unbalancing before the throw.

Controlling the opponent by gripping the head and underarm.

Chapter 7: Modern Olympic Wrestling

Modern Olympic wrestling includes two styles: Greco-Roman wrestling, and freestyle wrestling. The first modern Olympic Games were held in Athens, Greece, in 1896.[399] But the story of modern Olympic wrestling begins even earlier, in 1848 France, with the invention of Greco-Roman wrestling.[400] Catch wrestling, which came into vogue soon afterwards, had a tremendous influence on the development of freestyle wrestling.

The History of Greco-Roman Wrestling

Although Greco-Roman wrestling was first codified in 1848, the sport had existed for centuries in southern France.[401] The art was originally called "la luttes à mains platte" (open handed wrestling). It was also called "la lutte Romaine" (Roman wrestling) or "la lutte Grecque" (Greek wrestling). With time, the words Greek and Roman were combined and the art became known as Greco-Roman wrestling.[402] In Greco-Roman wrestling, the wrestlers are not permitted to touch their opponent's legs. They also may not choke or use submission holds. Therefore, Greco-Roman wrestling differed from the Olympic wrestling practiced in Ancient Greece.[403] In spite of having no connection to ancient Greek wrestling, the name Greco-Roman stuck.

Wrestling was very popular in France, and wrestlers performed in travelling circuses and other public exhibitions, not dissimilar to the way catch wrestling developed in the US. Eventually, a ruleset was agreed upon, and in 1848, the first world championship was organized

Greco-Roman wrestling matches can be won by a pin. In the absence of a pin, the win is determined by points awarded for throws, escapes, exposing your opponent's back to the ground, and throwing your opponent out of the wrestling circle.[404] Greco-Roman rules place many restrictions on competitors, such as how a wrestler may place his body position, how he can place his head in the clinch, how he can grip, etc. The modern Greco-Roman ruleset is one of the most complex of any sport.[405]

The wrestlers in the first world championship mostly came from Germany, Italy, Turkey and Russia. These wrestlers brought Greco-Roman wrestling back to their home countries, and as the art spread, more and more competitions were held.[406] Although this event was called a world championship, the entire world did not participate. Instead, the 1896 Olympic Games are considered to have been the first truly international Greco-Roman wrestling competition. However, as the Olympics was an amateur competition, and the best wrestlers were professional, the quality of the competitors was comparatively low.[407]

In America, professional wrestling tournaments became increasingly popular as a spectator sport, which people enjoyed betting on. There was, however, no unified American championship tournament.[408] Eventually, William Muldoon (1845-1933), a police officer from New York City, claimed to be the world champion.[409]

Wrestling in the first modern Olympics

Pierre de Coubertin of France, called the father of the modern Olympics, organized the first International Olympic Committee. Coubertin was impressed by the ancient Greek Olympic Games, and wanted to recreate the spirit of international sportsmanship and peace.[410] The committee decided that the modern Olympics would be held every four years, like its ancestor, and be open only to amateur athletes.[411] The Olympic congress chose ten sports for the first modern Olympic Games: athletics, wrestling, rowing, cycling, fencing, gymnastics, weightlifting, swimming, shooting and tennis.[412]

Pierre de Coubertin chose Greco-Roman wrestling for the first Olympics for several reasons, including the name, which he mistakenly believed associated Greco-Roman wrestling with ancient Greece and Rome.[413]

In the end, 241 male athletes from 14 countries participated in the first modern Olympics.[414] In the runup to the event, one reporter from the St. Paul Daily Globe predicted that "Never in the history of the world has there been an athletic event so notable and comprehensive as this one will be."[415] The first modern Olympics may very well be the first truly international event of any kind ever held.

The US was represented by 14 athletes from Princeton University. The rules of the first modern Olympics prevented women from competing.[416] Arriving at the first modern Olympics was difficult. Athletes had to travel across great distances, by sea and land. Transportation problems actually prevented two teams from arriving.[417]

Greco-Roman wrestling was the highlight of the first modern Olympics, just as it had been in the ancient Olympics.[418] Just like those early Olympics, there were no weight categories or time limits, and a wrestler was considered having lost if his back touched the ground.[419] Matches went on as long as they had to, until there was a winner. If no winner could be determined by the end of the day, the match could be halted and recommenced the next day.[420] There were only five competitors in wrestling in the first modern Olympic Games. Carl Schumann of Germany won first place, also winning three medals for gymnastics over the course of the games. Georgios Tsitas, a "pale wrestler" won second place and Greek Stephanos Christopolous won third place. British wrestler, Launceston Elliot placed fourth in wrestling and first in weight lifting. Popavicza of Hungary took fifth place.[421]

In the finals, Carl Schuhmann of Germany defeated the Greek wrestler, Georgios Tsitas, becoming "the first known Olympic wrestling champion since Aurelius Aelix of Phoenicia in 213 AD"[422]

After the First Olympics

In 1897, the first Greco-Roman wrestling world championships were held.[423] The competition was held in Cirque Royale De Bruxelles, and consisted of 118 wrestlers. Frenchman Maurice

90

Gambier was crowned the first champion.[424] The United States held its first national wrestling championship in New York City in 1888.[425]

Wrestling was not included in the 1900 Olympic Games in Paris.[426] Although wrestling had been dropped from the Olympics, professional wrestling remained a popular spectator sport in both America and Europe. Troupes of wrestlers travelled around Europe challenging "all comers." One reason why professional wrestling rather than the Olympic version remained popular was identified by famous French wrestler and trainer, A. Fénélon, who wrote in 1910 that the crowds preferred seeing the powerful muscularity and masculinity of professional wrestling, rather than the proper skill and technique of Olympic wrestling.[427]

In ancient wrestling history, Pankration gave way to catch wrestling, and by the end of the 1920s, catch wrestling had given way to a new American invention, freestyle wrestling.[428]

As stated earlier, catch wrestling was popular as a professional spectacle, but the problem with including catch in the Olympics was that catch had no fixed ruleset. Most of the experienced catch wrestlers travelled from town to town, wrestling in carnivals, with rules dependent on the location. This would not do for a legitimate international sport. Meanwhile, Greco-Roman wrestling now had a fixed ruleset, which allowed for its inclusion in the Olympics.

The problem with Greco, however, was that many spectators felt it was too restrictive, with no attacks allowed to the legs. This set the stage for the development of American freestyle wrestling.[429] Freestyle evolved directly out of catch wrestling. The name freestyle, meaning almost anything goes within the ruleset. Freestyle was exciting, like catch, in the sense that it allowed attacks to legs, but it was deemed safer because it did away with torture holds and submissions.

In Europe, Greco-Roman wrestling was the most popular wrestling style. In America and England, however, freestyle wrestling was growing in popularity.[430] Freestyle wrestling was introduced as the only wrestling discipline in the 1904 Olympics.

Since its inclusion in 1904, wrestling has been included in every modern Olympic Games.[431]

The 1908 Olympics were historically important because the Egyptian wrestler Ibrahim Mustafa became the first African wrestler to win an Olympic title.[432] Olympic Wrestling was truly becoming a global sport. A year later, in 1909, the first Canadian championships were held.[433]

In the 1912 Olympics, Greco-Roman wrestling was the only style featured. In the light heavyweight Greco-Roman wrestling contest, Anders Ahlgren of Sweden and Ivar Bohling of Finland wrestled for 9 hours, without a winner being declared. In the absence of a comprehensive set of rules, the judges awarded both men a silver medal.[434] Amazingly, this was not the longest bout. Another match, between Alfred Asikainen of Finland and Martin Klein of Estonia, lasted 11 hours.[435]

In addition to having no time limits, rulesets differed from country to country, and the Olympic committee had to sift through all of them to come up with a set of rules for the Olympics.[436] After the 1912 Olympics, one of the American wrestlers wrote, "I never saw so many injustices and so many rules broken in my life." Because of the fiasco of the 1912 Olympic wrestling, La Fédération Internationale de Lutte Amateur (FILA), or the International Federation of Amateur Wrestling was founded, to establish and enforce an international set of rules. Originally, FILA recognized and regulated both Greco-Roman and catch wrestling.[437] Today, FILA is one of the largest and most influential sports organizations in the world.[438]

Wrestling in the 1920 Olympic Games included many of the new rules established in 1908; such as five weight classes, time limits, judging and scoring, as well as prohibition of torture holds. The following year, FILA codified the ruleset with their "Rules of the Game."[439] This new set of rules marked the permanent transformation of catch wrestling into freestyle wrestling. Catch was dropped from the Olympics, and was never included again.

In 1922, the American Amateur Athletic Union (AAU) also dropped catch in favor of freestyle and Greco-Roman wrestling. American universities soon followed suit, doing away with catch, and adopting freestyle and Greco-Roman wrestling instead. In 1927, American collegiate wrestling rules were published, including the American collegiate style of wrestling but excluding catch.[440]

The 1952 Helsinki Olympic Games marked another great step in the international development of modern wrestling. Japanese wrestler, Shohachi Ishii, became the first Asian to win a wrestling medal at the Olympics.[441] The same year marked the first time that Russian wrestlers began to compete in the Olympics, quickly becoming recognized as one of the strongest wrestling countries. Other countries with high wrestling medal count include Cuba, Germany, Ukraine, and Poland.[442]

In the 1970s, the Olympics became more popular in America, and the American wrestlers began to excel. Although the US has produced many Olympic medal winners, US folk style wrestling remains the most popular wrestling art in America.[443] In addition to producing some of the most successful wrestlers, America also produced the heaviest wrestler ever to compete in the Olympics. American Chris Mason, who competed in the 1972 super-heavyweight freestyle competition, weighing 184 kg (405.5 Lbs).[444]

Historically, wrestling had been a sport only for men. But, in 1987, the first women's world championships were held.[445] In 2004, Women's freestyle wrestling was introduced to the Olympics.[446] As of 2015, Japanese female wrestlers had claimed four gold medals, Chinese two, and a Ukrainian and a Canadian had claimed one a piece."[447]

The Growth of Olympic Wrestling

The first modern Olympics, held in 1896, consisted of 250 male athletes, from 14 countries, competing in 43 events.[448] In the 2012 London Olympics, 204 countries were represented.[449] In contrast to 1896, the number of athletes competing had swollen to 11,000 across

300 events.[450] With the advent of television, combined with greater levels of prosperity around the world, the Olympics gradually became a truly global event. "The Olympics are the most anticipated international sporting event, viewed in person and on television by more than two billion spectators."[451]

While over 200 countries participate in the Olympics, the overall medal count is dominated by a small handful of powerful countries: US, UK, Russia, China, Germany and Australia. Russia, a leader in the wrestling medal count, has the highest percentage of wrestlers. Of the entire Russian Olympic team, 4 percent of the athletes are wrestlers.[452] The countries with the highest all-time Olympic wrestling medal count are The Soviet Union, with 68, and The United States, with 50.[453] The Olympic wrestling medal count of The Soviet Union is extremely impressive, considering that The Soviet Union hasn't competed in the Olympics since 1988.

The Soviet Union won 34 medals in Greco-Roman wrestling, Sweden 20, Finland 19, and Hungary 16. At Beijing 2008, Russia, won three gold medals, whereas Cuba, France and Italy each won one.[454]

The US, with 47 gold medals, is the Olympic leader in men's freestyle wrestling. The Soviet Union is next, with 28 gold medals. Modern Russia has won 13. Other notable wrestling nations include Turkey with 17 and Japan with 16. At Beijing 2008, the Russian wrestlers won in three of the seven categories. The former Soviet republics, Georgia and Uzbekistan won one medal each, as did Turkey and the USA.[455] Some smaller countries do particularly well in wrestling, because it is their national sport. Examples would be Iran, Turkey, and Mongolia.[456]

In February of 2013, The International Olympic Committee (IOC) announced that it would be dropping both Greco-Roman and freestyle wrestling from the 2020 summer games.[457] Fans and athletes around the world protested this decision, citing the fact that wrestling had not only been the main attraction of the ancient Olympics, but that it had been featured in every modern Olympics except 1900.[458] Many of letters and articles written in protest said that wrestling embodied the spirit of the first Olympics. "Undying spirit of pushing the limits, can we afford to exclude wrestling from the world's games?"[459] When comparing American scholastic or collegiate football spectatorship to wrestling, one will find paying crowds of thousands or even tens of thousands turning out to watch football, but sometimes only the athletes' families coming out to watch wrestling. By counting spectators alone, it would be easy to come to the erroneous conclusion that no one cares about wrestling. The outpouring of support, however, shows that people around the world respect the spirit and tradition of wrestling.

In addition to breaking tradition, the loss of wrestling would also adversely affect the medal counts of many countries, making the Olympics less egalitarian. Many of the former Soviet Republics, for example, are dependent on winning wrestling medals as a source of national pride. Georgia, for example only won seven medals in the London games, six of which were for wrestling. Similarly, for Azerbaijan, wrestling counted for seven of ten medals, and in Iran, six of twelve.[460]

Fortunately, the decision was overturned seven months later, and wrestling events were held in the 2016 Olympics and planned for the 2020 Olympics. The reinstatement of wrestling was achieved largely through the hard work and diligence of FILA and supporters around the world who wrote letters and organized protests.[461] The reinstatement of wrestling represented a courageous and coordinated international activity, an Olympic feat in itself.

Interesting Olympic Wrestling Facts

At the first modern Olympics in 1896 in Athens, Greece, the US team consisted of 14 male athletes.[462] In contrast, in 2012, "the USOC sent a total of 530 athletes to the Games, 261 men and 269 women, to compete in 25 sports."[463] More than one billion people from around the world watched the 2012, London Olympics on TV.[464]

In the history of Olympic wrestling, only 4 wrestlers have won titles in 3 Olympic Games: Carl Westergren of Sweden, who won titles for Greco-Roman wrestling in 1920, 1924 and 1932, Ivar Johansson, also of Sweden, who won titles for Greco-Roman and freestyle wrestling in 1932, and freestyle wrestling in 1936, Alexandre Medved of Russia who won titles for freestyle wrestling in 1964, 1968 and in 1972, Alexandre Karelin, also of Russia, who won titles in 1988, 1992 and 1996. "In 2002, during the World Championship held in Moscow, FILA awarded the title of Best Wrestler of the Century to both Russians: Alexandre Medved (for freestyle wrestling) and Alexandre Karelin (for Greco-roman wrestling)."[465]

Through 1912, the sport of wrestling was fought with controversy and scandal. The FILA was responsible for organizing and regulating the sport of wrestling. Today, the FILA represents 174 countries. In addition to overseeing Olympic wrestling, the FILA also governs the FILA Wrestling World Cup.[466] Thanks largely to FILA, both the sport of wrestling and the Olympics have grown tremendously.

Chapter 8: US Scholastic and Collegiate Wrestling

When it comes to the Olympics, the US has a very impressive record. The US has won more Olympic medals than any other country in history: 2,400 medals, with 976 gold.[467] Additionally, the US ranks second in overall medals for wrestling. The countries with the highest all-time Olympic wrestling medal count are The Soviet Union, with 68, and The United States, with 50.[468]

This success has created a great deal of interest in how the US selects and trains its athletes. In countries such as China, Vietnam, and many European nations, Olympic athletes are products of a sport school and sport university system, whereby a small number of elite athletes attend fulltime sports training (usually from a very early age), in lieu of traditional education. The US system is very different in that it is dramatically more inclusive, allowing millions of youngsters the opportunity to have regular training and competition, while continuing with their education. Young American athletes work their way up to different levels of competition, starting from school to state level followed by national level. This graduation to different levels of sport is also embedded in the American school system, with a continual increase in levels from junior high/middle school to university. It is at the top of this pyramid that Olympic athletes are selected.

Scholastic and Collegiate Sports Teams

According to National Federation of State High School Associations, more than 11 million high school students participate in scholastic sports teams. [469] Data from the National Collegiate Athletic Association states that more than 400,000 students participate in collegiate athletics.[470]

In contrast with the inclusive nature of the American sport system, modern China takes a very different approach. China utilizes a Soviet style system, whereby top athletes are created in sports schools and sport universities. Children as young as four are scouted, selected and introduced to the national sports training system. The best ones will receive a government salary to represent China in international competition.[471] One of the most famous government sponsored sports schools in the country is Li Xiaoshuang school, where most students board in order to train with the school's top gymnastics coaches. The staff are government employees, working under the General Administration of Sports. Headmaster Tian Hua says "the school is an integral part of the country's sports system."[472]

Unlike China, America does not have a system of sports schools and sports universities, nor do athletes reside in government sponsored live-in sports training centers. Instead, schools and universities have their own sports teams. The athletes attend the same academic classes as other students and train after class. High school athletes train about 2 hours per day, whereas collegiate athletes train about 4 hours per day. American universities offer 23 sanctioned sports, and high schools offer 16. At the high school level, the most popular sport is football, played by over 1 million high school boys across the country. The other nine most popular sports for boys are basketball, track and field, baseball, soccer, wrestling, cross country running, golf, tennis, swimming and diving. For girls, the most popular sport is basketball, played by nearly a half million American high school girls. The other most popular sports for girls are track and field, volleyball, softball, soccer, cross country running, tennis, swimming and diving, competitive cheerleading, and golf.[473]

Scholastic Sports

The term scholastic sports refers to interschool competition at the middle/junior high and high school levels.[474] When interscholastic high school sports began in the 1880s, they were originally sports clubs which catered almost exclusively to boys. Later, these sports clubs became part of the school curriculum. Formal, state scholastic sports programs started as early as 1895 in Michigan, followed by Indiana and New York in 1903. In 1921, the Midwest Federation of State High School Athletic Associations was formed, and two years later, the National Federation of State High School Athletic Associations was founded. The name was subsequently changed, in the 1970s, to the National Federation of State High School Associations.[475]

Over the next several decades, scholastic sports programs increased steadily. Although some opportunities were given to girls, most of these programs were focused on boys. In 1972, Title IX legislation of the Education Amendments was established to provide equal opportunity for both girls and boys in sports. Title IX was implemented in 1975, granting new opportunities to girls in sports.[476]

Today, The National Federation of State High School Associations is a private organization which oversees 16 sports for over 11 million boys and girls at 18,500 locations.[477] Among all of the sports on offer, wrestling is the sixth most popular sport for high school boys, with close to 275,000 participants.[478]

From this, we can begin to understand some reasons for the US's Olympics success. Although the US only has roughly a quarter of the population of China, US high school wrestlers outnumber the entire population of athletes across all sports and at all levels in China. Currently, it is estimated that across China, around 250,000 children are enrolled in sports schools.[479] In other words, the US draws its Olympic teams from a population of more than 11 million scholastic and collegiate athletes, whereas China is drawing from only a fraction of that number. For wrestling, the pool of athletes is over a quarter of a million people, from whom 20 will be chosen to fill spots on the US Olympic Wrestling Team.

Apart from producing a smaller number of athletes, the Chinese sports school system has been criticized for the low quality of education the athletes receive. The former Olympic diving coach, Yu Fen, is a harsh critic of the system, on the basis that upon leaving the sports school, most athletes are unprepared to earn a living.[480]

In America, scholastic athletes attend public high schools, where they are expected to pass the same courses and exams as non-athletes. Athletes who do not pass their courses can lose their sports eligibility. For example, the website of the Intercollegiate Athletic Association of Maryland details the requirements of eligibility for participation in high school sports. "Commencing with the date of enrollment at a member school, a full time student who is in good standing according to the policies of the particular member school...Students are considered full time and part of the school community when they take a majority of their academic classes on campus within their school, during the traditional school year."[481] Similar rules can be found in almost every state, showing that sport and academia have been intertwined in the American system.

Collegiate Sports

The main sanctioning bodies of collegiate sports are the National Collegiate Athletic Association (NCAA), the National Association of Intercollegiate Athletics (NAIA), and the National Junior College Athletic Association (NJCAA).

The US scholastic and collegiate sports system serves as a lengthy selection process for the Olympics and professional sports. According to the NCAA participation report, 450,000 students participate in NCAA sports teams in universities across the USA.[482] The best athletes from US junior high school or middle school teams compete for positions on high school teams. The best athletes from high school teams compete for positions on US collegiate teams. The best collegiate athletes will be awarded scholarships, which for many, are the only way they can afford the average $15,000 yearly tuition at US universities.[483]

Training on these teams is grueling, with athletes training up to 20 hours per week as well as competitions. An athlete can be dismissed from the team for failing to attend practices or for poor performance in competitions. If dismissed from the team, an athlete will usually lose his financial scholarship as well.[484]

To remain eligible to play collegiate sports sanctioned by NCAA, an athlete must remain an amateur athlete. Thus, they cannot receive money for playing sports. The long training sessions and demanding competition schedule make it difficult for athletes to keep up with their studies. To maintain their sports eligibility, however, they have to pass all of their courses, and maintain a satisfactory grade point average and earn at least 12 academic credits (4 complete courses) per semester.

Girls in Scholastic and Collegiate Wrestling

The number of girls competing on high school sports teams went from 290,000 in 1972 to 3.4 million in the 2016-17 school year.[485] While there is a greater gender balance across sports today than in the past, wrestling is still heavily dominated by boys. In the 2016-2017 school year, nearly 245,000 high school boys wrestled vs. 14,500 girls.[486]

The first high schools began permitting girls to wrestle in 1980, but they had to wrestle on the boys' team. Still today, some states allow girls to wrestle on the boys' team and to wrestle boys in championship matches. Other states have separate teams and divisions for girls.[487] Several US states now hold high school wrestling championships for girls; these states include California, Texas, Oregon, Hawaii, Massachusetts, Texas, Tennessee, and Washington.[488]

Although many wrestling teams allow girls, most schools do not have enough girls to field a team. As a result, most girls on wrestling teams in the US have to practice and compete with boys of the same weight.[489] In some states, such as Texas, Hawaii, and California, schools have separate wrestling teams for girls. In addition, as of 2007, the New York Mayor's Cup competition has had a girls' division.

As open as modern society is about the inclusion of women in athletics, there is still a certain level of cultural resistance when it comes to wrestling. In sports such as athletics or swimming, boys and girls are often treated the same. However, wrestling seems to have a very masculine perception. Parents worry that their girls will suffer broken noses, cauliflower ears, or concussions.[490] Many boy wrestlers do not like wrestling with girls. This is primarily because if a boy wins against a girl wrestler, he isn't seen as having accomplished anything apart from beating up a girl; if he loses, he is seen as a loser.[491]

New York is a state famous for wrestling and for progressive gender and race policies. Yet, even The New York City Department of Education did not form the first girl's wrestling team until the 2012-2013 academic year. However, since the introduction of the first girl's wrestling team, female wrestling in New York has exploded. Currently, 20 New York City schools have girl's wrestling teams, and girl's wrestling is going global. A team of New York City girl wrestlers even competed against wrestlers from 12 other nations in the prestigious Italian Grand Prix in Palermo, Italy.[492] The New York City team also placed fourth in the US Junior National Wrestling Championships. But, despite the success of girl's wrestling, there is still resistance to girl's wrestling. "In New York, there's a lot of parents who don't speak English, and don't understand what their daughter is doing. And also there's religious objections, and people who don't think it's appropriate because of their gender."[493]

At the tertiary level, according to National Collegiate Athletic Association (NCAA) data in the 2014-2015 academic year, 45.5 percent of collegiate athletes were female, with a total of over 219,000 women playing college sports.[494] The first university to offer women's wrestling was the University of Minnesota-Morris, in 1993.[495] Today, 27 colleges and universities sponsor women's wrestling teams. Additionally, the 30 colleges that comprise the National Wrestling Coaches Association, which have girls wrestling teams, offer wrestling scholarships.[496]

The Women's Collegiate Wrestling Association (WCWA) was formed in 2008, and governs all women's wrestling programs at NCAA, National Association of Intercollegiate Athletics (NAIA), and National Junior College Athletic Association (NJCAA) institutions.[497] The WCWA oversees freestyle wrestling competitions for women in weight divisions from 101 lb. to 191 lb.[498]

Women's collegiate wrestling is paying off in terms of helping the US Olympic medal count. In the 2016 Olympics, Missouri Baptist University women's wrestling team's Helen Maroulis became the first American woman to win a gold medal in wrestling.[499] At present, there is women's freestyle wrestling, but no women's collegiate or Olympic Greco-Roman wrestling, although there are now discussions about including women's Greco-Roman wrestling in the 2024 Olympics.[500] If women's Greco-Roman wrestling is accepted in the Olympics, it will most likely become a collegiate sport as well. Perhaps this could help to decrease the overall gender imbalance in US collegiate sports.

Title IX Regulations: Inclusion of Women in Collegiate Sports

The original intent of Title IX legislation was to offer athletic opportunities to everyone, regardless of gender, and to increase the participation of women in collegiate sports. In order for public universities to continue to receive government financial support, they had to comply with Title IX. This unfortunately had an unintended knock on effect for male participation in wrestling. This is because one of the fastest ways to increase the percentage of women in sports has been to simply cancel men's wrestling.[501] Since Title IX was implemented, more than 400 men's athletic teams have been eliminated. As wrestling has traditionally been an all-male sport, it has become one of the most common targets.[502]

Many coaches and athletes oppose Title IX, because it has negatively impacted sports.[503] An integral part of American wrestling culture is fighting. In this case, the coaches and wrestling associations are fighting to save wrestling in the face of Title IX. The National Wrestling Coaches Association (NWCA) filed a lawsuit against Title IX in 2002. Similar suits were filed by members of the College Gymnastics Coaches Association, the U.S. Track Coaches Association, and United States Diving Association. These suits called Title IX a case of reverse discrimination. Unfortunately, the NWCA's suit failed.[504]

Collegiate Wrestling Rules and Governance

In 1922, the Amateur Athletic Union (AAU), like the International Federation of Associated Wrestling Styles (FILA), dropped catch wrestling in favor of Greco-Roman and freestyle wrestling.[505] Prior to 1927, colleges used AAU rules. In 1927, collegiate athletic wrestling rules were published.[506]

The three styles recognized in US scholastic and collegiate wrestling today are: Greco-Roman wrestling, Freestyle wrestling, and folkstyle wrestling.[507] Greco-Roman wrestling forbids attacks to the opponent's legs. As a result, Greco-Roman wrestling utilizes more dramatic throws as a wrestler may not simply trip his opponent. He generally has to lift the opponent in the air to throw him. American folkstyle wrestling and collegiate wrestling are closely related to the international wrestling style of freestyle wrestling. All three styles allow attacks to the opponent's legs and share the same goal of winning by pin or by points.[508]

USA Wrestling is the national governing body for wrestling in the United States. The organization has over 160,000 members, charters over 3,000 wrestling clubs, and sanctions over 1,600 competitions.[509] "USA Wrestling oversees 70 regional and national tournaments, for children as young as age 9, in folkstyle, freestyle, Greco-Roman, and women's wrestling."[510]

There are over 350 collegiate wrestling programs in the US. Tertiary institutions are divided into Divisions I, II, and III, whereby Division I wrestling is considered the highest level of competition. The collegiate wrestling season starts in October or November and ends with the NCAA tournament in March.[511]

Of the two styles of international wrestling, freestyle is the most popular in the US as it closely resembles US folkstyle wrestling. Very few colleges and almost no high schools actually field a dedicated Greco-Roman wrestling team.[512] Teams will sometimes compete in Greco-Roman events, but most of their training and competition will be focused on folkstyle, at the high school level, or collegiate style, at the university level.

Both folkstyle and collegiate style wrestling in the US are similar to Olympic freestyle wrestling, but with significant differences in the scoring system. For a fall to be scored in collegiate wrestling, it must be held for one second, and at the high scholastic level, two seconds. Points are awarded for takedowns and reversals, but many of the spectacular throws which earn bonus points in international styles of wrestling are simply banned in scholastic and collegiate wrestling because of safety concerns. Wrestlers can earn points for escapes as well as time advantages for controlling the opponent. Folkstyle wrestling rules emphasize safety and strictly forbid brutality.[513]

The Business of College Sports

Some sports generate revenue for the universities, while others do not. Consequently, American universities tend to concentrate on revenue generating sports at the expense of Olympic sports. The only sports that generate significant sums of money for universities are football and men's basketball.[514] This money comes from several streams, including students, ticket sales, donations, media rights and branding rights. An example would be the University of Alabama which, in 2008, had total sports revenue of $123,769,841. That number was composed partly of donations, accounting for $29,860,400, Media rights of $8,825,964, and branding rights of $4,506,056.[515] Popular university sports teams are broadcast on TV, earning money through media rights. Team merchandise such as T-shirts, sweat shirts, and posters, also generates additional income.

The money earned through football and men's basketball is often used to support the rest of the athletic programs.[516] Tennessee, for example, in 2012, had a total sports revenue of $70,617,407, with American football generating $56,831,514, and Men's Basketball generating $13,785,893.[517] Budgets differ dramatically from university to university. University of Alabama had a total sports expenditure of $105,068,152, whereas University of Arkansas at Pine Bluff spent only $7,032,570. No matter how much or how little money a university has, it has to be spread across all of their athletic programs.[518]

During the past 30 years, NCAA Division I athletic departments have competed for money against men's basketball and football programs, often unsuccessfully.[519] Higher expenditure on football and basketball, and a focus on revenue generating sports programs, have led to a decrease in funding for non-revenue-generating, Olympic sport teams.[520] Wrestling has been the sport hardest hit by budget cuts. Looking at the NCAA program during the last 30 years, men's wrestling has suffered more budget cuts than any other Olympic sports program.[521] Since the 1988-89 school year, 101 men's wrestling programs have been cut. While overall total participation in NCAA sports has increased, wrestling participation has dropped by 26 percent in Division 1 alone.[522] However, increased participation in wrestling at the scholastic and club level suggests that wrestling participation has not dropped because of lack of interest, but rather, because of a lack of programs.

As universities compete in sports competitions with other universities in their geographic area, when one university cuts a sport, such as wrestling, it makes that geographical region less competitive. It also increases the cost of other universities maintaining teams, because now the teams may have to travel further to attend competitions. The increase in the cost of maintaining a wrestling program may serve as justification to close the program down. This closing of wrestling programs is surely damaging the US's competitive edge in Olympic wrestling.

In China, much of the training of Olympic athletes occurs in government sponsored sports schools. In the old days, all of these schools were free for those who were accepted. Today, most parents pay tuition fees for their children's training. The schools themselves, however, are not expected to earn money through sports competitions. Since the sports schools are not meant to generate money through sports, there is no predisposition to support one Olympic sport over another.

Life after College Sports

For the graduates of Chinese sports schools, the prospects are overwhelmingly dim. Chinese student athletes generally graduate severely under-educated, with often having no way of earning a decent living. One example would be Yang Wenjun, a Chinese gold medalist in flat water canoeing, who grew up in a sports school. He told the *New York Times* how he regretted missing out on a proper education: "As a child, I didn't learn anything but sport, and now what do I do? I can't do anything else. I have my own dreams, but it is very difficult. I don't have the foundation to make them come true."[523]

In contrast, students of the American system tend to leave much better equipped for life than their Chinese counterparts. In the US, many former wrestlers have taken up successful careers fighting in MMA.[524] Becoming an MMA fighter is an option for former collegiate wrestlers, but so is working as an accountant or marketing executive. Unlike in China's sport university system, US collegiate athletes are attending normal, academic universities, and may be majoring in any subject from teaching to engineering, computer science, French literature, or anything else that interests them. Most collegiate athletes will not make it to the professional leagues. In fact, the chances are generally less than 2 percent, with only baseball having a slightly higher percentage.[525] Fortunately for the remaining 98 percent, even athletes who do not become professionals have life career options. According to data published by the NCAA, "82 percent of Division I freshmen scholarship student-athletes who entered college in 2004 earned a degree. In Division II, 73 percent of freshmen student-athletes who entered college in 2004 graduated."[526] After graduation, they can go on to rewarding careers, and their glory days as collegiate athletes will be a pleasant memory.

Chapter 9: Disabled Wrestlers

[A note about this chapter: One of the mandatory courses for the PhD in *Wushu* was a course on disabled sports in China. The concept is so new to China that there were no disabled athletes at the sports university, and given that most buildings didn't have wheelchair access, it doesn't seem like they were expecting disabled athletes anytime soon.]

China is home to 83 million disabled people, but they are not nearly as visible as in Western countries, and report widespread discrimination. In traditional Chinese thinking, people believe that a family will be afflicted with a disabled child as a matter of karma, making up for a past transgression. Parents of disabled children even go as far as hiding them away so as not to bring shame to the family. The national university entrance exam, the *gao kao*, is proceeded by a medical exam, and disabled children are often barred from taking the exam and thus attending university.[527]

Given this embedded way of thinking, it was surprising when China was selected to host the Paralympics in 2008. One of the only high profile disabled people in China is Deng Pufang, the son of former leader Deng Xiaoping, who was crippled when he was thrown from a window during the Cultural Revolution. In 2008, Deng Pufang was president of the China Disabled Persons' Federation, and he told the press that he felt the Paralympics would help improve the situation for the disabled in China.[528]

Deng's words proved correct. People across China, both disabled and able bodied, were amazed to see the Chinese athletes win 89 gold medals. This was a turning point for the disabled in China, not only in the way they saw themselves, but also in the way they were viewed by society at large.[529] The Chinese government responded, and made the Paralympics a national priority. Consequently, with more government and public support, the

Chinese disabled athletes won 95 golds in the 2012 Paralympics and completely dominated in 2016, winning 107 gold medals.[530]

The Paralympics, like so many other areas of development, is something where China realizes they could benefit from the input of outside experts. One of the reasons why the Chinese government awards scholarships to foreign students is to encourage them to write papers and dissertations about how things are done in their home country. These papers and dissertations are then submitted to Chinese academic archives, where they become the basis for further research by Chinese scholars.

Addressing the very concept of athletes with disabilities was one of the most direct requests for research this author witnessed during his studies at the Shanghai University of Sport. All PhD students were made to attend a course on sports for the physically challenged. Afterwards, we were all asked to write a paper on disabled participation within our sport in our home country.

A second note about this chapter: For those who may see this chapter as a divergence from the history and comparison of wrestling, I would like to remind you that these athletes embody the truest spirit of the Olympic ideal: of man overcoming all obstacles to achieve their greatest potential. Athletes act as teachers: For every athlete wrestling on the floor, embracing the grind, there are a thousand spectators watching and learning. If an athlete who is missing a limb could drag himself to training and competition every day, then what excuse do you have?

What follows is the English language version of the paper I submitted about disabled wrestlers in the US.

"We Must Provide Equal Opportunity in Sports to Students with Disabilities," said *Arne* Duncan, Secretary of the US Department of Education. She was referring to a federal law, issued in 2011, which prevents schools from excluding students based on "intellectual, developmental, physical, or any other disability from trying out and playing on a team, if they are otherwise qualified."[531] This means that schools and universities must provide disabled students with sports opportunities, including wrestling.

Wrestling is a sport that is truly accessible to disabled athletes. As hearing is not a necessity for successful wrestling, it is a regular feature of The Deaf Olympics.[532] It is also a sport offered to the blind. According to the United States Association of Blind Athletes, wrestling is the sport most easily adaptable for the vision impaired.[533] The main change is a rule stating that the two wrestlers have to remain in constant contact. "This is done by touching fingertips; one hand up and one hand down. If contact is broken, the match is stopped and the wrestlers "touch up" and start again."[534] Blind wrestlers often wrestle sighted opponents. But whether both wrestlers are blind or just one, the opposing wrestlers must keep in constant physical contact with the blind wrestler. On the ground, this rule does not seem to cause many problems. In standing, however, some sighted opponents like to be able to hop around their opponent and attack from angles. This, of course, is forbidden when wrestling against a blind athlete.[535]

Inspirational Stories of Disabled Wrestlers

A blind New Jersey high school senior, Anthony Ferraro, placed fourth in the regional wrestling tournament, two years in a row. And now, he has been offered a spot on several university wrestling teams. American athletes and non-athletes alike take inspiration from people like Anthony. But Anthony remains very humble about the attention he receives. "People tell me I inspire them, and when someone tells you that, it's the best feeling in the world ... I never thought anyone would care about me and my wrestling, but now I see that I can help kids."[536]

Blind wrestlers even compete at the collegiate level. Jesse Gunter, a former state place-winner in high school, is now a wrestler at Baldwin Wallace University, where he has earned the titles of a two-time All-OAC (Ohio Athletic Conference) wrestler, and has qualified for the National Collegiate Athletic Association

(NCAA) Division III tournament. This is amazing, considering he has 0 percent vision in one eye, and only 10 percent vision in the other.[537] Jesse Gunter has also explained why some wrestlers don't like to wrestle against a blind opponent. The rule forcing them to keep contact may change their game strategy. He feels, however, that the rule improves the sport by forcing the opponents to simply wrestle, rather than dance.[538]

Wrestling is truly universal. "Wrestling is one activity that is available to anyone. In fact, you can be "differently abled" – blind, deaf, missing limbs, learning disabled, or a survivor of a near-fatal accident – and not only succeed, but become a champion."[539]

Anthony Robles, One-Legged Wrestling Champion

Anthony Marc Robles is a collegiate wrestling champion in spite of having been born without his right leg. When Anthony first began wrestling in high school, he was the smallest and worst on the team. Anthony credits his mother's encouragement for his success. She told him, "There is nothing wrong with you," and after hearing it over and over, he believed her. "Not many people believed that a tiny kid born with one leg, the worst wrestler in the city, would ever excel in such a demanding sport.[540] With the support of his mother and his coach, Anthony said he believed that he was unstoppable. Moving from last place to first, his wrestling record for his final two years of high school was 96 wins and 0 losses. He was also a 2-time Arizona State Champion and a high school National Champion.[541]

Despite Anthony's incredible success, he still experienced criticism. Anthony explained that his detractors claimed that he had an unfair advantage, because having one less limb made it difficult for his opponents to grab him. The other issue was that because wrestling is a weight class sport, a wrestler who is missing a leg, but weighs the same as his opponent would have a bigger, more powerful upper body. His response was, "The missing leg didn't seem like an advantage when I was being defeated every other match in ninth grade."[542]

Although he was an outstanding high school wrestler, university wrestling teams rejected Anthony because he was missing a leg. However, his mother had taught him to believe anything is possible, and he proved her right in this instance. He competed for a spot on Arizona State University wrestling team, one of the best in the country, and got in. He finished college as a 3-time All-American champion and the 2011 NCAA National Champion.[543]

For his achievements, Anthony was a featured guest on *The Tonight Show* with Jay Leno. In 2011, he was honored with The Jimmy V Award for Perseverance, which is awarded to a "member of the sporting world who has overcome great obstacles through physical perseverance and determination," He was also named Best Male Athlete with a Disability.[544] As a collegiate wrestler, he had a perfect record of 36 wins and 0 defeats. He won the Pac-10 conference (Western US Pacific conference) championship as well as the 2011 NCAA Division I Wrestling Championships. At the national championships he was named as the Outstanding Wrestler.[545]

Anthony recalls the life lesson he learned from wrestling "Although my competition days are over, I will continue to wrestle the challenges which life gives me. And I will always believe that I am unstoppable."[546]

Dustin Carter, Amazing Wrestler with No Limbs

When Dustin Carter was 5 years old, he had a blood infection and, in order to save his life, his hands and feet were amputated. When he first started school, he knew he would be a fighter, and nothing would stop his dreams. "I do not see myself as different,"[547] Carter said. "I like to fight. I hate that people feel sorry for me." He was initially a member of his high school football team, but then switched to the wrestling team to follow his true passion. He finished with a remarkable high school record of 41 wins and 2 losses.[548]

Dustin's coach, Scott Goodpasture, said, "Dustin Carter's life teaches us that we can rise to elite levels. His purpose: to inspire, to uplift and to move individuals."[549]

Alex Maughan, Wrestler with Down Syndrome

It is important to remember that not everyone can be a champion. Yet even without becoming a champion, disabled athletes show tremendous courage by training and competing in sports. Alex Maughan, a boy with Down Syndrome, is one such athlete, because not only did he train and compete in wrestling, but he inspired his teammates.[550]

Alex's Mom sent an email to Chris Babinski, the wrestling coach at Jordan High School in Sandy, Utah, telling him that she was looking for a place for her son to exercise. The coach responded, saying that Alex could join the team even though his condition made it impossible to legitimately "win" his matches. Alex's bravery inspired his teammates, who rushed to support him. His Mom cried at his matches because of the kindness of the other boys who had volunteered to wrestle Alex.[551] Alex's Mom said the other boys help Alex a lot. "They will say 'Alex, now roll me over.' They show Alex how to beat them."

Alex's teammates accepted and supported him, but when Jordan High was competing against another school, Coach Chris Babinski was concerned that he may not find a wrestler on the other team who was willing to "compete" against Alex. It turned out, however, that a boy instantly volunteered to wrestle Alex, because his own brother had Down Syndrome. This boy's selflessness moved the entire audience and showed the power that a disabled athlete can have to help those around him rise to their own full potential.[552]

In his final match, Alex's opponent Austin Davis, helped Alex win. Alex pinned Austin. When Alex wins, he raises his crossed arms over his head, making the sign of an "X," in imitation of his comic book hero, Wolverine from the X-Men.[553] One of Alex's teammates said "He makes wrestling a lot of fun. It's a whole new experience. He is a joy." Another of Alex's teammates said that Alex reminded him of his own nephew who had Down syndrome. "And Alex gives me a lot of hope that my own nephew can grow up and be just like Alex."[554]

Middle School Students' Sportsmanship

Most stories about disabled athletes are about people overcoming their disabilities in order to achieve something great. This story is a little different. It is about the valuable life lessons athletes with disabilities can teach to other children.[555] Jared Stevens has cerebral palsy, but he wanted to wrestle. His father asked the wrestling coach if Jared could practice. Eventually, he asked the coach if Jared could compete in a match.[556]

Jared's coach asked the coach of the opposing team if he had a wrestler who was kind and had a big heart. The coach asked 12-year-old Justin Kievit to be Jared's opponent.[557] Jared is confined to a wheelchair and has very little use of one arm and little or no use of his other arm. He had to be carried out to the center of the mat to compete. In the wrestling match, Justin Kievit allowed Jared to pin him. Kievit said "I didn't know what to do. I went over to shake his hand, but I saw he couldn't move. So I sat on the matt and pulled him over on me and slid under him." And Jared pinned Kievit, winning the match in just 18 seconds. Kievet said, "He looked at me with a cheerful face, right when the match was over, and that made me feel really good."[558]

Jared's Father said "The two words that come from this experience are courage and character." Jared Stevens, a boy with cerebral palsy, has courage to compete in wrestling. Justin Kievit, a young boy who wants to win wrestling matches, showed character by letting Jared beat him.[559] Kievet said, "Sometimes winning isn't the right thing and isn't always the most important thing"[560]

Disabled Fighters

The most famous handicapped fighter is the deaf wrestler and MMA Fighter, Matt "the Hammer" Hamill. Matt said that his motivation was to prove that a deaf person could be a professional athlete. To that end, his personal philosophy is simple: "I'm going to show up, and I'm going to win."[561]

According to Hamill, there are 100 million deaf people in the world, and he is the only one to ever fight in the Ultimate Fighting Championships (UFC), the highest level of professional MMA. When he was fighting, he claimed he was receiving 3000 emails per day from people who were inspired by his perseverance.[562]

Matt Hamill was born in 1976, completely deaf. His parents were simple, hard working people who just treated him like any other child. Interestingly, they never used sign language, instead speaking to him as they would to any other child. They also made him work on their farm, which served the dual purposes of giving him a "normal" childhood, but also making him physically strong, which later helped his wrestling career.[563]

Matt grew up feeling "normal."[564] Because of his parents, Matt Hamill could read lips and speak very well. The farm work and healthy farm food gave him tremendous physical strength, and his grandfather helped him join the wrestling team. At first, the coach didn't want to train Matt, because it was too difficult.[565] Hamill's coach had to write instructions on a small blackboard and show them to Matt. Sometimes Matt didn't know the drill was over, and he would attack his unsuspecting teammates. In time, the coach realized Matt would be a champion, and was happy to coach Matt.[566]

Matt Hamill was a farm boy, and one of the ways he trained was by "cow tipping." He and his friends would wrestle the cows and try to pin them to the ground.[567] His legendary strength led him to becoming a high school wrestling champion, and he received a wrestling scholarship to Purdue University. He failed his classes, however, because he couldn't understand his teachers. His parents, always supportive, mortgaged their house to pay his tuition at Rochester Institute of Technology (RIT), which had a deaf education program.[568] At RIT, he learned American sign language for the first time.[569]

Matt studied engineering at RIT, and was on the wrestling team. When Matt graduated with his bachelor's degree in electrical engineering, he had accumulated a wrestling record of 213 wins and

3 losses.[570] He became a three time NCAA Division III National Champion, and won a silver medal in Greco-Roman Wrestling and a gold medal in Freestyle Wrestling at the 2001 Summer Deaf Olympics.

Matt's journey to the UFC is equally as interesting. After college, Matt was working as a bouncer in a bar. Two big American football players started a fight and Matt beat them both, easily. Someone who saw the fight suggested he should fight in the Ultimate Fighting Championship (UFC).[571] Matt was chosen for the UFC TV show, The Ultimate Fighter, as the first deaf fighter to ever appear on the show. His wrestling skills stood out as being far superior to those of his housemates, and most of them commented on how unbelievably powerful his years of farm work and wrestling had made him. He was then selected to fight in the UFC, where he accumulated an impressive record of 12 and 8. To this day, he is the only deaf fighter to have fought in the UFC.[572]

Unsurprisingly, Matt's lack of hearing has had some negative impacts on his performance. When Matt is fighting, he can't hear his coach giving him instructions. He said that before the fight, he just goes over the game plan in his mind, but on the whole, being deaf is a disadvantage.[573] His coach said that it is difficult for him, because he can't shout instructions to Matt. He likened it to watching someone drowning and being unable to jump in and save them.[574]

Ultimate Fighter Matt "The Hammer" Hamill was born deaf, but he has not allowed his disability stand in the way of his dreams."[575] Matt Hamill's coach Duff Holmes explained that Matt is a hero to deaf people everywhere and he takes that very seriously.[576]

Two Friends with Disability Help each other

In 2009, an ESPN film crew travelled to an impoverished slum of inner city Cleveland, Ohio, to do a story about "Two high school wrestlers, one blind and one with no legs, discover the meaning of true friendship."[577]

Nineteen year-old Leroy Sutton was a senior and wrestler at Lincoln-West High School in Cleveland. When he was 11 years old, he was run over by a train and lost both of his legs. Leroy was forced to use a wheelchair, but he didn't want to. Instead, he determined to build up his arm muscles, so he could use his arms to move around.[578]

Leroy's training made his upper body incredibly powerful, and led him to becoming a champion wrestler. When he began attending a new school, the wrestling coach told him, "'You've been hit by a train. Nothing, no kid, no wrestler can beat you?'"[579]

The first opponent Leroy had to face at his new team was the best wrestler, Dartanyon Crockett, who was already a winner in multiple weight classes. Dartanyon said he had never faced an opponent like Leroy, saying "He was a complete powerhouse." Dartanyon said that Leroy was the strongest opponent he had ever wrestled, and that the two pushed each other to their limits, "and we didn't let each other give up."[580] After hours and months of practice together, Leroy and Dartanyon became best friends. Although Leroy weighed 77 kg,. Dartanyon carried him everywhere on his back. Even when they went to competitions, Dartanyon carried Leroy.

As wonderful as this friendship was, there was one more amazing aspect: Dartanyon was legally blind. Wrestling coach Justin Hons talked about how brave Dartanyon was: "You don't notice he is disabled. He doesn't ask for help."[581] Dartanyon's eyesight was so poor that when he wrestled, he only saw dark shapes coming at him.[582]

Dartanyon said, "God has given me a challenge. He will watch to see how I will react to this challenge…Will the challenge make me a strong person, like I am? Or will the challenge defeat me?"[583] In addition to blindness, Dartanyon had to overcome many difficulties. His mother died when he was a baby, and his father was both a drug addict and an alcoholic. When he was growing up, there was often no food in the house, and sometimes he had to sleep rough.[584]

Dartanyon competed at 85 kg, a very tough weight division in Ohio, one of the best states for high school wrestling. When Dartanyon wrestled, Leroy sat on the side of the mat and encouraged him. Dartanyon was very aggressive and had a reputation for using more strength than technique. His coach explained "He rarely waits for his opponent to attack first, because he might not be able to see the attack."[585]

Dartanyon's senior high school wrestling record was 26 wins and 3 losses, and he won the league championship in his weight class. For Leroy, wrestling was more difficult, because he had no legs and could not generate the leverage he needed to win most of his matches. Leroy did manage to win nine matches, the majority by pin. His coach said, "Watching him wrestle…has taught me how to stand in areas of my life that I wouldn't have wanted to."[586]

In the end, both boys graduated high school, a considerable achievement in itself, considering that for their part of Cleveland the graduation rate was only 40 percent.[587]

Leory said, "It was always my dream to walk across the stage at graduation." Just before he graduated high school, Leroy received a gift of prosthetic legs from a donor. At graduation the two insisted on receiving their diplomas together. So, for the first time, Dartanyon walked beside his friend.

After the ESP story ran, donors from all over the United States called in, pledging money to help the two young men attend college. Lisa Fenn, the story's producer, realized that without help the two would never know how to manage their money, college applications, financial aid, and their educations. Neither had a strong family to support them, so Lisa stepped in to fulfill that role.[588]

Before graduating, Leroy set an Ohio state record in bench press, 315 lb., as a member of the Lincoln-West power lifting team. After graduation, he placed 10th in the 2010 World Paralympics Powerlifting Championships in Malaysia. Thanks to the help of Lisa Fenn and kind donors, he graduated his BA from Collins College.[589]

Dartanyon Crockett went on to attend college at Pikes Peak Community college. Still an exceptional athlete, he switched from wrestling to judo and won bronze medal in the men's 90 kg division at the 2012 and 2016 Paralympics. Dartanyon is currently working on a bachelor's degree in social work. Additionally, he serves as an athlete ambassador for UNICEF, the Challenged Athletes Foundation, and the US State Department.[590]

Dartanyon's transition from wrestling to judo was part of a special program organized by USA Judo and USA Wrestling. As wrestling is not a sport featured in the Paralympics, disabled wrestlers are encouraged to switch to judo.[591]

Conclusion

One of the professors at Shanghai University of Sport said that China's goal in the Olympics is "Higher, faster, stronger, better," which is consistent with traditional view that sports competition is about winning medals. Yet, this does not reflect the true spirit of sportsmanship. Sports competition is about overcoming obstacles. It is about pushing yourself to your limits, not someone else's. Sports competition is truly about courage and building character.

All athletes with disabilities had to overcome obstacles in order to compete in sports. They showed great courage by even stepping onto the wrestling mat. Both athletes with disabilities and their teammates pushed themselves to their personal limits. Some became champions. All became better people. In every sense of the word, these athletes with disabilities embody the spirit of true sportsmanship.

Greco-Roman ground
technique.

Rolling the opponent to his
back.

As long as one arm is in, this is
a legal technique in western
wrestling.

Transitioning from a wrestling
takedown to a catch wrestling
neck crank.

Once you are in the air, there is no defense.

Pro wrestling is one of the modern evolutions of wrestling.

Pro wrestling does not use as many submissions as catch wrestling used to.

MMA is the form of modern wrestling which is closest to ancient Greek Pankration.

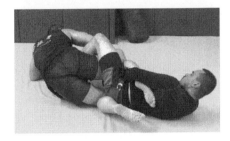

Submissions were used in Greek Pankration, catch wrestling, judo, jujitsu, sambo, and MMA.

Takedown from the ground.

Incredibly deep single-leg from
the ground.

Legal western wrestling
technique becomes a submission.

Chapter 10: Pro Wrestling

As "real" professional wrestling ended in the 1920s, "fake" World Wrestling Entertainment (WWE) style wrestling began to develop. From the humble beginnings of "worked" matches in small carnivals and fairs, professional wrestling entertainment developed into a multi-billion-dollar industry. With the rise of WWE style wrestling came the superstars associated with its success. The first TV wrestling star was Gorgeous George Wagner, who created his own costumes and persona. The first closed circuit TV wrestling star and internationally known wrestler was Andre the Giant. And the first pay-per-view megastar was Hulk Hogan.

From Sport to Entertainment

Americans have always enjoyed watching people fight. From the old days of bare-knuckle boxing to mixed martial arts, Americans love fighting.[592] The other great passion of Americans is the soap opera, which focuses on the love-hate relationships between complex characters which the audience comes to know and understand over a period of years. When you combine bloody battles and dramatic storylines, you get sports entertainment.[593]

During the mid-1920s, wrestling was real, but eventually, fans became bored. Matches could last for hours and end in a draw. Fans wanted something more exciting. They want to see speed, agility, skill, and gymnastics. To cater to this demand, professional wrestling switched from being a legitimate fighting sport to sports entertainment[594] This switch worked well for the fans, but because this new style of pro wrestling was scripted, with pre-planned outcomes, wrestling lost its credibility and its mainstream press coverage.[595]

In the 1920s, the wrestling promoters in the US began to capitalize on the early origins of pop culture by creating wrestlers who were characters that could be mass marketed. As in any epic battle, wrestling had to have heroes and villains. The heroes were called "baby faces." The villains were called "heels." The winner was picked in advance.[596]Pro wrestling was dominated by promoters who organized shows featuring the best catch wrestling.

The most famous promotion company was "The Gold Dust Trio," founded by Ed Lewis, Billy Sandow, and Toots Mondt. These men are credited with having invented time limits, pro wrestling holds, and tag team wrestling, where a team of two wresters would fight an opposing team of two wrestlers, alternately tagging each other in and out of the match.[597]The Goldust Trio also gave the referee the power to stop a match for a disqualification and added cheating tactics, where someone would distract the referee while another wrestler did something illegal. They created story lines for their wrestlers, as well as long running feuds, which sometimes ran for years. They also "raided talent," meaning that when they saw good wrestlers working for another promoter, they would offer him more money to come work for them.[598]

As wrestling became entertainment, the wrestlers became performers with bigger crowds, meaning bigger pay. The wrestler credited with having nearly invented the concept of a wrestler as a persona and as a self-promoter was "Gorgeous" George Wagner, who in the 1940s turned himself into the most hated and most highly paid wrestler in the world. He invented a pretty boy persona, a possibly homosexual character, who wore elegant robes, had bleach blond hair, made elaborate entrances, and had his butler spray perfume on the ring and the referee.[599]

Audiences hated George, and as a result spent a great deal of money to watch him lose. Thus, George became one of the first financially successful wrestlers. Eventually, creating these types of characters became the norm. Therefore, Gorgeous George was one of the characters who led professional wrestling to where it is today.[600]

Gorgeous George and his Influence on Professional TV Wrestling

One reason pro wrestling declined in popularity during the 1920s was because of the rise of radio. Families across America tuned in to hear the play-by-play coverage of baseball and the blow-by-blow of boxing. Wrestling was extremely difficult to call in that manner, and boring for the fans to listen to at home. However, with the rise of TV in the 1950s, wrestling once again became popular. In the early days, wrestling was perfect for TV, due to its small area of competition. In contrast, baseball was nearly impossible to televise. Baseball is played in large stadia outdoors, and would have required multiple cameras, zoom lenses, filters, and portable sound equipment. In the end, the nine players would have looked like blurry little specs on the tiny screens on those early sets.

Wrestling, however, was played indoors. Rings could even be constructed in TV studios, and the cameras could get right on top of the action. Wrestling matches only had two players, and with the close-ups and coverage, they both had the potential to become stars.[601] Gorgeous George has been called TV's first famous wrestling villain. TV made him a star, and in many ways, he made television.[602]

Gorgeous George's rise to prominence began in 1939. As a 24-year-old professional wrestler, George Wagner was already a brilliant self-promoter. He married his girlfriend in a wrestling ring. The wedding proved so popular with wrestling fans that George and Betty reenacted the wedding, again and again, in wrestling rings around the country.[603]

Soon after, George discovered the role of the "heel." Gorgeous George's wife had made a robe for him, similar to the robes worn by boxers. He wore that robe into the wrestling ring and meticulously folded it before his match started. When a restless fan scolded him for delaying the match, George jumped into the crowd and slapped the man in the face. The crowd went crazy, booing George. At that moment, George decided that making the audience hate him was a way of making himself unforgettable, and thus guaranteeing the promoters would call him back for more shows. "In wrestling they either come to like you or hate you. And they hated George."[604]

George decided to call himself "Gorgeous" George, to differentiate himself from other "tough' wrestlers. Instead, Gorgeous George tried to look pretty and clean. Before every fight, he meticulously styled his hair, using a hair net and bobby pins, and wore robes made of satin or silk. He was accompanied by a butler who would spray perfume on the ring, and on the referee. Often, his entrances were so dramatic that they took longer than his fights.

George's character and performance demonstrate the evolution of wrestling as sports entertainment. Other wrestlers soon followed Gorgeous George's lead and created personas, such as Antonio Rocco, whose trademarks were unusual submission holds and acrobatics.[605] Although there were imitators, Gorgeous George was the preeminent bad guy, doing everything he could to make the crowd hate him. "He always cheated -gouging eyes, biting ears, butting heads, punching kidneys, kicking crotches."[606] When he was winning, he gloated. When he was losing, he begged for mercy. He even cried when his opponents mussed his hair.[607] Gorgeous George understood the place that combat sports held in the American psyche, and he embodied everything that tough, strong, independent, masculine, apple-pie-eating, true American men were not supposed to be.

The most hated wrestler was often the most popular, if you counted by ticket sales. In 1949 alone, Gorgeous George sold out the Los Angeles Olympic Auditorium on 27 of his 32 appearances.[608] It was because of Gorgeous George that wrestling began to be shown on TV. As early as 1945, his fights were already being broadcast in California. "TV turned Gorgeous George in to a national star, even for people who didn't watch wrestling."[609] Many TV dealers displayed pictures of Gorgeous George in their shops, and TV sales skyrocketed. Gorgeous George helped to prove that television was going to be a viable medium of entertainment broadcasting, and in many ways, wrestling was "TV's first real success."[610]

Gorgeous George brought the pageantry to wrestling. He was the first wrestler to have his own entrance music, which again, worked well to appeal to a TV audience accustomed to stale matches and tired commentary.[611] Through TV, Gorgeous George had a huge impact on American pop culture. Heavyweight champion boxer Muhammad Ali reinvented his public persona after he happened to meet Gorgeous George on a radio show in Las Vegas in 1961. "That's when I decided I'd never been shy about talking, but if I talked even more, there was no telling how much people would pay to see me," Ali remembered. That's when he started calling himself "'The Greatest'...just like Gorgeous George.[612]

Gorgeous George created the concept of the villain being more popular and richer than the hero. Hulk Hogan, the most famous wrestler of the 1980s, said, that by watching Gorgeous George, he learned that wrestling was part live theater and part physical.[613] In many ways, one could draw a parallel between the gladiatorial battles of Rome and pro wrestling in that the audience played an active role in both – as, to some extent, it is the audience that decides what the competitors do. Hulk Hogan said that he based his actions on the crowd's reactions, and that's when he decided to switch from being a hero to being a villain.[614]

If one looks at the early cinema and TV codes in America, there were rules stating that good had to triumph over evil. The hero always won, and he could not be killed on camera. In contrast, the villain always had to be despicable. The censors evidently never had any control over wrestling, because Gorgeous George made the villain cool, perhaps for the first time in the entire history of American entertainment.

In spite of the Gorgeous George's antics, during the 1950s, the popularity of TV wrestling steadily dropped. George continued to wrestle until 1962, when a lifetime of heavy drinking finally caught up with him and he was forced to retire.. After mismanaging his money and two expensive divorces, he was broke. In 1963,

Gorgeous George, the man who had brought panache to pro wrestling, died of a heart attack at age 48.[615]

Wrestling continued for the next 30 years, but its popularity was low. There were a few regional wrestling TV shows, but wrestling still lacked any type of national organization The NWA existed, but it had little authority to govern the sport. Instead, the USA was divided into regional territories, each controlled by a small local wrestling production company.[616]

This system of regional territories continued until Vince McMahon, Jr., and his wrestling promotion, the WWF (World Wrestling Federation), changed wrestling forever. Originally called the WWWF (World Wide Wrestling Federation), the McMahon Company had been one of the country's four largest promotions which operated regionally, outside of New York.[617]

In an attempt to go national, McMahon began contracting local TV stations outside of his area to broadcast WWF programming. He also began inviting wrestlers from other regional promotions to work for him.[618] One of the wrestlers Vince McMahon recruited was the biggest wrestler who had ever lived, Andre the Giant. Standing at 2.1 meters (6'9") tall and weighing around 226 kg (498 lb.), this gifted wrestler and entertainer was often referred to as The Eighth Wonder of the World. From the 1960s to the 1980s, he was the highest paid wrestler in the world.[619] It was Andre who single handedly set the WWF on its meteoric rise, but it was Hulk Hogan who would take WWF to its peak.

The WWF grew and grew, absorbing smaller shows. Eventually, in 1987, they held the largest wrestling show of all time, "Wrestlemania III", the main event of which was Andre the Giant vs. Hulk Hogan. Attended by 78,000 people, it was the first wrestling show in history to break $1 million dollars in ticket sales. In addition to traditional ticket sales, Wrestlemania and other WWF productions had found a new revenue stream through pay-per-view, where people paid money to watch the event at home on cable TV.[620]

Wrestlemania III was a tremendous turning point in the development of wrestling in America. The event proved that wrestling had become an incredibly popular mainstream form of entertainment. It also made legends of both Andre the Giant and Hulk Hogan. The newspapers at the time exaggerated all of the statistics associated with the event. They claimed that 95,000 people were in attendance, and that Andre was 7 feet tall and weighed 525 pounds. They claimed that Hulk Hogan weighed 320 pounds and had 24 inch biceps.[621] While both men were huge, the media had turned them into impossible, mythical figures.

Hulk Hogan was the winner of his first bout; so, of course, a rematch was scheduled, which took place three months later. This bout, which Andre won, was broadcast live on TV to an audience of 33 million viewers (at the time 14% of the total population of the US).[622] However, because wrestling was not considered a legitimate sport, no sports journalists were in attendance to cover the event.[623] In spite of this, it can be said that in the late 1980s, wrestling had returned to the much admired place in society that it held during the Frank Gotch era of professional catch wrestling before 1925,

Andre the Giant

Andre the Giant (1946 -1993) was born as Andre Rene Roussimoff in Grenoble, France, to Russian parents. As a baby, he was diagnosed with a glandular disease which caused him to become abnormally large. By age 12, he was 190 cm (6' 2") and weighed 108 kg (238 lLb.). At the age of 17, when working as a furniture mover, he was recruited as a pro wrestler.[624] He originally went by the stage name "Andre the Butcher," but it was Vincent J. McMahon Sr. who dubbed him "Andre the Giant."[625]

"The big man loved two things: wrestling and booze – mostly booze – and his appetites were of mythic proportions."[626] He earned $15,000-$20,000 for a single appearance at Madison Square Garden, but had to spend most of it to settle his bar bills. "Vince McMahon Sr assigned a 'handler' to the Giant – long-time wrestler, manager, and road agent, Arnold Skaaland, whose only job when Andre was in town was to keep him out of serious trouble and to get him to the arena in time to wrestle."[627]

Andre the Giant was a legend in the days before YouTube. Today, fans can login and watch countless hours of cell phone video of their favorite stars. But in the 1970s, information about Andre was passed on from fan to fan.[628] Yet, the lack of video websites didn't prevent Andre from becoming one of the biggest stars in the world.

Earning $400,000 per year, Andre was named by the Guinness Book of World Records as the highest paid pro wrestler in 1974.[629] The Washington Redskins football team even offered Andre a tryout. Though most observers saw this as a publicity stunt rather than a serious offer, it still proves how popular the giant wrestler was. Other offers came for him to appear in movies and TV shows. In 1976, Andre played the evil Sasquatch (Big Foot) character on the incredibly popular TV show, *The Six Million Dollar Man*. That same year, André fought boxing heavyweight contender, Chuck Wepner, who later became the inspiration for the *Rocky* movie series. Sylvester Stallone, the creator and star of *Rocky*, was in the audience that night, and later recreated the match in his film *Rocky III*. In the film version, Rocky replaces Chuck Wepner, and Hulk Hogan plays the part of the giant wrestler, named Thunder Lips, the Ultimate Male.[630]

Given his size, traveling was a problem for Andre. When he was young, he drove a car with a sunroof, and stuck his head out the top so he would fit.[631] Flying was also difficult, because the seats and aisles were too small for him. He felt similarly cramped in cars, but to make matters worse, the same medical condition that made him a giant also caused him extreme pain in his knees, hips, and lower back. One of the reasons he drank so much alcohol was to cope with the pain.[632]

Being so large, Andre was an extremely recognizable star, and wherever he went, people crowded around him for autographs. Andre was even more popular in Japan, where "he was treated like a living god" and was paid thousands of dollars for a single appearance.[633] This was somewhat ironic, as Andre didn't like Japan. Everything was too small for him. The beds were like toys, and he couldn't always fit in the bathroom or the shower. He even had to rip the bathroom door off one hotel room and squeeze his body into the bathroom with his legs sticking out into the hotel room.[634]

In Japan, to make buses more comfortable for Andre, the promoters removed a number of seats to create a private sitting area where the big man could stretch out and sleep.[635] His eating and drinking habits just added to his fame. Andre's longtime friend has this to say about the Giant: "The legend that follows André around the food, the drink, he could do this, he could do that, He ate 16 steaks, 12 lobsters, drank a case of beer, 10 bottles of wine, and finished it off with a bottle of Jack Daniels. Well, I'm here to tell you: it's all true."[636]

He struggled daily with discomfort and indignity. On a daily basis, Andre was mobbed whenever he went outside. The shower only came up to his waist, and he couldn't dial the phone, because his fingers were too big.[637] In Japan, Andre saw a doctor for the first time, who told him that the same disease which caused his gigantic size would dramatically shorten his life, predicting that he would die before his fortieth birthday.

Professional wrestling is a brutal sport which takes a tremendous toll on a wrestler's body. When Andre finally submitted to having a back operation, a special operating table and equipment had to be constructed. The doctors were uncertain of how much anesthesia they would need to put him to sleep. The doctor asked Andre how much alcohol he needed to get drunk. The Giant replied that it usually took 2 liters of vodka. So, the doctor adjusted the anesthesia accordingly, and the operation was a success.[638] Five months after the operation, Andre the Giant wrestled a "body-slam" match against Hulk Hogan, and the fans went wild.

After Wrestlemania, Andre retired for good. The death of his father, in 1993, brought Andre back to France. He died there, later that year, at the age of 47.[639]

Gorgeous George is often thought of as being the first TV wrestler. Andre the Giant was the first world sensation, but when he lost his world wrestling title to Hulk Hogan, a new era began. This was the era of cable TV, pay-per-view, and WWF becoming a global company.

In 1984, the WWF took over the NWA's TV time slot in Atlanta. WWF offered larger salaries to wrestlers, to get the best wrestlers working in WWF shows. In 1985, they cemented their position as a global entertainment company when their wrestling event, "The War to Settle the Score," was broadcast live on MTV.[640] To expand the audience beyond the lower class, WWF made many changes to their wrestling. They created storylines, and also began dressing their wrestlers in elaborate costumes. They removed much of the violence and blood of wrestling, and increased the athleticism and acrobatics. By making these changes, WWF was able to appeal to a huge new audience of children.[641]

Children were a great market for the WWF, because they liked to buy T-shirts and toys with the wrestlers' images on them. Also, because children were too young to attend live matches alone, their parents came with them, which meant WWF could sell more tickets.[642] Thus, wrestling entered a new and incredibly profitable era of Hulkamania, named for the 1980s wrestling super star, Hulk Hogan.

Hulkamania!!!!

Hulk Hogan, born in 1953 as Terry Gene Bollea, made his professional wrestling debut in 1977.[643] At that time, wrestling did not have the national or international exposure it enjoys now. Instead, it was controlled by dozens of small, regional promotion companies, which paid the wrestlers very poorly. Consequently, Hogan was wrestling as many as 400 times a year for little compensation.

Hogan was becoming the superstar of the American Wrestling Association (AWA). But in 1983, the AWA made a mistake in letting Hogan sign a contract with the WWF. Around the same time,

Sylvester Stallone chose Hogan to play Thunder Lips, the Ultimate Male, in his movie *Rocky III*. Being associated with the *Rocky* film sparked public interest in both Hulk Hogan and professional wrestling. This was also the time when cable TV was spreading around the country, and as such, the WWF broadcasted Hogan's matches from coast to coast.[644]

By 1985, Vince McMahon had bought the WWF from his father. He now owned Hulk Hogan, the most popular wrestler in the world. His next move was to expand wrestling to pay per view (PPV).[645] This new medium paid off, and "Wrestlemania I" was watched by 400,000 viewers on PPV.[646]

In November of 1979, Islamic revolutionaries overran the US Embassy in Tehran, taking more than 60 Americans hostage. The hostages were held for 444 days, during which time, the American people felt violated, embarrassed, and injured. Those 444 days of despair, shame, and anger, which ended minutes after Ronald Reagan took the oath of office, received more press coverage than any event since World War II.[647]

As a brilliant promoter, Vince McMahon came up with the idea of having Hulk Hogan return to WWF to face off against the Iranian wrestler, The Iron Sheik.[648] Evoking images of America's humiliation at the hands of young religious extremists in Iran turned the match into an emotional affair, which pulled on the heartstrings and the patriotism of the American people. "When Hulk won the title, it set off a wave of patriotism, and a new cult called Hulkamania."[649]

No one could possibly have predicted the impact Hulkamania would have on America and on the future of wrestling. In his own words, Hulk Hogan explains how he felt. "Coming out with the United States flag and the US T-shirt, everybody was like, 'I hope Hulk really kicks this guy's butt.' Yeah, the people were very into the whole USA thing. They were chanting, 'USA, USA!'"[650]

With that single match, Hulkamania was born. Hulk Hogan went from wrestler to national hero. "They thought Hulk was defending our country."[651] Hulkamania also caused an explosion of interest in wrestling in general. Soon, TV wrestlers were household names, with their images on games, toys, clothing, and magazines. At the head of all of this new fandom was the national icon, Hulk Hogan, who was on everything from action figures to vitamins.[652]

The Hulkamania campaign was explicitly directed at children, with Hulk Hogan telling them to do their homework, study hard, exercise, take their Vitamins, and say their prayers. Hulk Hogan symbolized the powerful, good, moral spirit of American values, as well as the belief that good would always triumph over evil. Of course, Hulkamani made a lot of money for both the WWF and Hulk Hogan, but in an interview, Hulk Hogan explained that he really believed in the healthy lessons he was teaching American children. Hulk said that the character was completely planned to promote wholesome behavior, and that it was a great message to give to young people at that time. "It was a much better message than wrestlers of today, who give them two words: 'Suck it.' It was a great message, it was wholesome, it was the right thing to do."[653]

Although TV wrestling is "fake," the wrestlers still get hurt. Hulk Hogan has explained in numerous interviews over the last two decades that wrestlers get hit on the head with trash cans, tables, and steel chairs. When they jump off of a ladder or get tossed out of the ring, their bodies take a tremendous impact. During the early days of his career, when he was wrestling up to four hundred times a year, his body was damaged in every match.[654] Eventually, the constant battering of his body led Hulk Hogan to retire.

Shortly after retiring, the FBI called Hulk Hogan to testify about steroid use in pro wrestling. Hulk's public admission that he took steroids destroyed his image as a wholesome American hero and an inspiration for children. Hulk lost much of his income and endorsement opportunities because of it. Hulkamania was over.

Although he had lost his image, and in spite of years of accumulated injuries, there is an expression in the fight game: "A real warrior goes out on his shield." The idea is that no matter how damaged or defeated you are, you continue to fight. With this in mind, Hulk had a number of comeback wrestling matches, with various wrestling promotional companies, all of which were very successful, but never as successful as during the peak of Hulkamania.

Pro wrestling was dealt another heavy blow in 1985, when the New York State Government held a hearing to ban pro wrestling in the state. The government had two concerns about wrestling. Firstly, that it was violent and bad for children to watch; and secondly, that it was fake.[655] Several wrestlers were called to testify about whether or not wrestling was real. Most refused to state that wrestling was fake. because of an old wrestling code of conduct called "*kayfabe*, an old carnival term. In wrestling, it refers to the illusion that the characters and storylines are real"[656] In the old days, wrestlers stayed in character 24/7, and could be fired if they did anything that spoiled the illusion that wrestling was real.[657] After nearly a century, however, kayfabe came crashing down when a federal trial forced Vince McMahon to admit that wrestling was scripted.[658]

The law banning wrestling in New York did not pass, and the breaking of kayfabe also did not destroy the wrestling business. The WWF was renamed as World Wrestling Entertainment (WWE) because of copyright issues, but the new name worked well with the company's new stance. The WWE now officially recognizes that the wrestlers are entertainers following a script.[659]

From 1986 onward, mainstream media began reporting wrestling news. From that point on, WWE became first a national, then an international company.[660] When Vince McMahon faced a threat in the form of a competing wrestling organization, he simply bought it. By 2004-2005, Vince McMahon owned a monopoly on professional wrestling. He currently owns the rights to all of these promotional companies: WWE/WWF, WCW, ECW, AWA, and NWA footage, and any rights associated with those companies. "Vincent K. McMahon now owns Wrestling."[661]

A Brief List of Pro wrestling Techniques [662]

1. Boston crab
2. Iron Claw
3. Punch to the head
4. Forearm to the chest or back
5. Clothesline
6. Bouncing your opponent off the ropes
7. Running the ropes
8. Jumping off the top rope

Pro wrestling moves are designed to look painful, but inflict as little damage as possible. Pulling off a move and making it look plausible to the audience is called "selling it." Reacting to wrestling moves is a large part of the training that pro wrestlers undergo. For example, when they get hit in the back with a chair, they have to time it perfectly, so their legs buckle and they collapse. This movement serves the dual purpose of making it appear as if they have been injured, but it also dissipates most of the force of the blow.[663]

When the time limit is nearly up, the referee will tell the wrestlers to finish the match quickly by saying, "Bring it home!" Unlike in a movie fight scene, the whole match isn't choreographed, but the most difficult and dangerous acrobatic moves are carefully planned to avoid injury. Wrestlers also slow the pace of a match by jumping out of the ring or trash-talking (grabbing the microphone and talking to the audience, saying terrible things about their opponent). While one man is talking, both men are resting. The headlock and other wrestling holds are also used as resting techniques. A wrestling hold slows the action so both men can catch their breath.[664]

Often, pro wrestlers are actually hitting each other, but they do so in a way to minimize pain. For example, when they jump off the top rope of the ring and hit their opponent, they don't hit with an elbow or knee; instead, they hit with their thigh muscle. When they throw a punch, they open their hand just before impact, and their palm makes a tremendous sound when it lands on the opponent's chest. A punch may also turn into a forearm strike at the last second, which feels more like a loud slap than a sharp blow. Similarly, when they hit an opponent with a chair, they use the flat side.[665]

The ring is also designed to minimize injury. The ring floor is slightly padded and full of springs, so the flying leaps and body slams aren't as bad as they seem. Just before hitting the ground, wrestlers flatten out their bodies to distribute the shock more evenly. And when it looks like a wrestler is being dropped on the back of his neck, he is actually being dropped on his shoulder blades.[666]

The Piledriver is an extremely dangerous looking move, where one wrestler drives the other wrestler's head directly into the mat. However, the head never makes contact and the thighs of the thrower absorb the force.[667] Pro wrestling techniques are akin to magic tricks. The wrestlers use misdirection to fool the audience into believing someone is being very nearly killed.

This facade stretches to appearing that a wrestler is bleeding. There are two ways this illusion is created. One way is by using fake blood capsules, not dissimilar to the movies. The other way a wrestler can make it look like he is bleeding is by actually cutting himself. Wrestlers sometimes hide a small razorblade in their clothing or in their mouth. At some point during the match, the opponent will distract the crowd's attention. The wrestler lying on the ground, seemingly dead, will then cut himself on the forehead. The blood mixes with sweat and appears to flow freely. The wrestler then wipes it around with his hand to make it look even worse.[668]

Wrestling Hurts

In Hulk Hogan's own words, he described how much it hurts to be a professional wrestler. He also said that they have to endure this pain to avoid being fired. "You push yourself even when you're hurt, you think...*hurt me!* You go beyond human capabilities. I was always afraid to stop, because I didn't want to be replaced."[669]

Pro wrestling is one of the most physically demanding sports. In boxing or MMA, an entire career may only span 30 or 40 fights but wrestlers have thousands of fights by the time their ill health forces them to retire. Hulk Hogan recalls when he was starting out as a wrestler. "Wrestling twice on a Sunday, because every building sold out, flying 300 days a year, sometimes wrestling up to 400 times a year."[670] His wrestling career spanned four decades, and he was injured to some degree in every single one of those matches. Surprisingly, in the early days of his career, he was doing all of that travelling and wrestling for as little as one hundred twenty-five dollars a week.[671]

With the current WWE contracts, wrestlers don't have a retirement or healthcare plan to take care of them when they have to stop wrestling. Considering the amount of money that the WWE makes from the wrestlers, Hulk Hogan believes that there should be a risk and reward system in place. In the current system, the wrestlers take tremendous risks, but get very small rewards. "Our hard work, how much you work, how long you work, you should be rewarded"[672] According to Hogan, there have even been discussions about trying to form a union to protect the rights of the wrestlers.

The Culture of Wrestling

When Frank Gotch defended his title against George Hackenschmidt in Chicago in 1911, ticket sales totaled $87,000 (equivalent to over $2 million today[673]).[674]

In 1917, a time when the average American was earning a bit more than $12 per week, scalpers were charging $8 a ticket to watch the professional wrestling world championship between Caddock and Stretcher.[675] Wrestling has had a huge impact on American culture. While there have been ups and downs, periods of growing or waning popularity, it has always been there. The Gorgeous George wrestling era is credited with encouraging Americans to buy TVs and watch wrestling in their living rooms. The Andre the Giant era was marked the popularity of closed circuit TV. The Hulk Hogan era showed the power and money of pay-per-view and wrestling related toys and merchandise. While wrestling was big business prior to World War One, it became a billion-dollar business during and after the Hulk Hogan Hulkamania era.

In 1989, the owners of the WWF admitted to the New Jersey Senate that wrestling was fake.[676] This admission did not tarnish wrestling's image or turn away its millions of fans. If boxing or MMA had made a similar disclosure, the sports would likely have been destroyed. They would have lost all of their fans, and the lawsuits would have been endless. However, wrestling isn't quite a sport. It is some special form of entertainment which fits in its own unique category.

"In order to study a cultural phenomenon like professional wrestling, one must understand what it is. It is clearly unlike other activities that are in the category of sports; baseball and boxing, at least in theory, are pure contests."[677] Wrestling is a huge spectacle, like the gladiatorial games held in the coliseum, of Rome. "Cheerleaders, pyrotechnics, announcers, and half-time shows are not essential to the contest; but they are staples in today's sporting events." All of these elements, plus huge, well-trained wrestlers seemingly beating each other to death, results in tremendous ticket sales and a great deal of revenue for the leading organization in professional wrestling, the WWE (formerly WWF and WWWF).

While wrestling has fans in every country, the five countries where it is most popular are USA, Canada, United Kingdom, Japan and Mexico.[678] A large revenue stream for the WWE is from overseas shows and touring wrestling companies.

"During the summer months of 2012 (July, August and September), the WWE held 70 live events in the USA/Canada region and seven internationally, and were viewed by 450,000 fans.[679] The previous year, the WWE produced 80 live events internationally, reaching almost 500,000 fans with an average ticket price of US

$68.74. In North America (USA and Canada), 241 live events attracted 1,500,000 fans with an average ticket price of US$42.11. Total revenues from live events in 2011 was US$104.7 million.[680]

Through 1970s and beyond, "Gorgeous" George Wagner influenced wrestlers like "Superstar" Billy Graham, "Nature Boy" Ric Flair, and Jesse "The Body" Ventura to not only be good in the ring, but to have over-the-top personalities out of the ring. The wrestler's charisma contributed to his success and to the business overall. Fans wanted the ridiculousness of characters, not the oversized goons they saw back in the early days. These characters are what led to today's version of professional wrestling, including the immortal wrestlers such as Hulk Hogan, "Stone Cold" Steve Austin, and Dwayne "The Rock" Johnson.[681]

The popularity of "fake" WWE wrestling went beyond the wrestling shows on TV. From 1985-1986, the WWF owned a Saturday morning cartoon show called Hulk Hogan's Rock 'n' Wrestling, which featured cartoon versions of famous wrestlers such as: Hulk Hogan, Junkyard Dog, Captain Lou Albano, André the Giant, Wendi Richter, Jimmy "Superfly" Snuka, Hillbilly Jim, and Tito Santana. The evil wrestlers or "heels" were led by Rowdy Piper and consisted of Iron Sheik, Nikolai Volkoff, The Fabulous Moolah, Big John Studd, and Mr. Fuji.[682]

Wrestlers such as Hulk Hogan, Steve Austin, Dwayne Johnson, and others have gone on to successful careers in movies and TV.[683]

The following wrestlers have gone on to have careers in the movie industry: Dwayne "The Rock" Johnson, Andre The Giant, "Rowdy" Ronny Piper, Hulk Hogan, John Cena, Jesse "The Body" Ventura, "Stone Cold" Steve Austin, Tor "The Super Swedish Angel" Johnson, George "The Animal" Steele (Tie), William Scott "Bill" Goldberg, Toshiyuki "Harold" Sakata.[684]

Many "fake" wrestlers have also crossed over to the MMA freestyle fighting competition: Kazushi Sakuraba, Ken Shamrock, Masakatsu Funaki, Akira Maeda, Dan Severn, Kiyoshi Tamura, Kazuyuki Fujita, Nobuhiko Takada, and Antonio Inoki. Pro wrestler

Brock Lesnar won a victory at UFC 100 in 2009 to become the Ultimate Fighting Championship's UFC undisputed heavyweight champion.[685]

Jesse Ventura is arguably one of the most successful former pro wrestlers. In addition to having had a movie career, in 2002 he was elected governor of the US state of Minnesota.

Pro Wrestling Culture: The Violence of Pro Wrestling

The rise of wrestling-entertainment has also brought with it accusations of violence. In 2001, a 13-year-old boy in Southern Florida was sentenced to life in prison because he claims to have "accidentally" killed a 6-year-old girl while imitating "fake" wrestling techniques which he saw on TV.[686] In Louisiana, in 2013, a five year-old girl was killed by her 13 year-old brother, who was imitating TV wrestling techniques. To quote a news report, "Viloude Louis, of Terrytown, died Sunday of severe blunt force trauma that led to several internal injuries, including broken ribs, a lacerated liver, and internal bleeding." Local police arrested the 13-year-old brother, Devalon Armstrong, and charged him with second-degree murder. Armstrong told detectives he practiced "WWE-style wrestling moves" on his little sister. He repeatedly picked up the girl and slammed her onto a bed, and punched her in the stomach. The teenager also performed elbow drops – jumps where he landed on Viloude, leading with his elbow."[687] In 2012, in the same part of Louisiana, a 14-year-old boy was choked to death, by his 24-year-old cousin "just minutes after watching WWE's Wrestlemania 28."[688] In 2014, a 9-year-old was killed by his 16-year-old friend. Professional wrestling is being blamed again for the death of another child whose mother says he was imitating moves he saw on TV.[689] Unfortunately, these wrestling-related deaths continue.

Many critics have called for the abolishment of wrestling, arguing that it promotes violence. In defense of wrestling, however, these injuries happened because "despite warnings from professional wrestlers, imitation sometimes has deadly consequences." At the beginning of each wrestling broadcast, a warning message appears on the TV, telling viewers: "Do Not Try This At Home."[690] The WWE warns viewers that imitating professional wrestlers could lead to serious injuries. In the cases of two local victims, those injuries have been fatal.[691]

The WWE TV show, RAW, is rated T-14, which means that children under the age of 14 should not be watching the program. This information is displayed at the beginning of every broadcast. Many of the children who died were under the age of 14, and therefore, not part of the target audience of WWE.[692]

Despite the fact that WWE has published warnings telling children not imitate the wrestling techniques, and telling parents not to allow young children to watch, critics still call wrestling "savage." "Many scholars have condemned professional wrestling "for lacking any human dignity in its portrayal of violence and for fostering fighting among impressionable youth."[693]

Modern Rules of Pro Wrestling

"The most important thing to know about the rules of professional wrestling is that they can be changed, disregarded, made up on the spot, or broken at any time."[694]

1. Most matches have a time limit of 20 minutes.
2. Most matches are won by a pin or the best two out of three pins.
3. Wrestlers can also lose by submission.
4. A wrestler who is rendered unconscious (by a sleeper hold, for example) is assumed to have given up.
5. Wrestlers can lose by disqualification (DQ) (for using a weapon or for staying out of the ring for too long during a match)
6. A hold or a pin must be broken if the wrestler being pinned grabs the rope.[695]

The next evolution in the history of wrestling is MMA free fighting. MMA will be the subject of the next chapter.

Chapter 11: Wrestling in MMA

Mixed Martial Arts (MMA) is a combat sport which allows kicking, punching, wrestling, takedowns, knee strikes, elbow strikes, chokes, and submissions. The Ultimate Fighting Championship (UFC) is the largest and most prestigious MMA organization in the world. According to the unified rules of MMA established by the UFC, MMA fights can be won by submission, tap out, verbal tap out, knockout (KO), technical knockout (TKO), or judges' decision.[696] Under unified rules, referees have the right to call an end to a contest if one of the fighters is no longer able to "intelligently" defend himself. In the event of a referee stoppage, the fight is generally awarded to the other fighter.

Wrestling and MMA are related in that wrestling is one of the main skills of MMA. As a result, many American wrestlers have begun careers as professional MMA fighters as a way of earning a living. US Olympic wrestlers and hopefuls such as Randy Couture, Dan Henderson, Matt Lindland, Mark Coleman, and Tom Erikson all switched from wrestling to MMA as a way of earning money after their Olympic wrestling dreams ended.[697] Over the last three thousand years, wrestling has passed through various stages of development from ancient Greek Pankration to professional catch wrestling, from modern Olympic wrestling to WWE style professional wrestling, and onto present day MMA. MMA is the most recent stage of development in the sport of wrestling.

Pre-UFC MMA Fights

Modern MMA has its roots in Ancient Greek Pankration, which had very similar rules, including kicking, punching, wrestling, and choking.[698] The next step in the development of MMA came in the 19th century with the development of catch wrestling, which resulted in some of the first recorded mixed-style fights. These fights, frequently held in the USA, generally involved wrestlers and often called for wrestlers to compete in more than one style of wrestling, alternating after each round. Some of the styles included: catch wrestling, collar-and-elbow wrestling, Greco-Roman wrestling, Cornish wrestling, Cumberland wrestling, Westmorland wrestling, and even sumo.[699]

Other mixed bouts, often called "no-holds-barred" because they allowed wrestling submissions as well as punches, pitted boxers against wrestlers.[700] One such fight was when American catch wrestling champion William Muldoon fought against a boxer, Australian Professor, William Miller in 1888. The contest was meant to include two bouts, one of boxing, followed by one of wrestling. Professor Miller won a decision victory after 12 rounds of boxing, and the wrestling portion of the fight never took place because the police broke up the event, as prize fighting was illegal at that time.[701] The men were wearing 4-ounce gloves, exactly the same size as modern MMA gloves.

Muldoon also fought bare-knuckle boxing champion John L. Sullivan. The match was scored on the best two out of three falls. Sullivan scored the first fall, but eventually, as the *New York Sun* reported, "Wrestling Gladiator William Muldoon tossed Pugilist Gladiator John L. Sullivan…he just picked Sullivan up and slammed him to the carpet…the fall seemed heavy enough to shake the earth."[702] Just after the Muldoon vs. Sullivan fight, in Asia, mixed-style fights were being held which went by the Japanese name "merikan," suggesting that they recognized mixed fighting as "American-style fighting."[703]

Former world boxing champion Bob Fitzsimmons, who made history by winning titles in three weight divisions, fought William Muldoon's student, Greco-Roman wrestling champion Ernest Roeber. "Fitz took a punch or two. Then Roeber grabbed him, tied him into knots, and the show was over."[704] Predictably, Roeber took Fitzsimmons down and won the fight by way of submission, utilizing an arm lock.[705]

In 1883, the Olympic Athletic Club in San Francisco formed a martial art called Neo-Pankration, harkening back to Ancient Greek Pankration. In addition to Pankration matches, the club also held matches in "Roman cestus, a brutal form of boxing where the hands were wrapped in iron wool rather than gloves."[706] The Pankration matches featured catch wrestlers fighting against bare-knuckle boxers, but the rules only allowed open hand strikes.[707] Similar to modern MMA, Neo-Pankration included striking, throwing, and wrestling. The gloves proved to be a problem in these mixed-style matches, because boxing gloves were too bulky to allow for most grappling techniques.[708] Today, MMA fighters use fingerless gloves with padded knuckles to allow movement of the fingers. Even so, the gloves are still a controversial point, as they create greater chances for accidents and injuries. UFC commentator Joe Rogan has repeatedly spoken out against the gloves because the open fingered gloves frequently result in fighters taking an accidental finger poke to the eyes.[709]

In 1899, an English railroad engineer named William Barton-Wright wrote an article for *Pearson's Magazine*, entitled "A New Art of Self Defense." Previously, he had spent several years working in Japan, where he studied jujitsu with judo founder, Jigoro Kano. At that time, the terms judo and jujitsu were used interchangeably as Jigoro Kano's Kodokan judo was actually based on jujitsu. The new martial art which Barton invented was called bartitsu, which combined wrestling, boxing, jujitsu, savate (French style) kickboxing, and stick fighting.[710]

Barton brought jujitsu teachers K. Tani, S. Yamamoto, and Yukio Tani to London, where he opened a Bartitsu club. Arthur Conan Doyle was so fascinated with bartitsu that he even wrote it into the back story of his premier character, Sherlock Holmes. In *The Adventure of the Empty House*, Holmes employs bartitsu to overcome his arch enemy, Dr. Moriarty. Bartitsu later played a prominent role in the Sherlock Holmes movies starring Robert Downey Jr.[711]

In France, fights were held between wrestlers and savate fighters. Thanks in part to the Bartitsu Club, Japanese jujitsu became known in the West. In 1905, a match was held between savate master George Dubois and a jujitsu fighter, Ernest Regnier. [712] French Greco-Roman wrestler Ernest Regnier was a former student of the Bartitsu Club who had been trained in jujitsu under Taro Miyake and Yukio Tani. [713] In the fight, Dubois attempted a low kick to the legs of the jujitsu fighter. [714] This strategy is still employed in MMA today. Modern MMA fighters have learned that wrestlers are adept at catching high kicks and taking their opponents to the ground. Therefore, the low kick is a safer technique to use, as it is harder to catch. Eventually, the jujitsu fighter Regnier managed to take Dubois to the ground and used a submission technique to dislocate Dubois' elbow, "provoking such pain that Dubois, after attempting to stand for a second, then begs for mercy. The fight had lasted just 26 seconds, 6 seconds for the engagement itself." [715]

Most people would be shocked to learn that a mixed-style fight was once held at the White House. President Theodore Roosevelt (1858-1919) was a major fight fan who took lessons at the White House from various masters of boxing, wrestling, and martial arts. Among his favorite teachers was judo instructor Yoshiaki (Yoshitsugu) Yamashita. [716] Yamashita was not only a direct student of judo founder Jigoro Kano, but he was the nineteenth student to join Kano's Kodokan School when it opened. [717] The president was a former Assistant Secretary of the Navy, and took a particular interest in improving the US Navy's fighting capabilities. Consequently, he arranged for Yamashita to teach judo at the United States Naval Academy at Annapolis as a form of physical training and self-defense. The judo lessons were met with mixed results, as many Naval officers felt that judo was impractical and wrestling would be better. In order to decide which art was more effective, the President invited Yamashita back to the White House to fight middleweight catch wrestler Joseph Grant in 1905. [718]

According to a letter written by the President's son, Kermit, Grant quickly took Yamashita down and put him on his back; however, fighting comfortably from his back, Yamashita choked Grant into submission.[719] It is important to note that catch wrestling allowed submissions, but did not allow chokes, which at that time were called strangulations. Consequently, Grant did not know how to defend against them. Kermit observed that although Grant lost the second fall by way of elbow submission, Grant's wrestling ability, and strength to take a man down was at least equal to Yamashita's. According to Kermit, Yamashita looked worn out and hurt by the end of the match. [720]

The US Army had been considering bringing judo to the U.S. Military Academy at West Point. As a result of this fight, however, they decided to hire world champion wrestler Tom Jenkins to teach catch wrestling to the cadets.[721]

Mixed-style fights often had a unique rule set, such as limiting the combatants to open hand strikes. An example of this type of fight would be a 1912 fight between boxer "Denver" Ed Martin and wrestler Jack Leon, "The Russian Giant." In this fight, Martin was forced to slap the Russian every time he came in for the takedown.[722] Other fights allowed boxers to use boxing rules and the wrestler to use wrestling rules.

Jigoro Kano's students were travelling around the world, spreading judo/jujitsu, and taking on all comers. Possibly because of President Roosevelt's interest in the art, judo/jujitsu became well known, and mixed-style fights were being held across the entire United States. The first mixed-styles fights in Hawaii took place in 1916, where former Bartitsu club jujitsu instructor Taro Miyake defeated boxer Ben de Mello. Afterwards, mixed-style fights that pitted jujitsu against boxing and other martial arts were held in the islands.

Although mixed style fights were popular in America, the place where they really thrived was Japan, which is the birthplace of karate, judo, jujitsu, and sumo.[723] In 1924, a large scale mixed-style fight event was scheduled in Tokyo, and featured more than 30 fighters representing judo, jujitsu, and boxing. Back in America, mixed-style fights were being arranged between wrestler and jujitsu fighters, but nothing on the scale of the Japanese events.[724] This dynamic of the US and Japan undergoing the same evolution of martial arts at the same time would become particularly important in the 1990s, when modern MMA would develop in both places in tandem.

"Judo" Gene LeBell fought in the first televised MMA event in North America when he took on professional boxer Milo Savage.[725] Lebell was the national heavyweight judo champion in 1954 and 1955.[726] In addition, he had studied wrestling extensively, as well as karate, taekwondo, and kenpo. He was particularly pioneering in that he was always looking for ways to combine these arts.[727] In addition to freestyle wrestling, Gene had extensive knowledge of catch wrestling, as he grew up around the Los Angeles Olympic Auditorium, which was owned by his mother.[728] The auditorium frequently featured pro wrestling shows, and LeBell learned catch from the old time pros. Eventual, Gene would himself compete in professional wrestling, briefly winning the NWA world heavyweight championship belt.[729] LeBell is also credited with having taught judo throws and locks to Bruce Lee.[730]

LeBell's opponent, Milo Savage, was the fifth-ranked professional, light heavyweight boxing champion of America. Gene LeBell won the match in the fourth round when he took Milo Savage to the ground and choked him out. "The next morning, the newspaper headlines said, 'The Savage Was Tamed.'"[731]

The question of boxer vs. wrestler was so pervasive that even martial arts legend Bruce Lee addressed it. "The best fighter is someone who can adapt to any style." Perhaps that is why, in 2004, UFC President Dana White called Bruce Lee the "father of mixed martial arts."[732] In fact, in the opening scene of Bruce Lee's 1973 film, "Enter the Dragon", Bruce Lee defeats his opponent by taking him to the ground and submitting him. This scene demonstrates

Bruce Lee's awareness of the importance of combining ground fighting with punching and kicking, which is the spirit of MMA. At the time of his death, Bruce Lee's personal library consisted of more than 2,500 books; among them were books on wrestling and boxing, which he incorporated into his Jeet Kun Do style of fighting.[733]

Perhaps the most well-publicized mixed-style fight before the birth of the UFC was held in 1976, when three-time world heavyweight boxing champion Muhammad Ali fought against Japanese wrestling legend Antonio Inoki.[734] Apparently, the Japanese audience thought the fight was real; however, the Ali camp thought the fight was just meant to be entertainment. According to Ferdie Pacheco, Ali's doctor, "when we got over there, we found out no one was laughing."[735]

In a previous mixed-style fight, Inoki had defeated a judo Olympic gold medalist from Germany, Wilhelm Ruska. Inoki won by TKO and defeated Ruska with three submissions; however, suspicion was high that this fight was fixed, as were the roughly 20 other mixed-style fights Inoki fought.[736]

Many people consider the Ali vs Inoki fight as one of the most boring fights in history. The fight ran the distance, 15 rounds, with Ali landing only 6 punches. Inoki kept throwing himself on the ground to avoid Ali's punches. Laying on his back, Inoki would taunt Ali to come to the ground and fight him. While he was laying there, Inoki kicked Ali in the shins with his heavy wrestling boots. A similar technique is still used by Brazilian jujitsu practitioners in MMA today. They lie on their back to avoid punches while baiting their opponent to come to the ground and fight them. In the end, the match was declared a draw.

Inoki fought his final fight in 1998, when he was about 55 years of age. "Ali flew out from America to watch. After Inoki had completed his final victory, Ali climbed into the ring, and the two men hugged."[737]

Although this match was mixed, Inoki's early forays into mixed-styles fights helped the development of modern MMA.

"This fight is still important as it paved the way for both the sport of MMA and the participation of wrestlers in this new form of fighting competition."[738] In the US, mixed fights were also beginning to make headway. In the 1986 American pro wrestling event Wrestlemania 2, wrestler Rowdy Roddy Piper fought former pro-boxer and bouncer Mr. T in a boxing match. Piper lost by disqualification.[739] Piper was a student of Gene LeBell, and a strong supporter of both catch wresting and mixed martial arts.[740]

From Japan to Brazil, the Judo Connection

MMA in Japan can be traced back to Kodokan Judo founder, Jigoro Kano (1860-1938). Judo is a bridge connecting the development of wrestling in Japan, China, and the US. Judo is also the catalyst that spawned the creation of Brazilian jujitsu, which directly caused the rise of MMA.

Jigoro Kano modified jujitsu, the age-old martial art of the imperial army of Japan, and converted it to a civilian sport art. He removed what he believed were the most dangerous techniques to create a safe martial art which could be practiced by all people. Kano, himself a small man, concentrated on movements which required little or no strength, and allowed smaller men to defeat larger ones. Kano absorbed techniques from various other martial arts into his new style, which became judo.

Whereas Japanese jujitsu was an all-encompassing art which included kicking, punching, throwing, ground fighting, and submissions, Kano removed nearly all striking from judo, as well as much of the ground fighting and submissions. His rationale for doing this was because he felt that as a self-defense art, throwing was a better strategy, as the would-be victim could throw the attacker on the ground and then run away. The other reason was that Kano's own preference toward moves was affected greatly by physics and body mechanics. Throws executed correctly maximized the strength of the thrower, and reduced the need for size and power. Already, in the late 1800s, judo was selected as the official martial art of the Japanese police.[741] Judo allowed smaller police officers to control larger suspects, and allowed police to subdue attackers without hurting them or escalating the violence in a conflict.

After the turn of the century, Kano began sending his black belt students into the world to spread judo. This is how Yoshiaki (Yoshitsugu) Yamashita wound up teaching judo to President Theodore Roosevelt. Another of Kano's students, Mitsuyo Maeda, brought judo to Brazil in 1914. Maeda is one of the single most important individuals in the history of the development of MMA.[742] He was a Jiu-Jitsu champion who had been a student of Kano since 1897. When Maeda immigrated to Brazil in 1914, he was assisted by a successful Brazilian businessman, Gastão Gracie. In return for helping him get established in Brazil, Maeda taught Jujitsu to Gastão's oldest son, Carlos Gracie, who later taught jujitsu to his brothers. Helio Gracie (1913-2009) was the youngest of Gastão's eight children. A small, frail boy, Helio Gracie had difficulty executing the jujitsu moves taught by his older brother. As a result, Helio spent most of his time just watching his brothers practice jujitsu, rather than practicing himself. Away from prying eyes, Helio was busy modifying the jujitsu techniques to better match his frail physique.

The Gracies moved back to Rio in 1922, where Carlos opened the first Gracie jujitsu academy at 106 Marques de Abrantes Street in the Flamengo neighborhood.[743] One day, a student showed up at the jujitsu academy while Carlos was away. Helio taught the student his method of jujitsu, and the student was so impressed by Helio's skills that Carlos promoted Helio to instructor.[744] This new version of Japanese jujitsu became known as Brazilian jujitsu or Gracie jujitsu.

Carlos Gracie, as the leader of the family, issued "The Gracie Challenge," which was an open invitation to anyone to fight against a Gracie in a no rules, *vale tudo* (anything goes) style match. The winner would earn money, fame, and respect. The Gracie brothers fought countless matches against boxers, wrestlers, and Capoeira fighters. This tradition continued when Helio took over.[745]

Helio fought all comers to prove the effectiveness of his family's style of fighting. Helio and his Gracie jujitsu were undefeated until he fought champion jujitsu fighter and professional wrestler, Masahiko Kimura (1917 – 1993), who outweighed Helio by almost 80 pounds. By the rules of the fight, which would later become known as the Gracie rules, neither throws nor pins would count. The fight had to be won by submission or unconsciousness. Kimura won the match when he broke Helio's arm by utilizing a reverse ude-garami arm lock which, to this day, in Brazilian jujitsu is called the Kimura. Despite being the victor, Kimura was so impressed by the smaller man's skills that he invited Helio to go teach Brazilian jujitsu in Japan.[746]

Another of Helio's most famous fights came in 1955, when he was in his early forties. Helio accepted the challenge to fight Valdemar Santana, a former student of the Gracies. The match was a *vale tudo* contest. The fight lasted three hours and forty-five minutes.[747] Although Helio fought exceptionally well, Santana won by KO when he soccer-kicked a downed Helio in the face.[748]

There is a famous anecdote about the Gracie family, which says that when Helio's sons were going off to a fight, Helio would tell them, "I will give you $5 if you win, and $10 if you lose."[749] Helio wanted to teach his sons that a fighter learns more from his losses than from his wins.

Helio's two losses against Kimura and Santana did nothing to tarnish the Gracie name. In fact, both stories became part of the legend which elevated both the Gracie name and the art to mythical proportions, ultimately setting the stage for the birth of MMA.

Vale tudo to MMA in Brazil

In the early 20th century, *vale tudo* events were becoming popular at carnivals and festivals in Brazil. The fighters were fighting not only for themselves, but to prove that their martial art or their school was the best. The Gracies were instrumental in promoting these events, as it was their preferred method of advertising their style of jujitsu.[750]

Vale tudo fights gained popularity and were broadcast on a TV show called *Heroes of the Ring*. In 1959, in a *vale tudo* fight broadcast on national television, a Helio Gracie student, Joao Alberto Barreto, broke the arm of his opponent Jose Geraldo. Suddenly, the public turned against the sport of *vale tudo*, and later the style was banned in Rio. The sport had a resurgence in the 1980s, when Helio's son Rickson fought a highly publicized match in Brasilia before an audience of 15,000.[751]

With the rebirth of *vale tudo* in the 1980s, Muay Thai came to Brazil and helped further pave the way for the emergence of MMA. Muay Thai came via a man named Nelio Naja, "the father of Brazilian Muay Thai," who learned the art while he was in Thailand. Muay Thai, a striking art which includes kicks, punches, knees, elbows, and clinching, was combined with Brazilian jujitsu, and a new fighting style was born, which was called *vale tudo* or *luta livre* (free fighting).

Marco Ruas, one of the early *luta livre* champions, was a powerful Muay Thai fighter who taught a cross-training art that included Brazilian Jujitsu and Muay Thai.[752] Ruas went on to win the UFC 7 tournament, and this combination of skills became the combination favored by early MMA fighters.

In 1984, a mixed-style fight was held in Brazil, which was billed as *Vale tudo* "Jiu Jitsu vs Martial Arts." Several Gracie students fought against *luta livre* students at this event. The Gracie students often had better jujitsu skills than the *luta livre* students; however, the *luta livre* students used their Muay Thai skills to damage the Gracie students in standing. The *luta livre* students utilized their own jujitsu skills to avoid being taken down by the Gracie students, which is the exact strategy used by wrestlers in MMA today. Modern champions such as Chuck Lidell and Mirko Cro Cop were predominantly kick boxers; however, they had a wrestling background. The wrestling training allowed them to oppose takedown attempts by jujitsu fighters, and remain on their feet to continue punching and kicking. The fighting style of Chuck Lidell, an NCAA Division I wrestler, has actually been called using wrestling in reverse.[753]

Vale tudo eventually gave way to MMA, which was largely dominated by the Gracies and the *vale tudo* fighters. The history of MMA in both the US and Japan is closely tied to the Gracie family and their Brazilian Jujitsu. Helio's son, Rorion Gracie, helped create the UFC. Another of Helio's sons, Royce, won UFC 1, UFC 2, and UFC 4. Rickson and Renzo Gracie became famous fighters in early Japanese MMA. "From day one, MMA was linked to Brazilian jiu-jitsu."[754]

Development of MMA in Japan

The Gracie family and Brazilian jujitsu were not the only imports to Japan. Catch wrestling was also brought over and became part of the development of MMA. In 1972, catch wrestler Karl Gotch (not to be confused with Frank Gotch) was invited to Japan to teach Japanese wrestlers, including Antonio Inoki. In 1976, Inoki sponsored a series of mixed-style fights utilizing many of the moves he learned from Gotch.[755] Western martial arts such as catch wrestling heavily influenced Japanese professional wrestling and, eventually, Japanese MMA.

Gotch had a reputation for ferocity and skill. In his day, he had been a shooter, a real catch wrestler who, although competing in scripted fights, was capable of winning legitimate wrestling matches by submission. Because he was so ferocious, some American pro wrestlers and promoters were actually afraid to work with him. Gotch took that aggressive style and knowledge of submission holds and imparted it to the Japanese.[756] Several of Gotch's Japanese students formed the Universal Wrestling Federation (UWF) and *Shooto* or shoot fighting.[757] These early mixed-style fight leagues bore the direct mark of Gotch. The fights, while still scripted or worked, were more violent and more real than pro wrestling had been in Japan in the past, as they allowed some striking and utilization of submissions from catch wrestling.

In the 1990s, catch wrestler Billy Robinson from The Snake Pit, the birth place of catch wrestling in England, became the head coach of the UWF Snake Pit in Tokyo.[758] Two of Robinson's greatest students were MMA fighter and champion wrestler Kazushi Sakuraba, and Josh Barnett, a former UFC champion and world class grappling champion.[759] Josh Barnett, with an MMA fight record of 35 wins and 8 losses,[760] is one of the most outspoken proponents of catch wrestling and its importance in MMA. Barnett has been quoted as saying, "[Catch wrestling] is a root on the tree of MMA"[761] He is also quoted as saying, "Today's MMA, modern Olympic wrestling, WWE-style pro wrestling, and even the reality-based self-defense system of Krav Maga are all derivative of catch wrestling,"[762]

UWF, *Shooto*, shoot fighting rings, and Japanese Pancrase were all catch-wrestling based mixed-fight styles or fight leagues which popped up in Japan in the early 1990s. Japanese wrestler Akira Maeda started Rings, which claimed to offer real fights featuring fighters from different martial arts.[763] Pancrase was the invention of Masakatsu Funaki and Minoru Suzuki, two students of Antonio Inoki.[764] The name Pancrase was taken from Ancient Greek Pankration. Pancrase was a watered-down version of what would eventually become MMA, and combined some limited striking with catch wrestling. The fighters were bare-handed, and were only allowed closed fist strikes to the body and open-handed strikes to the face and head. Kicks were permitted to the head and body.[765] Some of the early UFC champions, including Ken Shamrock, Frank Shamrock, Josh Barnett, and Bas Rutten, got their start in Pancrase.[766] In addition to fighting in both Pancrase and MMA, Ken Shamrock was also a WWE wrestler. Josh Barnett has wrestled in several pro wrestling leagues in Japan and continues to wrestle in New Japan Pro wrestling (NJPW).

While these organizations offered mixed-style fighting, Japan was still in the early stages of developing MMA. These organizations did not permit closed-fist strikes to the face or ground, nor elbow strikes, which are characteristic if MMA fighting.

The other dissimilarity with these organizations is that they all evolved out of Japanese pro wrestling leagues, where fights were always scripted and outcomes predetermined. While these organizations claimed to be offering fair fights, it turns out that many of them were actually "worked" with predetermined outcomes.

In 1997, a new Japanese MMA promotion called Pride Fighting Championship held their first event.[767] The fights featured several prominent wrestlers, such as Dan Severn. Severn held world titles in wrestling, and also fought in Pride, UFC, and WWF. The event included a jujitsu vs wrestling match which featured Brazilian Renzo Gracie against pro wrestler Akira Shoji. The main event was also jujitsu versus wrestling, with Rickson Gracie facing Japanese wrestler, Nobuhiko Takada.[768] Rumors abounded that the Japanese mafia, the Yakuza, were the financial backers of the Pride Fighting Championships.[769] Many great wrestlers, such as Mark Coleman and Mark Kerr, were Pride fighters who also fought in the UFC. These fights were real fights with very minimal rules. Fighters could kick a downed opponent, strike on the ground, knee on the ground, and punch in the face with closed fists. At the time that Pride held their first event, the UFC was in turmoil and teetering on the brink of bankruptcy. For ten years, Pride was offering the biggest and best shows, paying the highest salaries, and gobbling up the best fighters. In 2007, Pride FC was purchased by Lorenzo Fertitta and Frank Fertitta III, co-owners of Zuffa, the owners of the UFC. After several scandals involving ties between Pride and the Yakuza, Pride closed down.[770] The closure of Pride left the UFC as the dominant MMA promotion in the world.

History of the UFC

"Although there are numerous MMA promotional companies in business today, the Ultimate Fighting Championship (UFC) continues to be the sport's premier league."[771]

In 1969, Rorion Gracie, son of Helio, moved to the United States and began teaching jujitsu out of his garage. His students often told him that teachers of other martial arts claimed jujitsu was a waste of time, so Rorion invited them to come and fight him. Rorion won all of these fights; however, he decided the world would never be convinced of the dominance of Brazilian jujitsu until the fights were televised and able to reach an audience of millions. This was the founding thought for the creation of the UFC.[772] Working together with Art Davie and John Milius, Rorion Gracie started UFC 1.

In 1993, the UFC held their first event in Denver, Colorado, before a crowd of less than 2,800 people.[773] The spirit of the early UFCs was to end the age-old question, which martial art would win in a fight. Consequently, UFC 1 featured fighters from a multitude of disciplines: sumo, savate, kick boxing, karate, jujitsu, boxing, shootfighting and taekwondo.[774]. There were no rounds, no time limits, no judges, and no score cards. Apart from prohibiting biting and eye gouging, there were very few rules. Fights had to be won by KO or submission.[775] The fights took place in an eight-sided cage (now known as the Octagon).[776]

The offbeat venue of Denver was a far cry from glitzy Las Vegas, where the events are held today, but the lack of rules in UFC fights meant that they could not be sanctioned by state boxing commissions; and in 1993, there were no other state commissions that regulated fight sports, meaning that, to be sanctioned, the UFC would have to adhere to boxing rules. Obviously, boxing rules would have defeated the purpose of the event. Colorado was finally chosen because it was one of the few states without a state athletic commission.[777]

Rorion chose his younger brother Royce to champion the family at UFC 1. Many people questioned this decision, as his brother Rickson was much larger and a well-established fighter in Brazil; however, Rorion wanted to use the UFC to make the point that a small, inexperienced fighter with a mastery of jujitsu could beat anyone.[778] Royce only weighed 77 kg (176 lb.), which was in sharp contrast to the average fighter, who was well over 90 kg (200 lb.), and the largest competitor, Teila Tuli weighing 200 kg (440 lb.).[779] Royce went on to win UFC 1, UFC 2, and UFC 4. These high-profile wins caused an explosion in interest in Brazilian jujitsu (BJJ), but the UFC itself was not doing well.

When the UFC first started, they billed themselves as being a violent fighting sport with no rules. True to their word, the early UFC events were incredibly barbaric, with a number of one-sided fights and competitors being beaten till they had to be carried out, as the referee stood idly by. As a result, there was a great deal of opposition to the UFC. In 1996, Senator John McCain called the UFC "human cockfighting," and urged state governors to ban the UFC.[780] Much of the UFC's income at that time came from television coverage; however, TV networks were unwilling to carry the UFC after the organization had been vilified. Opponents of the UFC sent letters to the governors of every state urging them to ban the UFC.

In response, the UFC began creating a set of rules so the sport could be regulated. In 1997, UFC introduced weight classes, and required fighters to wear fingerless gloves. Rules prohibiting hair-pulling, small-joint manipulation (meaning intentionally snapping a opponent's toes or fingers), headbutts, groin strikes, kicks to a downed opponent and strikes to the back of the head and neck were instituted.[781] Other changes included the addition of judges, time limits, rounds, and a 10-point must scoring system.[782] The 10-point must system was adapted from boxing, where the winner of a round must be given 10 points. The other fighter is given 9 or less points. In the event that there is no KO or submission, at the end of the fight, the score for each fighter is tallied and the fighter with most points is declared the winner.

Even with these rule changes, the UFC was nearly dead by 1998. However, Pride FC was growing, leading in terms of money and popularity. In Japan, Pride fighters became celebrities, even appearing in TV commercials. Where UFC 1 attracted a live audience of less than 3,000, a Pride event once attracted a live audience of 90,000. The Pride TV ratings were also exceptional, with nearly half of the Japanese population tuning in to watch the Pride New Year's Eve event.[783] This difference in success was partially due to demographics. Japanese fans came from the wealthier class, and Pride shows were attended by celebrities who wanted to be seen. UFC fans, on the other hand, were from the lower rungs of society.[784]

The UFC was trying to compete with Pride while trying to establish credibility with both American law makers and the public. Over the next three years, the UFC began trying to reposition itself as a sporting event instead of a blood sport. The referees were given the power to stop a contest if a fighter could "no longer intelligently defend himself" in order to increase safety. In 1999, the UFC established five-minute rounds. Finally, in the year 2000, the New Jersey's State Athletic Control Board sanctioned MMA, and the Unified Rules of Mixed Martial Arts were established.[785]

Still on the brink of death, the UFC was purchased in 2001 by Zuffa LLC, a company formed by former boxer Dana White, and casino moguls Lorenzo and Frank Fertitta III for $2 million.[786] Shortly after, the state of Nevada also sanctioned MMA, meaning fights could be held in Las Vegas. Deals between UFC and pay-per-view (PPV) TV soon followed, and created a new stream of income for the UFC.

The next tremendous financial boom for the UFC came in 2005, when they started the reality TV show *The Ultimate Fighter*.[787] The UFC was still recovering from bad publicity, and no TV channel wanted to pay to air *The Ultimate Fighter*. In fact, MMA was still illegal in many states. As a result, The UFC's owners, the Fertitta brothers, paid for the production using an estimated ten million dollars of their own money.[788] Luckily for the UFC and the Fertitta brothers, the show was an instant success.

The Ultimate Fighter Show (TUF) featured 16 fighters living in a house together for a period of weeks, competing in an elimination tournament. The fighters were divided into teams headed by a celebrity coach. Each episode showed the teams' training, as well as showing the tedium and monotony of the being locked in a house with 16 fighters, and no TV, no video games, no books, and no magazines. Each week, there was one fight challenge where the loser was sent home.[789] The two coaches for Season One were UFC champions Chuck Liddell and Randy Couture. In the show's finale, the two coaches would fight. TUF became a powerful advertising tool for both the UFC and for specific fights, building interest and generating ticket sales long before the fights took place. The live finale of TUF Season One attracted an audience of 2.6 million viewers on Spike TV.[790]

The weeks of competition in the fighter house also set the stage for the coaches' fight. The match "between the two coaches, Chuck Liddell and Randy Couture, was the highest-grossing live gate the organization ever had and scored 280,000 PPV buys."[791] Along with the success of the TV show, UFC began to buy up competing MMA networks.

At the time that UFC was growing into the largest, most profitable fight organization that had ever existed, in Japan, Pride was the subject of newspaper stories claiming that the organization had close ties to the Yakuza. Pride lost its TV audience and, in 2007, was bought by the UFC. Other UFC purchases included Strikeforce, World Extreme Cage Fighting (WEC), and World Fighting Alliance (WFA).[792]

As a result of the unified rules, Senator John McCain softened his harsh opposition to the UFC, telling NPR: "They have cleaned up the sport to the point, at least in my view, where it is not human cockfighting any more. I think they've made significant progress."[793]

The success of both MMA and the UFC has spawned an entire industry of products ranging from a chain of UFC brand martial arts clubs to grappling shirts, workout clothing, hand raps and gloves.[794]

Today, MMA is one of the fastest growing sports in the world.[795] Analysts say that MMA is already more popular among suburban youth than boxing, hockey, and professional basketball.[796]

Additionally, MMA has transcended the status of a spectator sport and become a participation sport, with fans joining gyms and learning to wrestle and fight. MMA has also spawned interest in grappling, and most MMA schools offer wrestling classes. Schools have also popped up across the United States to teach Brazilian jujitsu or offer training for grappling competitions.

The UFC earns a significant amount of money through "pay-per-view shows, event gate receipts, and various merchandising and product-licensing agreements."[797] As of 2014, MMA was sanctioned in most US states, with the exception of New York and very few others.[798] In 2016, New York finally ended the ban on MMA.[799] The same year, the WME-IMG group bought most of the shares of the UFC for a whopping $4 billion.[800]

Wrestlers in MMA

The UFC was conceived to end a debate over which martial art would beat which martial art in a fight, and which was the best martial art in the world. For decades, people had suggested that karate would win because of the powerful kicks, or taekwondo because of the speed, or kung fu because of its fluidity, or boxing because of its powerful punches. When the first several UFCs were held, people were shocked to find out that Brazilian jujitsu, which no one had ever heard of, was the martial art that dominated over the other styles.

Brazilian Jujitsu expert, Royce Gracie, the youngest and smallest son of the founder of Brazilian Jujitsu, Helio Gracie, won 3 of the first 4 UFCs, going on to become the first UFC Hall of Fame inductee.[801] Through the efforts of Royce and others, the early UFC era was dominated by Brazilian Jujitsu practitioners. After seeing a small man dominate over a much larger, ferocious opponent, Brazilian jujitsu was awarded almost mythical reverence; however, reign of the Brazilian jujitsu fighters was put to an end by American wrestlers. Once American wrestlers entered the UFC, "wrestlers won five of the first 10 UFCs."[802] Wrestlers turned the tide, and have become the dominant force in the UFC through today.

Wrestler Dan "The Beast" Severn

"Standing 6'2", weighing a stout 250 pounds, and sporting a ferocious mustache, Dan Severn was the UFC's original big scary wrestler."[803]

Dan "The Beast" Severn was one of the first decorated US wrestlers to compete in the UFC. In 1994, at age 37, with very little MMA training, he entered UFC 4 and won two of the three fights necessary to be crowned champion. "Severn came in with zero knowledge of anything other than grab, pick up and slam" his opponents."[804] Using these crude, but effective methods, he won his first two fights in a combined time of less than three minutes.[805]

Growing up, Severn and his four brothers were all all-American wrestlers, meaning that he qualified as one of the top 8 wrestlers in the nation in their weight category.[806] In high school, Severn won the national wrestling championships twice. He set eight national records and was inducted into Arizona State University's Wrestling Hall of Fame.[807] After graduating from university, in 1982, Severn continued competing internationally in wrestling, traveling all around the world, including Japan, Hungary, Cuba, France, and Turkey. He won a number of international titles. And back in the US, he won 13 National AAU wrestling championships.[808]

Beginning in 1998, Dan Severn participated in thousands of pro wrestling matches across 30 separate professional wrestling organizations, and "held the National Wrestling Alliance (NWA) heavyweight title for longer than any other previous champion."[809] He even wrestled in the prestigious WWF (later WWE).

Severn has been one of the most active MMA fighters who ever lived. In 2011, Dan Severn became the second MMA fighter in history to achieve his 100th win. Having passed the age of fifty, Dan

Severn continued to fight an average of four times per year.[810] His MMA career achievements include: two eight-man tournament wins in the UFC, and a UFC Superfight Championship title.[811] According to Sherdog, the most widely accepted registry of MMA fight records, Dan Severn's final professional MMA fight record is 101 wins, 19 losses, and 7 draws.[812]

Dan Severn's basic MMA fighting style seemed to be to take his opponents to the ground, violently, using his powerful wrestling skills. He rarely shot low for a single leg or double leg takedown. Instead he would use more of a Greco-Roman upper body wrestling style. Next, he would lie on his opponent, essentially pinning him. Severn maintained top position, holding the opponent down, which is a skill developed through years of wrestling competitions. The win would usually come from striking or choking his opponent.[813]

No one could have predicted it at the time; however, but Dan Severn would be the first in a very long list of American wrestlers to dominate the sport of MMA.

Wrestler Mark "The Hammer" Coleman

At 6' feet tall and 220 pounds of solid muscle, UFC Hall of Famer, Mark Coleman was an incredibly powerful wrestler who had an almost unstoppable single-leg takedown.

In 1996, Mark Coleman, fought in UFC 10. Coleman's MMA strategy was to use his powerful wresting style to take his opponent down. His wrestling style was more like freestyle wrestling, and he is said to have had one of the most powerful single-leg takedowns in MMA. Next, he maintained top position, but different from Severn, he did not just lie on his opponents. He postured up and rained down powerful punches till the opponent was unconscious or forced to tap out.[814] This new style of fighting was called "Ground and Pound," and Mark Coleman, as the inventor of the style, became known as the "Godfather of Ground and Pound."[815]

Coleman was a 1988 Big Ten Wrestling Champion, and made the 1988 All-Big Ten selection.[816] He was a two-time conference champion when he wrestled at Miami University, and he later won an NCAA championship after transferring to Ohio State University. In 1991, he placed second in the FILA wrestling World Championships. In 1992, he was an Olympic wrestling team member, representing the US at the Barcelona Olympics, where he placed 7th overall.[817] He won gold medals at the Pan American championships in 1990, 1991, and 1992, and won a gold medal at the Pan American games in Havana, in 1991.[818]

Coleman tried, but failed to obtain a place on the US Olympic team in 1996. "At the Olympic trials, a manager (Richard Hamilton) came to me, Mark Kerr, and Tom Erikson (three powerhouse wrestlers who didn't make the team), and slapped a contract in front of me. UFC 10 was in 30 days."[819]

Mark Coleman described his early fighting strategy. "I had a simple game plan for every opponent. Take him down and pound the crap out of him. I worked hard, but I was scared. After signing the contract, fighting scared and I only had 30 days."[820] Coleman wound up winning both the UFC 10 and UFC 11 championships. In 1997, at UFC 12, Mark Coleman defeated fellow wrestler, Dan Severn, and became the UFC world heavyweight champion. Among other high-profile wins, in 2000, he won the Pride Grand Prix in 2000, where he had been a tremendous underdog. He identified this victory as one of his greatest accomplishments.[821] In 2008, Mark Coleman was inducted into the UFC Hall of Fame.

During the early days of Mark Coleman's MMA dominance, head-butts were still allowed in MMA. But once head-butts were banned, Coleman was at a tremendous disadvantage. "Head-butts were a great equalizer to combat the guard game. Later, wrestling shoes were banned for competition, which was a rule that hampered wrestlers' takedown ability."[822] Many wrestlers felt that without the shoes they could not get sufficient traction to develop enough speed for their blinding takedowns.

Much of the action of MMA in the 1990s and beyond has been an ongoing rivalry between wrestlers and jujitsu practitioners. One area where wrestlers are superior to most other fighters is in their ability to take the opponent to the ground. Jujitsu fighters, however, often do not mind being taken to the ground, and fighting from bottom position. In the pre-rules days of MMA, wrestlers like Coleman or Mark Kerr would take their opponents down and hit them with headbutts. Once headbutts were prohibited, the wrestlers were forced to use hand strikes on the ground, which often left them open to submission attempts from the jujitsu fighters.

Wrestler Mark "The Smashing Machine" Kerr

Mark Kerr was one of the early stars of MMA. He is credited with being one of the first wrestlers to pursue a well-rounded fight strategy, which including punching and kicking. "While many wrestlers stuck with the skills that brought them to the game, Kerr branched out into submission grappling and was nigh unbeatable."[823] Kerr was an excellent wrestler and, weighing 255 pounds of solid muscle, possibly the most powerful fighter who has ever fought in MMA.

In high school, Kerr was an Ohio State wrestling champion. At Syracuse University, Kerr was the Division I champion as well as a Division I All-American in 1992. In 1993, he placed 7th in the FILA World Championships for freestyle wrestling.

In 1994, Kerr won the USA Senior Freestyle wrestling Champion.[824] He also won three professional submission grappling tournaments: weight class champion in Abu Dhabi in 1999, weight class champion in Abu Dhabi in 2000, and absolute champion in Abu Dhabi in 2000. He won the ADCC 2001 and 2003 Superfight championships.

Kerr "entered the world of mixed martial arts to earn money and still have the ability to compete at a high level."[825] In 1997, Mark Kerr travelled to Brazil, where he won his first MMA fights. In fact, he fought in a *vale tudo* tournament in which he won three successive fights and became the overall champion.[826] Mark went on to win the UFC 14 and 15 tournaments, defeating a total of four opponents in a total time of less than six minutes. Around the same time, UFC was being banned in most US states, and losing PPV dollars. So, Mark Kerr and many other MMA fighters headed to Japan, where fights were plentiful and well-paying.[827]

Later that year, Mark Kerr fought and won in Pride Fighting Championships 2, 3, 4, and 6. Through 1999, he amassed a list of 11 consecutive wins and was completely undefeated.[828] Sadly, he later destroyed himself with drugs and had to retire from fighting. Nevertheless, Mark Kerr proved wrestling's dominance in MMA.

Wrestler Dan Henderson

Dan Henderson has been considered as one of the most successful wrestlers in MMA. As an MMA fighter, Henderson amassed the following titles: Strikeforce Light Heavyweight Champion, champion of Pride Fighting Championships, UFC 17 Middleweight Tournament Winner, the 1997 Brazil Open Lightweight Tournament Champion, the RINGS King of Kings 1999 Tournament Winner, and the 2005 PRIDE Welterweight Grand Prix Champion.

His success in MMA is heavily attributed to his long and successful wrestling career. In 1988, Henderson was the junior national champion in both Greco-Roman and Freestyle wrestling. As a member of the Arizona State University wrestling team, he qualified for the 1993 NCAA championships. He was the national Greco-Roman wrestling champion in 1991, 1993, and 1994. He won the senior national champion in 1993, 1994, and 1997. Henderson was a member of the US Olympic team in 1992 and 1996. In 1995, he won a bronze medal in the Pan-American games, and a gold medal in the 2000 Pan-American Championships. He is considered to be the second most highly decorated wrestler in the UFC.[829]

Dan Henderson is "the only man to hold two major titles in different weight classes simultaneously…This Greco-Roman wrestler is the gold standard for crossover wrestlers entering MMA."[830] While utilizing his wrestling ability to control his opponents, Henderson has won most of his fights by KO. Some experts suggest that Greco-Roman wrestlers have stronger hip power than other athletes, making them able to punch harder.[831]

At the beginning of 2016, when Henderson was 46 years old, he was still ranked among the top ten in the world. After losing a rematch fight with British fighter Michael Bisbing, Henderson finally announced his retirement from the UFC. His career record stood at 32 wins and 15 losses.[832]

Wrestler Randy "The Natural" Couture

Randy "The Natural" Couture, also called "Captain America," is one of the most amazing MMA fighters who has ever lived. Randy has won more UFC titles than any other person. At the age of 43, he held the age record as the oldest fighter to ever win a UFC championship.[833]

While his career record is 19 wins and 11 losses, 15 of Couture's fights were title fights.[834] He was the three-time UFC Heavyweight Champion, two-time UFC Light Heavyweight Champion, an Interim UFC Light Heavyweight Champion, and was the UFC 13 Heavyweight Tournament Winner. Couture was inducted as the fourth member of the UFC Hall of Fame.[835]

In high school, Couture tried to win a place on the wrestling team at 71 kg (158 lb.), but he was defeated. So, he challenged at 141, 148, 158, then 168 pounds, and eventually won a spot on the team at 80 kg (178 lb.). To make weight on fight day, he would drink gallons of water. He said that constantly fighting larger guys helped him when he later joined the UFC and had to fight against unlimited heavyweights.[836] In those days, the heavyweight division had no upper weight limit. Couture once faced WWE wrestler Brock Lesnar, who outweighed him by 20.5 kg (45 lb.).

When Couture was in the US Army, he won the military world championship in Greco-Roman wrestling at 82 kg (180.5 lb.). After leaving the army, he received recruitment calls from numerous universities.[837] While he was older than most university students, the

NCAA subtracted military service years from a wrestler's age. It turned out that because Couture had never wrestled at the college level before, he still had four years of eligibility.

In addition to his successful collegiate wrestling career, Couture won a gold medal in the 1991 Pan-American Games. In the Pan-American Championships, he won silver in 1992, gold in 1991, silver in 1990, bronze in 1997, and silver in 1998. He won a bronze medal in the FILA Wrestling World Cup in 1991, and again in 1992.

"Adversity comes in all shapes and sizes. Over the last eleven years, my opponents have gotten younger and fresher, while I just seem to get older. As one of the lighter competitors in the heavyweight division, I've stared across the cage at monsters 40 to 60 pounds heavier than me, thinking to myself, how am I going to get out of this one? It's just the nature of the game. The truth is, we all face adversity in our lives, through our work or our relationships with family and friends. No one is immune."[838]-Randy Couture

Although Couture is one of most revered former UFC champions, he is not listed as one of the ten most highly decorated wrestlers in MMA.[839]

Wrestler Daniel Cormier

Daniel Cormier's current MMA record is 19 wins with 1 loss and 1 no-contest.[840] In all of his first 15 fights, Cormier was never taken down.

Daniel Cormier is considered to be one of the most highly decorated wrestlers in the UFC. His wrestling credentials include a high school wrestling record of 101 wins and 9 losses. He won a bronze medal in the world championships in 2007, gold in the 2003 Pan-American Games, bronze in 2007, and gold in the 2002 Pan-American Championships. He was also a member of the 2004 US Olympic Wrestling Team.[841]

For many great wrestlers, MMA represented an opportunity to earn money. For people like Cormier, the UFC also offered a second chance at being a champion. In 2004, Cormier placed 4th in the

Olympics. In 2008, he was slotted to represent the US again; however, he was unable to compete for medical reasons. In the weeks leading up to his first UFC title fight, Cormier said, "For a long time I thought the Olympics was it; I represented America, and nothing would match that. But as I get closer to this fight, this feels bigger. So many people are watching. And the ability to make money is life changing."[842]

Wrestling Coaching Strategy Applied to MMA

Watching a modern MMA fight, one would see many of the same elements of wrestling one saw in catch wrestling matches of the 18th and 19th century, including the escapes, reversals, double-leg takedowns, single-leg takedowns, leg sweeps, suplex, and submission locks of catch wrestling.[843] Because catch wresting and MMA are so closely related, many of the training techniques used today represent a return to the past, to the days when Martin "Farmer" Burns (1861 – 1937) was considered the best catch wrestling coach.[844] As a coach, Burns believed that each wrestler needed to be treated as an individual with his own, unique training routine. "Each wrestler has to develop skills on their own."[845] As MMA contains elements of boxing, wrestling and even Muay Thai, one of the first rules of being a good MMA coach today is to treat each fighter as an individual and customize the training regime to capitalize on each fighter's strengths. This type of personalized training is in sharp contrast to how most coaches trained their fighters in the 19th and 20th centuries, or how many wrestlers are trained today in China.

Modern MMA coaches generally recognize that there are strikers – fighters who like to punch and kick – and grapplers, or fighters who want to wrestle. Both kinds need to be trained differently. There is some overlap in training, as all MMA fighters need training in the rudiments of both striking and wrestling, as well as how to cross the cage, close distance, and engage with the opponent. For the grappler in particular, all of these skills have to be learned before he can even be in position to apply a submission hold and win the fight. Burns, as well as some of the better catch wrestling coaches of the day, realized this nearly a century ago. "There is wrestling and then there are wrestling holds. You have to learn to wrestle before you can apply the holds. You know you have three basic styles of wrestling: let's go out there and pin the other man, let's throw the other man – which is basically Greco-Roman, or let's submit the other man. So amateur wrestling is the basic thing you need to know as far as I am concerned."[846] Today, great coaches use the phrase, "position before submission," meaning a fighter has to first know how to take his opponent down and immobilize him before attempting to end the fight with a submission hold. The skill that allows a fighter to take his opponent to the ground and pin him is wrestling.

Why Wrestling Works in MMA

"Whether we call it judo, jiujitsu, sambo, Greco-Roman, freestyle or submission, we're talking about the same thing: wrestling."[847] "There's no secret that wrestling is a huge part of the grappling game and if you're able to master that – a lot of your troubles are gone."[848]

In the early days of MMA, a black belt in Brazilian jujitsu was considered the best base for a fighter to have. As the sport evolved, a base of high school or collegiate wrestling seems to be more valuable. "Of the ten UFC champions or contenders for the vacant title, seven are former All State or All-American wrestlers. By contrast, only two are BJJ black belts."[849]

The first wrestlers in the UFC were people such as Dan Severn, Don Frye, Mark Coleman and Mark Kerr. Later, other wrestlers came and continued the trend of wresters in MMA, including Kevin Randleman, Randy Couture, Tito Ortiz and Matt Hughes. These wrestlers embodied the power and strength of wrestlers, and the ability to lift, slam and control an opponent. More recent champions and contenders Rashad Evans, Cain Velasquez, Ben Askren, Daniel Cormier, and Gray Maynard continue to prove that wrestling is an important base for MMA training.[850]

"Wrestling dictates where the fight takes place. If you are a good striker with no takedown defense, you will lose. If you are great at Brazilian jujitsu, with no takedowns, you will lose. You have to be able to wrestle."[851]

All MMA fights begin with the two opponents standing. Once the referee signals the beginning of the match, the fighters are free to punch, kick or wrestle each other. Some fighters prefer to take the opponent down and fight on the ground. This is where a wrestler has an advantage because wrestlers specialize in taking opponents down and dominating them from top position on the ground. Other fighters prefer to remain standing and kick and punch; however, wrestlers control where the fight goes. Although the opponent may prefer to kick and punch, whether or not he is able to remain standing depends on whether or not the wrestler can take him down. Former UFC champion Chuck Liddell was a very unique case. He was a former wrestler who preferred to stand on his feet and kick and punch. He is said to have used "wrestling in reverse." In other words, because Chuck Liddell's wrestling was so good, he was able to sprawl, defend the takedown and remain on his feet, kicking and punching his opponent, and frequently winning by KO or TKO. These types of fighters "made a career out of defensive wrestling by using their sprawl to keep the fight on the feet where they have lethal striking abilities. But what if he does want it to go to the ground? He can make that happen as well by using takedowns and clinch work."[852]

Strength is another huge advantage which wrestlers have. Greco-Roman wrestlers in particular are extremely strong. Because of the rules, Greco-Roman wrestlers are forced to execute all of their throws using upper body grips as opposed to leg trips or sweeps. After years of training, this gives them phenomenal power. Much of their practice involves battling for hand position, including double underhooks, where they have both arms inside of the opponent's arms and grip his body. This makes Greco-Roman-trained wrestlers particularly good at clinch fighting.[853]

While most of the UFC champions have come from an American collegiate wrestling background, the UFC is international, and successful fighters have come from all over the world, bringing a variety of wrestling styles with them. The wrestling styles that have had success in the UFC are: Greco-Roman wrestling, Judo, Freestyle wrestling, Russian Sambo, Catch wrestling, Shoot wrestling, Pancrase, Shootfighting, Shooto RINGS, Shoot Boxing, and Combat Submission wrestling.[854] Two of the single most successful fighters of all time, Dan Henderson and Randy Couture, were both champions in Greco-Roman wrestling.[855]

The culture of both wresting and of wrestling training lends itself to MMA. "Besides conditioning, physical toughness, and the sado-masochistic streak, wrestling primarily requires technique. The key lies in concentrating all your bodyweight against a single point on your opponent's body."[856]

The training and mentality of wrestling translated well into MMA. Wrestling is a culture of pain. In the words of former UFC champion Forest Griffin, "How do you develop this kind of toughness? The answer is simple – do things that make your body and mind scream at you to quit, but don't…You prove to yourself that pain is just that, pain. You can walk away from it afterward knowing that you surpassed a barrier that makes most humans give up."[857]

Wrestling has been called the most exhausting form of fighting because you are engaged every second.[858] In boxing or kick boxing, the opponent can circle away or jab when he needs a break. In wrestling, he is in constant physical contact with his opponent, working his muscles, and carrying the opponent's weight. In jujitsu, the opponent in the down position may be catching his breath or fighting defensively; however, in wrestling, the fighter in the down position only has seconds to escape. Wrestling is work from the time the bell rings till the time the round ends.[859]

The culture of the American wrestler is an aggressive culture, which is embodied in Iowa wrestling and the great coach, Dan Gable. "The Iowa style of wrestling: pressing the attack, pushing, mauling, wearing down the opponent with superior conditioning, and picking his bones in the last period. It was the domination principle: Gable-coached wrestlers crushed their opponents, humiliated them on the mat and on the scoreboard."[860] This aggressiveness, combined with an incredible work ethic, is one reason why American wrestlers have done so well in MMA.

Ten reasons why wrestlers make the best MMA fighters:

1. Wrestling workouts are harder than any other athletic workout.
2. Wrestlers control their opponent better.
3. Wrestlers know how to cut weight.
4. Wrestlers know how to take fighters down.
5. Wrestlers know how to eat right.
6. Wrestlers hate to lose.
7. Wrestlers are used to hard contact.
8. Wrestlers work harder than any other athlete.
9. Wrestlers dominate on the ground.
10. Wrestlers are the toughest guys at school.[861]

Wrestlers are used to tough, punishing workouts. In his book, *Becoming the Natural*, Couture described his life as a junior high school wrestler. "The workouts were grueling, even for a team of energetic twelve-year-olds. We started with jumping rope and then did pushups and calisthenics. When we were worn down enough and gasping for each breath, we'd wrestle each other."[862]

Wrestlers often engage in sparring only after becoming completely exhausted. This type of training prepares them well for fights in an MMA cage where the five-minute rounds can sap a fighter's strength. There is an old fighters' saying that MMA fighters like to quote, "Fatigue makes cowards of us all." When you are tired, you cannot defend yourself, and you certainly cannot attack. Therefore, the fighter with better fitness will be in a much better position to win.

Wrestling workouts are so difficult that when Couture joined the army, he found boot camp easy. "The army was just one big exercise in physical fitness. It was countless push-ups, running in bulky combat boots in formation, and obstacle courses every day – and I felt right at home compared to the grueling physical training of any wrestling."[863]

MMA training is largely based on wrestling training. MMA fights are three five-minute rounds, and title fights are five five-minute rounds. Fighters need incredible cardio endurance to actively fight for that length of time. They also need strength to get through the wrestling, and toughness to withstand the punches and kicks. Being kicked and punched when one is already physically exhausted can break the spirit. MMA is one of the few sports where a competitor can voluntarily quit. Being completely depleted physically, and having a powerful opponent lying on top of you while reigning down blows with his elbows, knees, or fists can make giving up seem like an attractive option.

Development of Wrestling through MMA

As the sport of MMA has developed over the last 22 years, the fighters and techniques have evolved. As a result, certain techniques have become almost obsolete, such as the single-leg takedown. All fighters now train in the single and double leg takedown; therefore, a single-leg takedown has a lower chance of success today than it did two decades ago.[864] Part of the development of wrestling has been to move on to other throws rather than remaining with the single and double which every MMA fighter knows how to counter. "Wrestlers are some of the most difficult fighters in MMA to actually take down and then control."[865]

Previously in MMA, fighters were trained to never turn their back to an opponent. Today, the turtle position is becoming more common in MMA to help fighters avoid having an opponent roll them on to their back, take side control or full mount in order to hit them with punches or elbow strikes. Wrestling trains fighters to easily control an opponent in these positions and flip them on their back. Another special skill which wrestlers possess is the ability to scramble on the ground and take the top position. Unlike in Chinese wrestling, when a Western wrestler is thrown to the ground, he continues to fight. In MMA, this means when a Western wrestler is thrown to the ground, he scrambles to get on top of his opponent and hold him in side control or pin. From this position, it is easy to punch the opponent in the face until he is knocked unconscious, or until he willingly concedes.[866]

One of the weaknesses of wrestling is the wrestling stance. In striking arts such as boxing and kick boxing, the left foot is forward. In wrestling, the right foot is forward. Many wrestlers have trouble learning to box or kick box, because they feel awkward standing with the left leg in front. It is also difficult for them to transition from a left leg lead to a right leg lead during the fight. They box with their left leg forward, but when they attempt to take their opponent down they put their right leg in front. This can be a clumsy and time wasting change.[867]

Another disadvantage for wrestlers in MMA is that in wrestling, the fight ends 3 seconds after their back touches the ground; however, in MMA, a fighter can continue fighting indefinitely while lying on his back. Wrestlers do not have experience fighting while lying on their back. This makes them vulnerable to opponents who can put the wrestler in this unfamiliar position.[868]

On the ground, both freestyle and Greco-Roman wrestlers are adept at controlling their opponent. Their disadvantage on the ground is that they have a lack of joint submissions.[869] Brazilian jujitsu specializes in joint submission techniques; however, Greco-Roman wrestling usually only contains about three or four submission techniques. The biggest disadvantage of Greco-Roman wrestling is the lack of lower body attacks. In Greco-Roman wrestling, it is illegal to attack the opponent's legs with either the hands or feet. As a result, Greco-Roman wrestlers are neither good at using these types of attacks nor at defending against them when they transition to MMA. In Chinese wrestling, there are certain attacks which Chinese wrestlers have no answer to, because those attacks do not exist in Chinese wrestling. The limitations of the arts are the limitations of the rules. The rules determine which techniques are practiced and which are used.

While facing opponents trained in other martial art styles, wrestlers have been able to adapt their moves. Couture was known as the inventor of "dirty boxing." Dirty boxing consists of holding an opponent in a clinch, or gripping the back of his head while hitting him with short boxing punches, mostly upper cuts and hooks. This technique is called "dirty boxing," because holding and hitting is against the rules in the sport of boxing.[870] Mark Coleman invented the "ground and pound" simply by pinning his opponents and striking them with punches, elbows, and headbutts. Both "dirty boxing" and "ground and pound" are striking techniques which were invented in order to adapt to MMA. Those techniques were then picked up by non-wrestlers and have now become standard tools in the arsenal of all MMA fighters. Once again, this demonstrates that Western wrestling is constantly evolving, morphing into something very different than it was forty years ago.

As much as MMA is helping wrestling to evolve, MMA is also beginning to negatively impact the US performance in amateur wrestling. In the Beijing Olympics, the US only won one gold medal in wrestling. Historically, remaining in wrestling meant constant training and suffering in a life of poverty; therefore, many wrestlers see a switch to MMA as a chance to capitalize on their skills and earn money. This has depleted the number of potential US Olympic wrestlers over time, and organizations have sought to rectify this. To keep wrestlers in wrestling, USA Wrestling introduced the Living the Dream Medal Fund, whereby wrestlers competing in the Olympics will be paid bonuses by USA Wrestling and private donors in the amount of $250,000 for a gold, $50,000 for a silver, and $25,000 for bronze.[871]

MMA and Pro wrestling

During the nearly 25 years of the UFC, the sport of MMA has shared a number of wrestlers with the WWE and the world of pro wrestling including: Nobuhiko Takada, Bobby Lashley, Dan Severn, Kiyoshi Tamura, Alberto Del Rio, Kazuyuki Fujita, Chael Sonnen, Ken Shamrock, Masakatsu Funaki, and Kazushi Sakuraba.[872] Others MMA fighters who performed in pro wrestling include: Josh Barnett, Don Fry, Paul Varlans, Brian Johnson, Tank Abbott, Tim Sylvia, Kevin Randleman, and Tito Ortiz.[873]

The most famous crossover from pro wrestling to MMA was Brock Lesnar. Lesnar was a former WWE superstar who switched to the UFC, where he amassed an MMA record of only 5 wins and 3 losses.[874] At university, Lesnar was a former NCAA Division I Heavyweight Wrestling Champion.[875] Shortly after joining the UFC, Lesnar was able to secure the UFC heavyweight championship.

While MMA attracts wrestlers and gives them an opportunity to earn money, many MMA veterans go to pro wrestling as a way of earning even more. UFC Hall of Fame member Ken Shamrock left the UFC to perform in the WWE. "Ken Shamrock brought a unique style to the pro wrestling milieu in 1997, combining wrestling with martial arts acumen to produce a new kind of gladiator – a combatant whose martial arts agility would launch a mini-revolution in the wrestling world."[876] Shamrock was said to have earned more in his first year of pro wrestling than the he did during his entire MMA fighting career.

MMA careers are often short, painful, and not very lucrative. The bottom level matches in the UFC do not earn millions per fight; however, the MMA fighters are under exclusive contracts, and can only fight in the UFC usually no more than three to four times per year. With paydays sometimes as low as $10,000 per fight, and only three to four fights per year, the average MMA fighter does not earn much.[877] In an interview with former UFC champion, George St-Pierre told the *MMA Hour*, "Most fighters in the UFC, they are starving."[878]

According to the Bleacher Report in 2016, the average pay for UFC fighter was $42,000, including bonuses, for the year. Top fighters such as McGregor and Rousey can earn up to $3 million for a single event, but 79 UFC fighters earned only $20,000 in 2016. Thomas Almeida was paid only $25,000 for his fight on UFC Fight Night 88, and Nunes earned only $100,000 for winning the UFC women's bantamweight title. Before McGregor became a top fighter, he was still working part-time at Subway, the sandwich franchise, because his fight income was only $18,000.[879]

Comparing the salaries of the top athletes in both UFC and WWE, WWE pays much better. WWE champion John Cena earns around $3 million per year.[880] In contrast, Georges St-Pierre, one of the most famous and popular UFC champions of all time, has lifetime earnings of $4,457,000.[881]

In conclusion, both MMA and WWE represent the most recent evolutions of wrestling. Both have provided a professional venue for wrestlers to earn a living while continuing to wrestle. MMA also has a negative impact on wrestling in that it draws Olympic hopefuls away from amateur competition. In the long run, WWE is the more lucrative opportunity for wrestlers; however, whether UFC or WWE is better for the sport of wrestling is questionable.

And so, Western wrestling continues to evolve and develop while Chinese wrestling takes a very different path.

Chapter 12: Chinese Wrestlers

Author's note:
The interviews were all conducted in Chinese, and have been
translated.

"We can see that Chinese wrestling arts are the progenitors of all
martial arts."[882]
Wrestling master Tong Zhongyi (1878-1963)

According to Chinese scholars, wrestling styles vary from country to country, but the basic concept of all wrestling, including Chinese wrestling, is two wrestlers trying to throw each other to the ground.[883] For this reason, most traditional wrestling styles across the globe do not have a complex rule system or require a win by pin. Generally, in traditional wrestling, when one wrestler has thrown the other to the ground, this is the win or, slightly more complex, the winner is determined by the best two out of three falls. The simplest forms of wrestling techniques originated in primitive times, when people used wrestling as a means of survival either during hunting or inter-tribal conflicts.[884] Nearly all mammals engage in wrestling play. In addition to being a form of entertainment, wrestling helps to develop the fighting and even killing skills of young mammals who will one day grow into providers and protectors of families. Human wrestling followed a similar path. However, as societies became more advanced, various martial arts began to develop, with wrestling among them.[885]

Chinese traditional wrestling has been called China's oldest martial art. It is commonly called Chinese style wrestling or *Shuai jiao*. In Chinese, practitioners often refer to it as *guojiao* (国角), meaning "country wrestling," as opposed to international wrestling, which would mean Olympic style Greco-Roman and freestyle wrestling. The current version of Chinese traditional wrestling has been influenced over the centuries by several other wrestling styles, including many ethnic styles. China is home to 56 ethnicities, and their wrestling styles are showcased in the Ethnic Games. These games include Mongolian, Uyghur, Hui, Korean, Tibetan and Yi styles.[886] All of these, plus Northeast Asian and probably central Asian wrestling styles, and possibly even judo, left their mark on the development of Chinese traditional wrestling. The old masters who preserve the heritage of Chinese wrestling say that although Chinese wrestling was influenced by other nations' styles, the Chinese style remains Chinese in every aspect, from the dress, the culture, and the rules, to the competition, the origin of the techniques, and the training.[887]

Chinese wrestling has been developed over centuries, and through many Chinese dynasties. During the Qin and Han Dynasties, the wrestling style was called "angle-of-arrival" (jiǎo dǐ角抵). During the Tang and Song Dynasties, the names sumo (xiāng pū相扑) as well as hand-strike (shǒu bó手搏) or wrestling (Guàn jiāo掼跤) were used. After 1949, international wrestling, freestyle, and Greco-Roman were introduced into China and Chinese traditional wrestling took the name "Chinese style wrestling" (Zhōngguó shì shuāijiāo中国式摔跤).[888] While the name, some of the rules, and dress changed over the centuries, the goal of Chinese wrestling remained the same: to throw the opponent on the ground.

The Chinese have a saying about wrestling: they say wrestling went from military to entertainment, to competition, to folk sport.[889] Wrestling was once taught only to palace guards and soldiers. During the Qin Dynasty, wrestling became a performance art. During the Tang Dynasty, the performance achieved a peak, and working as a wrestling performer became a fulltime job. For the first time, wrestlers actually trained specifically for the shows. This wrestling culture continued into the Song Dynasty when competitions, rather than performances, became more common.[890]

Many traditional Chinese wrestling authors refer to takedowns as "tripping" techniques (*Àn jiāo bàn* 按跤绊). Chinese wrestlers are absolute masters of tripping and leg sweeping techniques, which is one reason why they are able to continue to compete into their sixties. Tripping and sweeping require much less energy and muscular power than the aggressive throws and slams of Western wrestling. Additionally, as the rules of Chinese traditional wrestling prevent the thrower from going to the ground with his opponent, a trip or a sweep is a good way for the thrower to remain on his feet.

Author Luo Li classifies Chinese tripping techniques into two categories: offensive wrestling, and counterattack wrestling (Jìngōng jiāo bàn hé fǎngōng jiāo bàn liǎng 进攻跤绊和反攻跤绊两). Just as in Western wrestling, Luo Li explains that some of the counters can be used to simply stifle a takedown attempt or to buy time; these types of defense techniques can be called leg-blocking or "taking the back."[891]

Other counters can be used to attack the opponent, such as a reversal. A common reversal in Chinese wrestling is the cross-leg-hug (pántuǐ lǒu 盘腿搂), whereby the defender crosses his own legs, twisting his body down in a corkscrew, and then explodes into a powerful throw. This cross-leg hug or *pantui* is one of the basic exercises included in Chinese *jibengong*, the basic set of traditional exercises. Traditional practitioners will do hundreds or even thousands of these movements each day to increase their flexibility, strength, and balance. A unique feature of Chinese wrestling is that because it exists in the same culture as Chinese Kung Fu, the practice is largely designed to be done alone. Many of the best traditional wrestlers practice alone 90 percent of the time, doing countless repetitions of the *jibengong*, and then only wrestle a live opponent once a week. On Sundays in Beijing, it is common to find groups of old men wrestling in the park.

Wrestling master 王文永 Wang Wenyong (1933–) is one of the most respected wrestling teachers and authors in Beijing. In his book, *China Wrestling Celebrity Record* (中国摔跤名人录), he profiles a number of famous wrestlers including his teacher, Jin Baosheng (金宝生), who was born in 1909. When Wang Wenyong was young, he saw the powerful Jin Baosheng standing on a hill. He asked people who this Oak tree of a man was, and someone told him that it was Jin Baosheng, a famous wrestler. Before Jin Baosheng accepted Wang Wenyong as a student, he said, "If you can accept and follow the ways of old school wrestling, I can make you a man."[892] The book talks a great deal about the almost mythical physical strength of the old wrestlers, like Jin Baosheng, who were said to have followed superhuman strength training routines. The book also stresses the respect that was given to the wrestling teachers in those days. This feature of respecting the master carries forward until today.

The descendants of Grand Master Wang Wenyong refer to their Chinese wrestling style as Kung Fu wrestling. This is an acknowledgement of the close tie between Chinese wrestling and Shaolin kung fu. In kung fu circles, it is always important to honor one's lineage. This means the students honor the teacher, have a special respect for the teacher's training brothers, and pay homage to the teacher's teacher. One former student, Meng Shifu (孟师傅), currently has a wrestling school in Beijing. In traditional thinking, although Jin Baosheng is long dead, the current batch of students at Meng Shifu's wrestling school would consider Jin Baosheng their great grandfather.

Interview with Meng Shifu, June, 2016

Meng Shifu (孟师傅) began training in traditional Chinese wrestling under Grand Master Wang Wenyong when he was 9 years old. "At that time, we all worked while teaching. We got up at four o'clock in the morning to practice basic wrestling exercises (*jibengong*), and then worked during the day, and then practiced wrestling at night."[893] The traditional respect and hierarchy which Wang Wenyong discussed in his book is still alive at Meng Shifu's school. The students all call each other "training older brother or younger brother (*shi xiongdi*师兄弟)." The students call the teacher *shifu* (师 父), a word which has the meaning of both teacher "shi (师)" and father "fu (父)." They call the master's contemporaries (the master's training brothers) great uncle/master (*shiye*师 爷), and they call Wang Wenyong a name which connotes both grandfather and grand master (*daye*大爷).

In his interview, Meng Shifu explained his conception of Chinese wrestling.

"The goal in Chinese wrestling is to throw your opponent. If the opponent grabs me, then I use his grip to throw him. The technical requirements are very high, so the basic skills (jibengong) must be solid.

"The rules of Chinese wrestling are to make the opponent touch any part of his body, except his feet, on the ground, using techniques which are highly ornamental and in such a way that the opponent is not injured. Wrestlers in the West generally cannot grab the clothing. They grab the body or the waist, the physical requirements are higher in Western wrestling. Western wrestling is quite powerful, but not as aesthetically beautiful as Chinese wrestling.

"Western wrestling evolved from classic wrestling, Chinese wrestling evolved from the Chinese martial arts. Wrestlers learned the essence of Chinese martial arts. Since Chinese martial arts are mainly for performances nowadays, there is antagonism against Chinese wrestling."[894]

While most of the Chinese martial arts practiced in China today, such as *Wushu* performance and *Tai chi*, are no longer used for fighting, *Sanda* and wrestling still are. As a result, *sanda* and wrestling share the commonality of being somewhat marginalized in China's traditional martial arts community. However, Meng Shifu feels that *Sanda* and wrestling originated as martial arts and should still be accepted today.

Hhe accuses those who oppose the inclusion of wrestling of "lack of attention to traditional Chinese," and that by rejecting the fighting component of Chinese martial arts, modern Chinese were losing part of the essence of the arts.

As for the future survival of Chinese traditional martial arts, Meng Shifu said, "Chinese wrestling has not yet entered the Olympic Games. I hope that by having wrestling matches between China and the West, we can learn from each other, or that we can integrate a new type of wrestling with uniform rules so that we can enter the Olympic Games later."[895]

Interview with Chinese Traditional Wrestling Master He Yanzhong (何彦忠)

(Telephone interview from Shanghai University of Sport, June 2016)

He Yanzhong (何彦忠) is a 60-year-old wrestling master of the same lineage as Meng Shifu, teaching Kung Fu wrestling in Beijing. He Yanzhong explained his conception of Chinese wrestling:

"Wrestling is a simple word, but the connotation is deep. Chinese wrestling contains elements of aesthetics, psychology, and mechanics, plus offense and defensive. Chinese wrestling is an old tradition in China. It is not an imported sport like wrestling, judo, or taekwondo. It incorporates martial arts, like the hands of Tai chi, and the waist rotation and foot sweeps of kung fu. The techniques are different from Western wrestling. The equipment is also different. We use traditional hand weights to build strength.

186

"Our effort is to preserve traditional Kung Fu-based wrestling. Today, wrestling has become a fitness workout, a way to make money. But, we inherited and now we need to carry forward the ancient traditions."[896]

"There are deep cultural connotations contained in Chinese wrestling. We focus on friendship, friendship forever. We have a rule, better to lose a match, than to hurt someone. This is Kung Fu wrestling. It is our martial art, and martial arts have virtue. We want to predict the opponent's movements and to win, using artistic technique."[897]

He Yanzhong told an anecdote: "Chinese-style wrestling is the quintessence of wrestling. Many years ago, a number of European countries were invited to fight in Yanqing. We were thinking that if we let them win a few rounds, they would fall in love with our Chinese wrestling. Our national champion deliberately lost to the foreigners, which gave the wrong impression. When a foreigner wins, he feels that the Chinese people are incompetent and weak. He thinks that he beat you, which hinders the Chinese. This is the impact of the Western world."[898] It is clear that Chinese traditional martial arts feared influence from abroad. Additionally, as Chinese wrestling is a non-Olympic sport, it is often an afterthought for government funding, and is extremely vulnerable to being displaced by a foreign martial art such as Olympic wrestling or MMA.

"China has not paid enough attention to traditional sports. For so many years, we have lost a lot of our heritage." He Yanzhong's words were common among Chinese traditional wrestlers. Not only is there a lack of government support for the traditional art, but also a lack of press coverage, and only the smallest interest among young people to take up the art. However, despite adversity, he also expressed a glimmer of hope. "I am optimistic about the future development of China. I am very happy to inherit the traditional skills and kung fu. We must promote China's traditional sports."[899]

To help preserve China's cultural heritage, He Yanzhong teaches wrestling for free in Beijing. "I think it would be a sin if we lose these traditions. If the heritage does not pass to the next generation, we must apologize to our ancestors."[900]

He Yanzhong concluded with, "This is my family. I am willing to carry forward with Chinese wrestling, to contribute to it, even if minimally."[901]

In addition to Chinese traditional wrestling, China is home to another grappling art, *Shaolin chin na*, a very old form of Chinese kung fu which is similar to *hapkido* or *aikido*. It primarily focuses on joint locking techniques. Technically, *chin na* belongs to Shaolin Kung Fu; however, the grappling component shares a close relation to wrestling.

In Chinese traditional martial arts, it is believed that "A proficient martial artist must acquire four basic categories of fighting techniques: kicking (ti 踢), punching or hitting (da 打), wrestling (shuai 摔), and joint locking (*chin na* 擒拿). Wrestling was designed to fight against kicking and punching. *Chin na* was created to counter wrestling."[902] Shaolin monk Shi Deyang wrote a book on Chinese *chin na*, discussing its effectiveness as a standup grappling art and also describing a small number of Chinese *chin na* that were used in ground fighting. According to Shi Deyang, *chin na* was taught to high level students of the Shaolin Temple.[903]

Traditional wrestling master Tong Zhongyi (1878-1963), in his book, *The Method of Chinese Wrestling,* said that "Chinese pugilistic and wrestling methods were often taught together. In addition, Chinese pugilistic and wrestling arts also included locks and holds."[904] This suggests that Chinese strikers were taught wrestling, and that *chin na* was taught to both wrestlers and strikers. This also supports what Meng Shifu said about the current Chinese martial arts having evolved from actual fighting arts.

The joint locking techniques of *chin na* are against the rules of both Chinese *Shuai jiao* wrestling and *sanda*, but, the throws of *chin na* are identical to both. At Shanghai University of Sport *Wushu* Institute, it is mandatory for all PhD *Wushu* students to take a class in Chinese *sanda ge dou* (散打挌斗), an older style of *sanda*, which includes ground fighting techniques based on *chin na*.

Since these Chinese joint locks and submissions existed, one would have to ask why did they disappear from Chinese wrestling? Also, at Shanghai University of Sport, as well as at the Shaolin Temple, *sanda* fighters are trained separately and even live separately from the *Wushu* and Tai chi practitioners, although all three arts belong to the *Wushu* Institute. The wrestlers, including Chinese traditional wrestlers, are completely separated, existing in the college of modern sports training rather than *Wushu* Institute. In terms of numbers, of the roughly 7,000 students at Shanghai University of Sport, at least half have attended *Wushu* classes including Tai chi, *Wushu* performance, and *sanda*, whereas only about 20 attend Chinese traditional wrestling.

Another anomaly is that while martial art, almost by way of definition, means a fighting art, why is it that the wrestlers and the *sanda* fighters fight, but the *Wushu* and Tai chi practitioners do not?

Professor Dai Guobin and Luo Yuanzhou

In an interview, these questions were presented to Professor Dai Guobin (戴国斌), Dean of the *Wushu* Institute of Shanghai University of Sport, the only university in China which offers a PhD in *Wushu*. At age 54, Professor Dai Guobin, in addition to holding a PhD and being an acclaimed martial arts author in China, is a lifelong practitioner and teacher of martial arts, particularly his family's style of Tai chi and *Wushu,* which he learned from his father.

Professor Dai: "While Shaolin martial arts are traditional martial arts, with the foundation of the People's Republic of China in 1949, a new era of modern martial arts began. It seems that very little happened with martial arts during the early years of the new China. It was only in 1970 that the new China began to explore the nature of martial arts. In that year, Zhang Zhijiang began the Central Martial Arts Institute to promote the development of martial arts. Part of his plan for modernization was to use competition to demystify the arts.

His goal was to make them actually fight and separate legend from reality. For this purpose, he promoted the use of *sanda*. At the same time, in Shanghai, Wang Jingwei proposed that martial arts competitions should be more performance oriented routines. He, therefore, organized a *Wushu* performance competition at Wujiaochang Jiangwan Stadium."[905]

"And so the two roads formed in the end leading separately to *Wushu* (martial arts routine) and *Sanda*."

"The debate was taken again in the 1980s, and the same two camps were formed, one proposing *Wushu* performance, and one proposing *sanda* fighting."

Professor Dai Guobin stressed: *You have to keep the routines, however, because if you take the routines away, there would be no difference between Chinese martial arts and Western boxing.*[906]

The biggest difference between Western martial arts and Chinese martial arts is that in Western martial arts, there is no performance, only fighting. But what is art? What is Chinese martial art? For the Chinese martial artist, he has solved the problems of getting enough food and clothing, and planning for his future. After that, he can fight. My master Wang Peisheng said he could put a man down cleanly, but he said "my fight is a thug, who hits."

It seems that Professor Dai Guobin believed that fighting was an essential component of martial arts, but that fighting was thuggish and uncultivated, whereas *Wushu* and Tai chi performance represented a higher order of civilization, as they were art. Among *Wushu* experts, there seemed to be an ongoing debate about whether or not *sanda* and wrestling should be included in martial arts at all.

Luo Yuanzhou (罗源周), who earned his Master's degree in *Wushu* performance at Shanghai University of Sport, said he believed *sanda* is a martial art and should be included in the canon of Chinese martial arts.

"Mr. Cai Longyun said, martial arts developed along two lines. The first is a martial arts routine, which is similar to dance. Then the other is to fight, that is, offensive and defensive fighting, similar to the current *Sanda*.[907]

"*Sanda* techniques are based on actual combat, and there are no routines. *Wushu* performance routines are exaggerated offensive and defensive actions with some artistic features added.

"*Sanda* strategy lies in concealment. The aim is to defeat the opponent. So, the action will be small, more sudden, subtler. *Wushu* routines are overt, magnified, beautiful and artistic. Routines include offensive and defensive movements, advance and retreat. Like a drama, *Wushu* routines have a plot arrangement. You attack, I defend. I attack, you defend. It has ups and downs.[908]

"Since ancient times there have been many changes in the martial arts. The current traditional martial arts focused on exercising the body, physical fitness, and then combat and self-defense. But now the competitive martial art is the pursuit of performance. The movements have become higher, more difficult. The goal is to be more beautiful. It is not the same orientation as before."[909]

"I think wrestling is also part of martial art. If two opponents are far apart, they can strike with their arms and legs. And then close in, they can use wrestling and throwing. In fact, wrestling is a kind of martial arts, which is used under a different situation. Two people pressed close together, they cannot kick, but they can use the hook and the clinch, wrestling techniques. Besides, 70percent of the wrestling movements come from the *Wushu* routines."[910]

Luo Yuanzhou loved traditional martial arts history. Particularly the Shaolin Temple. "Martial arts can be traced back to the Shaolin Temple. In China, there are more than 130 kinds of martial arts, but they all come from the Shaolin Temple, so they have many similar techniques. There is a saying in China that your ultimate attainment of martial art is the same whether you follow boxing or Tai chi or *sanda* or wrestling. In the end, it is about redirecting the force of the opponent.

"Western wrestling: I only practiced a little at Shanghai University of Sport, so I don't know as much. Perhaps the greatest feature of Western wrestling is power. If you're strong, both opponents will use brute force, and whoever is stronger will eventually win. But Chinese wrestling is not the same. For example, if you push forward, I will redirect your power and use your power to put you down. Chinese wrestling focuses more on skill, or leveraging force, to change the direction of your force, and then counter-attack.

"In Chinese martial arts we have pushing hands (推手tui shou). You do not feel tired when you play push hands, the way you do when you practice Western wrestling. In Western wrestling, you will feel tired after one or two rounds, because you will fight with your own strength. But push hands is not the same. It is more homeopathic. You use leverage, and your force is borrowed.

"The elderly can do pushing hands or Chinese wrestling. The older the skill, the deeper the understanding. This is why martial artists in China respect older people. It takes time to polish these skills. This type of muscle strength may differ from the skill in the West. Muscular strength may degrade as you age, but skill is a magical thing. It's not muscle-specific, meaning your muscular strength may not be there, but your skill may still be strong.

"The perception of strength in China and the West is not the same. The exertion of power in the West may be the exertion of a muscle mass, but in Chinese martial arts, no matter what action one takes, the entire body is exerting force, and the muscle strength of the whole body concentrates on a single point. That is to say: Chinese martial art can mobilize not only the muscles, but also chi... the breath and mind working in cooperation. When you want to throw this punch, there is no other thought in your mind, only this punch. You only think of this punch, every cell in your whole body is mobilized."[911]

Professor Dai Guobing

"Is *sanda* art? Can *Wushu* fight? *Wushu* used to be able to fight, but the true essence has been lost. *Wushu* performance is a series of stances, standing like a flower. But with *sanda*, you always have an opponent before you, and you are always growing. And when you do not train with a human opponent, you hit the sandbag, and even that is fighting, because then the sandbag is the opponent.

"In Chinese martial arts, there is also an opponent, but the opponent is imaginary, or internal, or spiritual. But Western martial arts always need an external opponent to fight with. Many people have tried to understand why Chinese martial artists chose an artistic life. I believe it is because Chinese society, in an ancient era, had already solved the problems of normal life, and already become an advanced society. The Chinese from an advanced society were not easily satisfied. I eat this apple. Not only do I make the farmer plant the apple for me, but also, I need an artist to draw the apple.

"The Art of martial arts and its social development has reached another state. We Chinese today already have a well-to-do society. The ancient Chinese society was the world's most developed country, a bit like the United States today. The Tang, Song, Han and Ming dynasties were highly developed. They had military forces, economic power, and even culture. In this developed country, one would not seek to fight. Fighting is not good-looking, right? Instead, martial art was very artistic. Martial art had beauty and precision. Because of the pursuit of art, of the beauty of this pursuit, *Wushu* developed into performance routines.

"Historically, the principle of education of scholars in the Western Zhou Dynasty was civil and military advancement. Therefore, education in China started from Confucius. National education is better than private education, because all people have the right to enjoy education., Confucius educated his students with both civil and military education. Therefore, martial arts as an education means that one also upholds the great education of China in both civilization and war. In the New China, there is a comprehensive development of morality. Therefore, when a teacher of martial arts cultivates his disciples of martial arts, he must add in the cultural component.

"It is necessary for the martial artist to understand boxing, as well as calligraphy and poetry. And you must practice several hours per day. If you wish to learn Tai chi, you have to practice 3000 times to lay down a foundation. Being a professional martial artist is like being a professional athlete. You must have a half day of practice, and a half day of reading and education. Even when we sleep, we should sleep in accordance with martial arts.

"Before the founding of the Republic all arts which were related to the military were considered martial arts, including wrestling and archery. In Tianjin, in the early 1950s and again in 1995, there was a national martial arts competition which included archery, wrestling, and other martial arts. Archery, Wrestling, boxing, and even bayonet training were considered martial arts, because they were related to fighting or to the military. By this definition all kinds of fighting, empty-handed striking, throwing or punching should be included in martial arts. And they should be able to fight against each other.

"It is because of these fights that Chinese people understand the limitations of martial arts. *Wushu* is too routine. *Sanda* is too narrow. Qigong is not a martial art, because Qigong is related to health and falls under the General Administration of Sport. The dragon and lion dances are also martial arts."[912]

Sometime after the formation of the Republic in 1948, wrestling was no longer classified as martial arts, and as a result, wrestling is generally included in the modern sports training departments. However, there is a shift back towards incorporating traditional wrestling into the same department as the martial arts. Consequently, the *Wushu* Institute at the Shanghai University of Sport is looking to recruit students and build a traditional wrestling team.

One of the issues in developing a Chinese traditional wrestling team within the *Wushu* Institute is that the current batch of wrestlers all come from an international wrestling background. The members of the Chinese traditional wrestling team are mostly students who graduated from a sports high school, majoring in international wrestling. Many of them came to the sports university as members of the Greco-Roman team, and were later cut from the team, for injury or lack of performance, and were then shifted to the Chinese traditional wrestling team. In fact, only one member of the team came from a sports school where he specialized in Chinese wrestling.[913] As a result, the actual wrestling being done on the team is highly influenced by international wrestling. Additionally, it is all but impossible for *Wushu* students from a Tai chi, performance, or even a *sanda* background to join the team, because there would be a complete mismatch in skill levels. According to Professor Dai Guobin, a number of *Wushu* students have expressed an interest in learning traditional wrestling, but they are intimidated by the size, power, and ability of the current crop of wrestlers.

Modern Olympic Style Wrestling in China

In 2004, Wan Xu won China's first ever Olympic wrestling gold medal in women's freestyle wrestling. Wang Jiao won a gold medal for China in 2008 for women's 72 kg wrestling. The 2016 Olympics marked only the 10th appearance of the People's Republic of China since its founding in 1949, and China's first medal in the 2016 Olympics was a bronze, taken by Sun Yanan for women's Freestyle 48 kg wrestling.[914] To date, China has won a total of 22 medals for wrestling, with only 2 golds, which were both won in women's freestyle wrestling.[915]

Based on the most recent survey of data, the total number of wrestlers in China in 2013, including both Olympic wrestling and Chinese traditional wrestling, was less than 1,400, with a breakdown of 601 in men's international wrestling, 215 in women's international wrestling, 403 in men's Chinese style wrestling and 158 in women's Chinese style wrestling.[916] Only about 24 sports universities fielded a wrestling team.

Most of the current Chinese wrestlers are the byproduct of the sports education system in China. Whereas US schools aim to balance academic and athletic training, sports schools in China focus primarily on sports education. Children are selected at a very young age, some as young as 6 or 7 years old, to be sent to a sports school where they train full-time in a single sport. Students are often chosen by recruiters who usually determine the sport the student will pursue.

As of 2015, across China there were 1,435 sports schools, with somewhere between a quarter and half a million children attending.[917] At the tertiary level, there are 32 undergraduate and vocational schools categorized as sports schools, 14 of which offer a bachelor's degree. The total number of students pursuing a bachelor's degree at sport universities is 14,766.[918]

The top five sports universities in China in order of ranking are: Beijing Sport University, Shanghai University of Sport, Tianjin Institute of Physical Education, Wuhan Institute of Physical Education, and Chengdu Institute of Physical Education.[919]

In 2017, there were 50 universities in total with a Wushu Department offering a major in martial arts.[920] University admissions in China are generally based on the National Higher Education Entrance Examination (*gaokao*), a grueling two-day exam which determines the entire future of a young person. Admission to a pure sports university can be based on athletic performance alone, for international and professional champions, or a combination of athletic performance and an athletic *gaokao,* which is considered much easier than the National Higher Education Entrance Examination for academic purposes.[921] Many of the schools with *Wushu* departments were not sports universities, but multidisciplinary universities which included the *Wushu* department as a sub-unit of the physical education department. The official major is generally called a *Wushu* and Ethnic Traditional Sports major, and it is divided into: *Wushu* performance routine (武术套路), *Sanda* (武术散打), Tai chi quan (太极拳), and Chinese-style wrestling (中国式摔跤).[922] Shanghai University of Sport is the only university in China which offers a PhD in *Wushu*. The PhD program at the Shanghai University of Sport Wushu Department celebrated its 20th anniversary in 2017. To date, 101 candidates have graduated the program, including 16 international students.[923]

Students at sports universities are admitted as part-time athletes or professional team athletes based on academic test scores and an evaluation of their proficiency with their sport's key skills. With high test scores and low physical scores, students can be admitted as *sanda*, judo, or wrestling majors, where they train part-time and study full-time. Alternatively, as professional team athletes, they train twice a day and receive minimal education in academic subjects. At the Shanghai University of Sport, professional team athletes officially received three hours of general education classes; however, these lessons generally occurred at 7:00 pm, after a full day of training. The performance standard for these classes tends to be low, as the focus for the professional team athletes' education was on training in their sport. Some athletes reported having been given all of the exam answers, and they simply had to copy them over and sign their name on the answer sheet. Others were not capable of copying the answers, so another student helped.

Asked about the differences between the training of Western and Chinese athletes, Lukai, a student at the Shanghai University of Sport stated, "Chinese athletes may sometimes be forced to enter training. Maybe they are not necessarily interested in the sport. And probably in the West, the athletes join more out of interest." In sports beyond *Wushu*, it often seems to be the case that students practice their sport because a recruiter placed them in that sport. Lukai, for example, had never heard of judo and never thought about wrestling till a recruiter selected him for a sports school. "Some Chinese athletes enter sports training because their families are poor. Training in sports may be a way out. So, the starting point for the Western and Chinese athletes is not the same." Chinese Olympians receive money from the government and often receive government jobs and payments for life.

Some recruiters convince poor parents that their child is special, and the he or she could be the next Yao Ming.

Lukai explained that the training in the West was also different than in China. "Western athletes have many specialized coaches who teach them different things, such as conditioning, strength, and skill. In China, many athletes are only trained by a single coach. So, the West is more professional."[924]

Interview with Zhengtong (郑通), wrestling major, Shanghai University of Sport

From the age of nine, Zhengtong (郑通) began living in a sports school, training in Greco-Roman wrestling. He won a high school national championship and was given the opportunity to live at Shanghai University of Sport and train with the professional wrestling team. He was eventually admitted to the university as a professional wrestling team member; however, he was later cut from the team do to a severe back injury. Afterwards, he remained at the university as a wrestling major and as a member of the Chinese traditional wrestling team.

Zhengtong said that Greco-Roman wrestling and Chinese wrestling are as different as "boxing and wrestling." Of the two, he prefers Greco-Roman, because "Greco-Roman wrestling is more interesting, more coherent, more technical. It includes ground fighting, as well as standing wrestling. In Chinese wrestling, as soon as your knee touches the ground, it's over. Chinese wrestling is just too limiting."[925]

He explained, *"Greco-Roman wrestling is much more popular than Chinese traditional wrestling. Provincial Greco-Roman competitions can have three or four hundred entrants, but Chinese wrestling may just have eight. In national Greco-Roman competitions, there might be 79 people in a single weight division. In Chinese wrestling, sometimes not even eight. Not many sports schools offer Chinese wrestling, because there is less government support for non-Olympic sports. So, I don't see Chinese wrestling developing in the future.*

"Even the training is different. Greco-Roman focuses on strength training. Chinese wrestling focuses on technique. But the Chinese wrestling is just about pulling on the clothes. If I take off the jacket, they can't throw me. It's like judo. The coaching strategies are also different between the Greco-Roman and Chinese wrestling coaches. The coach for the Greco-Roman team is a friend. We had a good relationship. He treated us well. But the traditional wrestling coach was very strict."[926]

Zhongtong said he did not regret having grown up in a sports school, because he hated studying and loved wrestling. When asked if he was sad to be graduating and no longer wrestling, Zhengton said, "Since I was nine years old, the only thing I ever did was wrestle." He seemed as if he was ready for it to be over.

Interview with Yang Wenbin (杨文斌), Wrestling Major, Shanghai University of Sport

Yang Wenbin began Greco-Roman wrestling at age ten. In junior high school, he won the Shanghai Municipal Games wrestling championship, and placed ninth in the nationals. He was invited to join the professional Greco-Roman wrestling team at Shanghai University of Sport, but because of injury, he was moved to the Chinese traditional wrestling team.

After three years of training in Chinese wrestling, Yang Wenbin explains that his wrestling style is still heavily influenced by Greco-Roman wrestling, a sport he lived and trained with for over ten years. Leg hooking is a major component of Chinese wrestling, which Yang Wenbin found difficult to adopt. Moving from Greco-Roman to Chinese wrestling meant going from a wrestling style where leg attacks are not permitted at all, to one where leg attacks are a significant part of the game. On his own admission, he didn't hook legs at all. He was still using his Greco-Roman skills, frequently lifting and tossing his opponents.

"Few elements of Chinese and Western wrestling are related," explained Yang Wenbin. "Chinese style wrestling focuses more on standing grappling. As soon as the opponent has three limbs on the ground you win points. Greco-Roman wrestling also includes kneeling techniques."[927] In the Greco-Roman style, a wrestler may take one or sometimes even two knees, grab his opponent around the waist or the waist-and-arm, and throw him or lift-and-throw him. These types of moves require tremendous strength combined with advanced technique. The reason the Greco-Roman wrestlers became frustrated in Chinese wrestling was because the second they took a knee, they had lost the round.

"Chinese-style wrestling uses more of a dragging motion, dragging the opponent's body past the center of gravity. In Chinese wrestling, you pull the opponent's clothes and trip his legs, or use a single or double leg takedown. Western wrestling puts more emphasis on direct physical confrontation."[928]

Chinese wrestling also has a cultural component. *"Chinese wrestling emphasizes courtesy. As the wrestlers step into the circle, they first salute the judges, then the referee, then each other. In international wrestling, the wrestlers exchange only a simple handshake before beginning.*

"The training is more advanced in the West. Physical fitness is a profession. Physical trainers focus on comprehensive quality, and a professional nutritionist plans the diet in accordance with the physical training program. These are things that China's athletes lack."[929]

Yang Wenbin echoes the sentiments of all traditional wrestling proponents on why the sport is not growing. "Chinese sports which do not go to international competitions are lacking government support, and have very low popularity. In order for Chinese wrestling to develop, the cultural heritage aspect should be emphasized."

For Chinese wrestling to grow, Yang Wenbin felt that "Chinese wrestling doesn't need to be changed. It just needs more people to join. The reality is that in China, not many people think that wrestling is fun. This is related to the different cultural traditions of

China and the West. In Western nations, maybe people like fighting sports more. MMA and these fight sports are developing rapidly in the West." Yang Wenbin sees that MMA may be the savior of wrestling in China. "In China, those who really like fighting may lead the development of wrestling."[930]

For any sport to develop and grow in China, it needs government support. Xi Jinping has stated that he sees sport as an integral part of achieving the China dream and improving China's position in the world. At the 18th National Party Conference, he put forth his plan to increase mass sports, calling for China to have 435 million people regularly doing physical exercise by 2020.[931] Hopefully, this push for sport will result in more emphasis being placed on traditional sports and more money going to the promotion of traditional wrestling. At the same time, President Xi Jinping is calling for the development of "Olympic spirit." He has also supported China's bid to host the 2022 Winter Olympics.[932] This could mean that China will continue to pour money into Olympic sports, including international wrestling, while ignoring traditional wrestling.

Beyond Amateur Wrestling

Some very limited attempts have been made to create local pro wrestling shows and organizations in China; however, they have been largely unsuccessful. WWE hit a peak in 2015, and has been on a fast and steady decline since then. MMA is growing very slowly in popularity, but is still dramatically less popular than WWE, and is only 1 percent as popular as the NBA.[933] In a presentation at the *Wushu* Institute of Shanghai University (SHU), of roughly 25 undergraduate students in attendance, not one had heard of MMA, UFC, or WWE.

In 2016 Bing Wang, who wrestles under the name Tian Bing, became the first Chinese wrestler to headline for the WWE. In April 2017, he made history by competing in WrestleMania 33, the first Pay-Per-View (PPV) TV broadcast in China, and with Mandarin commentary.[934] Bing Wang was trained and competed in Japan before returning to China.

WWE is a foreign trend, and one theory on foreign trends being picked up in China is that Chinese business people are smart and driven by earning a profit. If they see that money can be made with a project, they will go forward with it. Another theory is the "build it and they will come" theory, which suggests that if pro wrestling existed in China as a way of earning money, then athletes would begin seeking training. According to a Forbes Magazine article, the numbers for WrestleMania 3 were staggering and clearly demonstrate that a great deal of money could be earned through the wrestling business. The fee to watch WrestleMania on PPV was $59.99, and WrestleMania 2 was purchased by 1.82 million viewers. Ticket prices to see WrestleMania 3 live ranged from $38–$2,130. WrestleMania 2 was attended by a live audience of 101,763 fans. A subscription to WWE Network costs $9.99 a month and has an average of 1.41 million paid subscribers. Merchandise sales for WrestleMania 31 hit $4.55 million.[935]

In 2016, hoping to capitalize on China's tremendous market potential, the WWE held tryouts in Shanghai and eventually signed seven Chinese wrestlers: Big Boa, Gu Guangming, Gao Lei, Zhao Xia, Wang Xiaolong, Yifeng and Cheng Yuxiang. The Chinese wrestlers were scheduled to attend the WWE Performance Center in Orlando. Perhaps banking on the hometown appeal of these wrestlers, the WWE signed a PPV contract with China for the shows Raw and SmackDown LIVE, which will be broadcast in Mandarin.[936] Unlike American fans, who pay $9.99 a month, the Chinese fans will be charged a subscription of $3 a month. The Mandarin shows will also be broadcast on phones and media devices.[937]

At the end of 2016, wrestling had some more increase in popularity with the release of the Bollywood block buster, *Dangal* (*Shuai jiao* Baba 摔跤爸爸). *Dangal* was the highest grossing non-Hollywood film in Chinese history. Both the Chinese public and critics loved the movie, and on the Chinese social media platform, Weibo, many Chinese were expressing a similar sentiment: namely, that China has great sports stars, and yet China has thus far been incapable of making such a great movie.[938]   This suggests that the "Build it and they will come" theory might be correct. At present the interest in wrestling appears to be low, but if more Chinese media, particularly movies, promoted wrestling, perhaps interest would grow.

Chinese Athletes in MMA

Most of the professional MMA fighters in China come from a *sanda* background. Vaughn Anderson, an American MMA fighter, was a coach of the Xian Sports University MMA team in 2015. The team was composed of *sanda* fighters and, at the time, was the most successful MMA team in China.[939] Vaughn said, in an interview with *Bloody Elbows*, that he was one of four coaches who basically fills in the missing pieces of a *sanda* fighter's game. He teaches the fighters submissions, ground and pound, and fighting off the cage. He also goes with the fighters and corners them in competition.[940]

The Xian Sports University's *sanda* team has produced several *sanda* based Chinese MMA stars in the Ranik Ultimate Fighting Federation (RUFF), China's first large scale MMA promotion, which began in 2011. Xian fighters who have won honors in China include Wang Guan and Zhang Meixuan.[941] Another Xian fighter, Jumabieke Tuerxun, was signed to the UFC, but lost all three of his fights.[942]

One Chinese UFC fighter with a wrestling background was The Mongolian Wolf, Tiequan Zhang, who grew up with Mongolian wrestling.[943] At age 16, he won the Inner Mongolian Wrestling Championships, and was invited to train and compete with a top *sanda* academy. Cross training in MMA, he was also the first person in China to receive a brown belt in Brazilian Jiu-Jitsu.[944] Tiequan "The Wolf" Zhang finished with a professional record of 15 and 4, finally retiring from the UFC in 2012 after three consecutive losses.[945]

In 2013, the TV show *The Ultimate Fighter China* ran on Liaoning Television with Vietnamese-American wrestling and *sanda*, with MMA champion Cung Le as the head coach.[946] However, according to Baidu trends, there was no major spike in MMA popularity during 2013-2014. The fact that it would be years before the UFC returned to China suggests that the results were not encouraging.

MMA took a dip in popularity in 2015, when Chinese fighter Yang Jian Bing died as a result of dehydration caused by an extreme weight cut.947 MMA took another major blow in 2017 after a video showing a Tai chi master, Wei Lei, who accepted a challenge from 38 year-old MMA fighter Xu Xiaodong, went viral. The one-sided fight lasted roughly 20 brutal seconds during which Xu Xiaodong pounded the Tai chi master mercilessly and emerged completely unscathed. Afterwards, there was outrage in China as the martial arts associations, as well as the government, saw the incident as an insult to Chinese martial arts and to the Chinese cultural heritage as a whole. A follow-up fight, scheduled against another Tai chi master, was halted by the police before it took place. Since then, the General Sports Administration has issued edicts banning unlicensed fights.948 Some of the traditional martial arts masters were pushing for a complete ban on MMA and other foreign martial arts. While this has not occurred, the incident resulted in the attachment of bad connotations to the name MMA.

By the fall of 2017, the UFC was back in China, signing the first female Chinese fighter, Yan Xiaonan, who is a *sanda* fighter.949 Later the same year, UFC Fight Night 122 was held in Shanghai. This was the first UFC event on the mainland, and it drew a sellout crowd of 15,000, which was the largest attendance at any fight event in Chinese history. Five of the eight Chinese fighters won their matches, including Yan Xiaonan. Song Kenan won his fight in just 15 seconds, which was his 9th straight first-round KO victory. Wang Guan defeated Ultimate Fighter star Alex Caceres. Li Jingliang, whose skills are listed as *sanda*, wrestling, and jujitsu, won the "Performance of the Night" bonus for a first round stoppage, which was his second straight fight night bonus.[950] According to Chinese media, creating a local hero will be the key to the future success for the UFC and MMA in China. As of now, Li Jingliang is poised to be that hero.[951]

Even the weigh-in attracted a crowd of 10,000 which is a complete first in China. Weigh-ins are generally not televised, and no one attends one live.[952] According to Chinese sports media, the Chinese who attend local fight events are older men from blue collar backgrounds, whereas those who attended the UFC were white collar workers from first and second tier cities. Apparently, building popularity in China means striking a difficult balance between local and foreign. Chinese media reported that 300 million Chinese watch the American NBA, but "no one cares about the Chinese Basketball Association (CBA)." Similarly, there are fans who will watch UFC who would never consider watching a local fight promotion. The key to success seems to be having Chinese fighters in a foreign event.[953]

Chapter 13: The Final Comparison

"There is only one type of body, 2 arms, 2 legs, etc., that make up the human body. Therefore, there can only be one style of fighting. If the other guy had 4 arms and 2 legs, there might have to be a different one."

–Bruce Lee

Both Chinese and Western wrestlers share a common physiology, and yet their wrestling styles are quite distinct. Any technique that works against a Chinese wrestler would also work against a Western wrestler, and vice versa; however, techniques used in Chinese and Western wrestling differ. The rules differ, the historical development differs, and, in the modern world, Western wrestling evolved into two styles of Olympic wrestling and then into the WWE and MMA, while Chinese traditional wrestling remained mostly unchanged.

The purpose of this research was to discover why Chinese and Western wrestling differ, and culture is the prime cause. The culture of the West, particularly the United States, is one which is more prone toward competition, aggression, and fighting. Boxing, predating the first Olympics, has always been a feature of Western society. China has no such history of combat sport. Particularly from the 19th Century until today, fight sport, whether wrestling, boxing, or MMA, has become a billion-dollar industry in the United States; however, it has only recently begun to emerge in China.

Chinese martial arts stress performance routines, whereas Western martial arts stress combat. Western martial arts do not have a performance routine component. Even in "the old days," when Chinese Kung Fu still contained the fighting elements, there were no records of large scale fighting competitions or professional prize fights similar to what is experienced in the West.

Western wrestling dates back to the Greek and Roman Empires. Rome was a massive military power which conquered lands far from home, and built one of the largest empires ever in existence. By 700 BC, the Chinese had already begun building a wall around their territory. This suggests they were playing a defensive rather than an offensive strategy, planning to maintain the land they had rather than expand. During the 15th through the 19th centuries, European countries began sending out their conquistadores, explorers, soldiers and colonizers to co-opt lands on other continents. China's only major sea voyage was that of Zheng He, which occurred during (1371–1435), and did not return with any colonized land.

Western countries tend to specialize in high contact sports and adopt these as "top sports." These sports, such as football, hockey, or rugby, are highly popular across the country and have high number of players. In China, the de facto national sport is ping pong, and other popular participation sports in include badminton and basketball. In short, Western children grow up playing rough, aggressive games, and this culture carries over to the wrestling style. Conversely, Chinese ping pong and badminton are polite games of skill, where the loosing opponent remains uninjured. This culture of non-contact, skill-based sport influenced the Chinese wrestling style.

Historically, the earliest forms of both Chinese and Western wrestling evolved out of pure human fighting in the most primitive of eras. As Chinese society evolved, martial arts developed and the wrestling styles became more scientific. In China, the development of Kung Fu contributed to the development of scientific wrestling. In ancient Greece, the development of Pankration contributed to the development of wrestling. Wrestling in both China and the West was taught to the military. In both regions wrestling became sport, then entertainment.

In a superficial way, one could say that both styles followed a similar path of development; however, upon closer inspection, there are significant differences at each stage of development. When wrestling became a sport in China, competitions were held locally in villages and cities, at the provincial level, and possibly at some type of national championships. Chinese wrestling competitions did not go beyond China's borders. In Greece, the Olympics encompassed multiple city states as it did in Roman times. Eventually, the Olympics and Olympic wrestling expanded to the world with 206 countries participating in the 2016 Rio Olympics.[954]

When Chinese wrestling became entertainment, it was featured in shows at public fairs and festivals. When Western wrestling became entertainment, it grew from being a major sport which filled stadiums in the late 19th century, to a principle feature of early television, to becoming a multibillion dollar business with both WWE and UFC having estimated worth of around $4 billion each.[955]

The levels of violence and aggression are not the only cultural difference between Chinese and Western wrestling. A personality of pride helped drive the popularity of the art in the West, whereas in China, the athletes come from a long tradition of quiet humility. In Ancient Greece, wrestlers and Pankration fighters fought in the nude. In the days of professional catch wrestling, and on into the WWE and MMA today, the athletes are shirtless, proudly displaying their muscles. Chinese wrestlers wear a jacket, concealing their build. Even the singlet worn by international wrestlers is more revealing than the long trousers and jacket worn by Chinese wrestlers. Part of the appeal of Western wrestling is the cult of masculinity: powerfully built men fighting to defeat each another. This has a broader appeal than two polite strangers pulling on each other's jackets in a park in Beijing on a warm Sunday.

In the West, stars of WWE and MMA participate in celebrity culture, with fan bases able to follow them through interviews, press conferences, and events. Chinese wrestling evolved out of kung fu, a quiet and humble pursuit with no competitions or public fights, and largely practiced in a monastery on a mountain. With such a pedigree, it is difficult to draw a crowd.

Finally, the concept of cultural heritage in China and the West differs. Although Western wrestling has a history which stretches back for centuries, it is a history of constant evolution and change. Western wrestling absorbed features and techniques from many arts along its journey and also transformed itself to appeal to people in changing eras and through changing media. One the other hand, Chinese traditional wrestling is traditional and thus, almost by definition, cannot change. The living Chinese masters fear that influence from Western wrestling or from modern/foreign fight sport will destroy their cultural legacy, So Chinese wrestling, while exported in some limited way to foreign countries, remains Chinese and unaltered.

Implications for the Future of Chinese Wrestling

China winning the 2008 Olympic gold medal count was a boon for the development of sport in China, with both the people and the government attaching the concepts of national strength and pride to success in international sports. The government is now investing more money in the development of Olympic athletes, which will hopefully have a trickle-down effect in helping to grow Chinese traditional wrestling. Universities across China are adding more *Wushu* programs to their curriculum to preserve their cultural heritage. While these programs generally do not include Chinese style wrestling, they should help to increase interest in the martial arts in general, which may also help Chinese style wrestling. In this new era of internationalization, both the WWE and UFC have recruited wrestlers from China. So far, it seems that having Chinese wrestlers on the card will help attract Chinese viewers. Once again, this may have a residual effect of increasing interest in wrestling in general, and possibly even in Chinese traditional wrestling.

Both inside and outside of China, as people read *The Wrestler's Dissertation*, perhaps they will become interested in and begin practicing Chinese style wrestling. So, buy a copy for a friend and help promote the art.

Glossary of Chinese Terms

Phonetic	Chinese character	Pinyin	Translation
Anjiao ban	按跤绊	Àn jiāo bàn	tripping techniques or trip wrestling
Chin na	擒拿	Qínná	Joint locking techniques
da	打	Dǎ	punching or hitting
Fangongjiao banliang	反攻跤绊两	fǎngōng jiāo bàn liǎng	anti-attack trip tripping or counter attack
Daye	大爷	Dàyé	Both grandfather and grand master – one's teacher's teacher
Guanjiao	掼跤	Guàn jiāo	An old name for Chinese style wrestling
guojiao	国角	guó jiǎo	National wrestling, another name for Chinese style wrestling
jiben gong	基本功	jīběngōng	basic movements, wrestling exercises
Jiaodi	角抵	jiǎo dǐ	angle-of-arrival" an ancient Chinese wrestling style
Jinggong jiaoban	进攻跤绊	Jingong jiaoban	Offensive trip or offensive attacks
Kuai jiao	快跤	Kuài jiāo	fast wrestling
Pantui lou	盘腿搂	pántuǐ lǒu	cross-leg-hug
sanda	散打	Sǎndǎ	Chinese kickboxing with takedowns
sanda gedou	散打挌斗	Sǎndǎ gé dòu	A type of Chinese kick boxing which includes both takedowns and ground fighting submissions
Sanshou	散手	Sàn shǒu	Another name for *sanda*, Chinese kickboxing with takedowns
Shi xiongdi	师兄弟	Shī xiōngdì	"training older brother or younger brother

210

Shifu	师 父	Shī fù	A martial arts master - Has the meaning of both teacher shi 师 and father fu (父)
Shiye	师 爷	Shīyé	Great uncle/master - the master's contemporaries (the master's training brothers)
Shanghai University (SHU), *Wushu* Institute	上海大学武术学院	Shànghǎi dàxué wǔshù xuéyuàn	The Wushu Department of Shanghai University (SHU) (unrelated to Shanghai University of Sport (SUS)
Shanghai University of Sport (SUS), Wushu Department	上海体育学院武术学院	Shànghǎi tǐyù xuéyuàn wǔshù xuéyuàn	Shanghai University of Sport (SUS) Wushu Department
Shoubo	手搏	shǒu bó	A Chinese wrestling style which includes kicking and punching
Shuai jiao	摔跤	Shuāijiāo	Chinese style wrestling
Shuai Jiao Baba	摔跤爸爸	Shuāijiāo bàba	The Indian wrestling movie "Dangal" literally, "Wrestling Father"
Tai chi quan	太极拳	Tàijí quán	An internal Chinese martial art characterized by routines composed of slow, precision movements
Ti	踢	Tī	kick
Tui shou	推手	Tuīshǒu	pushing hands
Wushu	武术	wǔshù	Martial arts, especially Chinese martial arts
Wushu sanda	武术散打	Wǔshù sǎndǎ	The official name of the sanda major at sports universities
Wushu taolu	武术套路	Wǔshù tàolù	Wushu performance routine
Xiangpu	相扑	xiāng pū	"sumo" Tang dynasty wrestling style
Xingli	行礼	Xínglǐ	Salute
Zhongguo shi shuaijiao	中国式摔跤	Zhōngguó shì shuāijiāo	Literally "Chinese style wrestling"

Author Bio

Antonio Graceffo PhD, China-MBA, works as an economics researcher and university professor in China. He holds a PhD from Shanghai University of Sport Wushu Department where he wrote his dissertation "A Cross Cultural Comparison of Chinese and Western Wrestling" in Chinese. He is the author of 8 books, including *Warrior Odyssey* and *The Monk from Brooklyn*. His regular column, *Destinations*, has been running in Black Belt Magazine since 2009. He has fought professionally as a boxer and MMA fighter as well as fighting as an amateur in boxing, *sanda*, and wrestling. Having spent over 16 years studying martial arts in Asia, he holds black belts in Cambodian Bokator, Filipino Kuntaw and Cambodian traditional kick boxing. In Malaysia, he was the first non-Malay to be awarded the title of Pahlawan Kalam (warrior of Silat Kalam). Currently, he is pursuing a second PhD in economics at Shanghai University, specializing in US-China Trade, China's Belt and Road Initiative, and Trump-China economics. His China economic reports are featured regularly in The Foreign Policy Journal and published in Chinese at The Shanghai Institute of American Studies, a Chinese government think tank.

ENDNOTES

[1] Jiang Lingling. New era of Chinese wrestling development countermeasures, Network wealth, 2009,

(江玲玲."新时期中国式摔跤发展的对策研究."网络财富, 2009年)

[2] Wei Yungui, "The Characteristics of Chinese Wrestling." Journal of Anhui University of Technology, 2006.

(魏云贵."中国式摔跤的特点."安徽工业大学学报,2006.)

[3] Wu Baokun and Li Long. "Chinese wrestling technical principles interpretation." Fighting martial arts science, 2007.)

(邬宝坤,李龙." 中国式摔跤技术原理解读." 搏击·武术科学, 2007.)

[4] Wu Baokun and Li Long. "Chinese wrestling technical principles interpretation." Fighting martial arts science, 2007.)

(邬宝坤,李龙." 中国式摔跤技术原理解读." 搏击·武术科学 2007.)

[5] Wei Yungui, "Characteristics of Chinese Wrestling." Journal of Anhui University of Technology, 2006.

(魏云贵."中国式摔跤的特点."安徽工业大学学报,2006.)

[6] Wei Yungui, "Characteristics of Chinese Wrestling" Journal of Anhui University of Technology, 2006.

(魏云贵."中国式摔跤的特点."安徽工业大学学报,2006.)

[7] Li Guoan, "China's ancient wrestling development history." Wuhan Institute of Physical Education, 2004,

(李国安."我国古代摔跤运动发展史略."武汉体育学院院报 , 2004.)

[8] Li Guoan, On the Development of Ancient Wrestling in China. "Journal of Wuhan Institute of Physical Education, 2004,

(李国安."我国古代摔跤运动发展史略."武汉体育学院院报 , 2004.)

[9] Luo Li, Zhang Xuezheng. "Chinese style wrestling technology comparative analysis and research." Shenyang Journal, 2008,

(罗利 , 张学政."中国式摔跤跤绊技术对比分析与研究."沈阳学报, 2008.)

[10] Li Guoan, A Brief History of the Development of Ancient Chinese Wrestling. "Wuhan Institute of Physical Education, 2004,

(李国安."我国古代摔跤运❏ ❏ 展史略."武❏ 体育学院院❏, 2004.）

[11] Wei Yungui, "The Characteristics of Chinese Wrestling." Journal of Anhui University of Technology, 2006.

(魏云贵."中国式摔跤的特点."安徽工业大学学报,2006.)

[12] Wei Yungui, "The Characteristics of Chinese Wrestling." Journal of Anhui University of Technology, 2006.

(魏云贵."中国式摔跤的特点."安徽工业大学学报,2006.)

[13] Li Guoan, "China's ancient wrestling development history" Wuhan Institute of Physical Education, 2004,

(李国安"我国古代摔跤运动发展史略"武汉体育学院院报，2004年)

[14] Shengze Tong, "Chinese Style" Wrestling Sports Status and Development Countermeasures. "Anhui Yunke Magazine, 2004.

(盛泽堂.""中国式"摔跤运动现状及发展对策."安徽运科杂志，2004.)

[15] Dong Chen, Journal of Jilin Institute of Physical Education, 2013

(董辰."高校体育教学中的中国式摔跤研究."

吉林体育学院学报，2013.)

[16] Li Guoan. A Brief History of the Development of Ancient Wrestling in China. Journal of Wuhan Institute of Physical Education,

(李国安。我国古代摔跤运动发展史略"武汉体育学院院报，2004年)

[17] Dong Chen, Journal of Jilin Institute of Physical Education, 2013

(董辰."高校体育教学中的中国式摔跤研究."

吉林体育学院学报，2013.)

[18] Jiang Lingling. "New era of Chinese wrestling

(江玲玲."新时期中国式摔跤发展的对策研究."网络财富,2009年)

[19] Luo Li, Zhang Xuezheng. "Chinese style wrestling wrestling technology comparative analysis and research." Journal of Shenyang, 2008,

(罗利，张学政."中国式摔跤跤绊技术对比分析与研究."沈阳学报 2008.)

[20] Dong Chen, "Chinese Style Wrestling in College Physical Education." Journal of Jilin Institute of Physical Education, 2013,

(董辰."高校体育教学中的中国式摔跤研究."
吉林体育学院学口 ， 2013.)

[21] Jiang Lingling. "New era of Chinese wrestling
(江玲玲."新时期中国式摔跤发展的对策研究."网络财富,2009年)

[22] Luo Fuyu. "Chinese wrestling development status and development countermeasures." Shanghai Institute of Physical Education, 2009

(罗富玉."中国式摔跤发展现状及发展对策研究."上海体育学院,
2009)

[23] Shengze Tong, "Chinese Style" Wrestling Sports Status and Development Countermeasures. "Anhui Yunke Magazine, 2004.

(盛泽堂.""中国式"摔跤运动现状及发展对策."安徽运科杂志, 2004.)

[24] Wang Luyao. "Chinese wrestling into the Olympic Games Development Strategy Research. "Wuhan University of Science and Technology, 2009.

(王路遥."中国式摔跤进入奥运会的发展战略研究."武汉科技大学,
2009年.)

[25] Su Hongtao, Ma Jianguo, Zhu Jianliang. Reflections on the Development of Chinese Wrestling. Journal of Capital Institute of Physical Education, 2004,

(苏鸿涛, 马建国,朱建亮."中国式摔跤发展的思考."首都体育学院学报,
2004年.)

[26] Dong Chen, "Research on Chinese Wrestling in College Physical Education." Journal of Jilin Institute of Physical Education, 2013,
(董辰,"高校体育教学中的中国式摔跤研究"吉林体育学院学报, 2013.)

[27] Dong Chen, "Research on Chinese Wrestling in College Physical Education." Journal of Jilin Institute of Physical Education, 2013,

(董辰,"高校体育教学中的中国式摔跤研究。"吉林体育学院学报,
2013.)

[28] Dong Chen, "Chinese style wrestling in college physical education teaching." Journal of Jilin Institute of Physical Education, 2013

(董辰."高校体育教学中的中国式摔跤研究."

吉林体育学院学报，2013.)

[29] Su Hongtao, Ma Jianguo, Zhu Jianliang. Reflections on the Development of Chinese Wrestling. Journal of Capital Institute of Physical Education, 2004,

(苏鸿涛,马建国,朱建亮."中国式摔跤发展的思考.

"首都体育学院学报,2004年.)

[30] Dong Chen, Study on Chinese Wrestling in College Physical Education. Journal of Jilin Institute of Physical Education, 2013.

(董辰."高校体育教学中的中国式摔跤研究." 吉林体育学院学报,

2013.)

[31] Dong Chen." Chinese style wrestling in college physical education. "Journal of Jilin Institute of Physical Education, 2013.

（董辰 "高校体育教学中的中国式摔跤研究 "吉林体育学院学报,

2013.)

[32] Shengze Tong, "Chinese Style" Wrestling Sports Status and Development Countermeasures. "Anhui Yunke Magazine, 2004.

(盛泽堂.""中国式"摔跤运动现状及发展对策."安徽运科杂志, 2004.)

[33] Li Shiying. "*Sanda* technology classification and its application research." Journal of Beijing Sport University, 2005 ,

(李士英."散打技术分类及其应用的研究."北京体育大学学报,2005.)

[34] Li Shiying, "*Sanda* technology classification and its application research." Journal of Beijing Sport University, 2005,

(李士英."散打技术分类及其应用的研究."北京体育大学学报,2005.)

[35] Hao Xinyan, "International Development of Chinese Wrestling." Sports Science and Technology, 2007.

(郝新燕."中国式摔跤运动的国际化发展研究."体育科技 , 2007.)

[36]Terry, S, Origins of Wrestling, Livestrong.com, Jan 15, 2014,

http://www.livestrong.com/article/339526-origins-of-wrestling/

[37]Dellinger, B, The Oldest Sport, National Wrestling Hall of Fame

http://www.mtlsd.org/district/athletics/wrestling/stuff/the%20oldest%20sport.pdf

[38]Carroll, S, Wrestling in Ancient Nubia, Journal of Sport History, Vol. 15, No. 2 (Summer, 1988),

http://wysinger.homestead.com/nubiansport.html

[39]Squared Circle of Wrestling, Wrestling In Prehistory, History, And Mythology, June 15, 2013,

http://www.squaredcircleofwrestling.com/2013/06/15/wrestling-in-prehistory-history-and-mythology/

[40]Olympic.org, Ancient Olympic Games

http://www.olympic.org/ancient-olympic-games?tab=the-sports-events

[41]ancientolympics.arts, Pankration, Ancient Olympics,

http://ancientolympics.arts.kuleuven.be/eng/TC007cEN.html

[42]Perseus.tufts, Milo of Kroton, Athletes' Stories,
http://www.perseus.tufts.edu/Olympics/milo.html

[43]perseus.tufts, Theagenes of Thasos, Athletes' Stories
http://www.perseus.tufts.edu/Olympics/theag.html

[44]Jones, T, The Pugilist at Rest: Stories,Little, Brown and Company, 1994

[45]Semaan, J, Roman Gladiator Games: the Origins of MMA, Part Two, Bleacher Report, Jun, 2008
http://bleacherreport.com/articles/30004-roman-gladiator-games-the-origins-of-mma-part-two

[46]Sparta Club, The history of the Greco-Roman wrestling,
http://sparta-club.org/eng_about_history.shtml

[47]Launchpad, Catch Wrestling, constantaggression.com, Sep, 2014
http://www.constantaggression.com/catch-wrestling/

[48]Launchpad, Catch Wrestling, constantaggression.com, Sep, 2014

http://www.constantaggression.com/catch-wrestling/

[49]Olympic.org,Wrestling Reco-Roman Equipment and History

http://www.olympic.org/wrestling-greco-roman-equipment-and-history?tab=history

[50]Nash, S The Martial Chronicles: The Forgotten Olympic History of Catch-As-Catch-Can Wrestling, Bloody Elbows, Aug, 2012

http://www.bloodyelbow.com/2012/8/13/3238285/martial-chronicles-olympics-history-catch-wrestling

[51]Frankgotch.com, Frank Gotch, Biography,

http://www.frankgotch.com/biography12.html

[52]Nash, S, Wrestling with the Past: The Man of a Thousand Holds, Cageside Seats Features,Oct, 2012

http://www.cagesideseats.com/cageside-seats-features/2012/10/18/3518600/pro   wrestling-history-earl-caddock-man-of-thousand-holds

[53]Nash, S, Wrestling with the Past: The Man of a Thousand Holds, Cageside Seats Features,Oct, 2012

http://www.cagesideseats.com/cageside-seats-features/2012/10/18/3518600/pro   wrestling-history-earl-caddock-man-of-thousand-holds

[54]Nash, S The Martial Chronicles: The Forgotten Olympic History of Catch-As-Catch-Can Wrestling, Bloody Elbows, Aug, 2012
http://www.bloodyelbow.com/2012/8/13/3238285/martial-chronicles-olympics-history-catch-wrestling

[55]WWE, Gorgeous George, Superstars, WWE.com
http://www.wwe.com/superstars/gorgeousgeorge

[56]Biography Channel, Andre the Giant, Jan. 1999
https://www.youtube.com/watch?v=LZbmR8rnJvk

[57]Lifetime TV, Hulk Hogan, Biography
http://www.lifetimetv.co.uk/biography/biography-hulk-hogan

[58]UFC, The Fighter The Sport The UFC The Fan Glossary, history, UFC.com
http://www.ufc.com/discover/ufc

[59]Thomas, L, Technique Talk: Josh Barnett's pushing and pulling for catch wrestling's respect, MMA Fightmag, Sep, 2014

http://www.mmafighting.com/2014/9/7/6093013/technique-talk-josh-barnett-on-catch-wrestlings-place-in-the

[60]Wrestlingassistant.com, (2014). Throw Styles. [online] Available at: http://www.wrestlingassistant.com/C5B.html [Accessed 15 Nov. 2014].

[61]UAE Wrestling, From Brawling to Wrestling, History, uaewjif.com http://www.uaewjjf.com/index.php/wrestling/wrestling-history.html

[62]Dellinger, B, The Oldest Sport, National Wrestling Hall of Fame http://nwhof.org/stillwater/resources-library/history/the-oldest-sport/

[63]FILA, Roots and history of Olympic wrestling, Filla-official.com http://www.fila-official.com/index.php?option=com_content&view=article&id=14&Itemid=100246&lang=en

[64]Squared Circle of Wrestling, Wrestling In Prehistory, History, And Mythology, Squared Circle of Wrestling, June 15, 2013 http://www.squaredcircleofwrestling.com/2013/06/15/wrestling-in-prehistory-history-and-mythology/

[65]Carroll, S, Wrestling in Ancient Nubia, Journal of Sport History, Vol. 15, No. 2 (Summer, 1988).

[66]Carroll, S, Wrestling in Ancient Nubia, Journal of Sport History, Vol. 15, No. 2 (Summer, 1988).

[6767]FILA, Roots and history of Olympic wrestling, Filla-official.com

http://www.fila-official.com/index.php?option=com_content&view=article&id=14&Itemid=100246&lang=en

[68]Sherman, M, Techniques of the Ancient Wrestlers, Amateur Wrestling News, January 7, 2000, http://www.wrestlingassistant.com/AncientWrestlers.html

[69]Carroll, S, Wrestling in Ancient Nubia, Journal of Sport History, Vol. 15, No. 2 (Summer, 1988).

[70]Steve Craig, Sports and Games of the Ancients, 1961, Greenwood Press, Westport, Connecticut, p. 10

[71]UAE Wrestling, From Brawling to Wrestling, History, uaewjif.com
http://www.uaewjjf.com/index.php/wrestling/wrestling-history.html

[72]Penjak, A and Karnincic, H Sport And Literature: An Overview of the Wrestling Combats in the Early Literary, International Journal of Humanities and Social Science Vol. 3 No. 5; March 2013

[73]UAE Wrestling, From Brawling to Wrestling, History, uaewjif.com
http://www.uaewjjf.com/index.php/wrestling/wrestling-history.html

[74]UAE Wrestling, From Brawling to Wrestling, History, uaewjif.com
http://www.uaewjjf.com/index.php/wrestling/wrestling-history.html

[75]Penjak, A and Karnincic, H Sport And Literature: An Overview of the Wrestling Combats in the Early Literary, International Journal of Humanities and Social Science Vol. 3 No. 5; March 2013

[76]Penjak, A and Karnincic, H Sport And Literature: An Overview of the Wrestling Combats in the Early Literary, International Journal of Humanities and Social Science Vol. 3 No. 5; March 2013

[77]USA Today, Wrestlers at Ancient Olympia thinking of sport's future, July 21, 2013
2013-7-21-ancient-olympia-wrestling

[78]Penjak, A and Karnincic, H Sport And Literature: An Overview of the Wrestling Combats in the Early Literary, International Journal of Humanities and Social Science Vol. 3 No. 5; March 2013

[79]Miller, C, Submission Fighting and the Rules of Ancient Greek Wrestling, Judo Information, May, 2004, http://JudoInfo.com

[80]Penjak, A and Karnincic, H Sport And Literature: An Overview of the Wrestling Combats in the Early Literary, International Journal of Humanities and Social Science Vol. 3 No. 5; March 2013

[81]Arvanitis, J Pankration, Boxing and Wrestling: 3 Combat Sports From Ancient Greece, Black Belt Magazine, March 23, 2011

[82]Arvanitis, J Pankration, Boxing and Wrestling: 3 Combat Sports From Ancient Greece, Black Belt Magazine, March 23, 2011

[83]Miguel Piernavieja del Pozo, Wrestling in Antiquity, 1973, Olympic Review, http://library.la84.org/OlympicInformationCenter/OlympicReview/1973/o re70/ore70k.pdf

[84]UAE Wrestling, From Brawling to Wrestling, History, uaewjif.com
http://www.uaewjjf.com/index.php/wrestling/wrestling-history.html

[85]Squared Circle of Wrestling, Wrestling In Prehistory, History, And Mythology, Squared Circle of Wrestling, June 15, 2013

http://www.squaredcircleofwrestling.com/2013/06/15/wrestling-in-prehistory-history-and-mythology/

[86]Dellinger, B, The Oldest Sport, National Wrestling Hall of Fame
http://nwhof.org/stillwater/resources-library/history/the-oldest-sport/

[87]Penjak, A and Karnincic, H Sport And Literature: An Overview of the Wrestling Combats in the Early Literary, International Journal of Humanities and Social Science Vol. 3 No. 5; March 2013

[88]Wrestlings Best, Amateur Wrestling Collectibles Gallery Ancient Coins
http://www.wrestlingsbest.com/collectibles/wrestuffcoins001.html

[89]Mihoces, G, Ancient text proves wrestling is oldest sport on record, USA Today, 10/18/2011

http://usatoday30.usatoday.com/sports/olympics/story/2011-10-18/wrestling-artifact-history/50817198/1

[90]Mihoces, G, Ancient text proves wrestling is oldest sport on record, USA TODAY, 10/18/2011

https://usatoday30.usatoday.com/sports/olympics/story/2011-10-18/wrestling-artifact-history/50817198/1

[91]Mihoces, G, Ancient text proves wrestling is oldest sport on record, USA Today, 10/18/2011

http://usatoday30.usatoday.com/sports/olympics/story/2011-10-18/wrestling-artifact-history/50817198/1

[92]Malice, Professional Wrestling in the United States of America, The Wrestling   Game,
http://www.thewrestlinggame.com/wrestling/articles/the_history_of_pro fessional_wrestling_part_1.asp

[93]Miller, C, Submission Fighting and the Rules of Ancient Greek Wrestling, Judo Information, May, 2004, http://JudoInfo.com

[94]Miller, C, Submission Fighting and the Rules of Ancient Greek Wrestling, Judo Information, May, 2004, http://JudoInfo.com

[95]Squared Circle of Wrestling, Wrestling In Prehistory, History, And Mythology, Squared Circle of Wrestling, June 15, 2013

http://www.squaredcircleofwrestling.com/2013/06/15/wrestling-in-prehistory-history-and-mythology/

[96] United World Wrestling, History of Wrestling , 2017, https://unitedworldwrestling.org/fa/node/997

[97]Arvanitis, J Pankration, Boxing and Wrestling: 3 Combat Sports From Ancient Greece, Black Belt Magazine, March 23, 2011

[98]Arvanitis, J Pankration, Boxing and Wrestling: 3 Combat Sports From Ancient Greece, Black Belt Magazine, March 23, 2011

[99]Arvanitis, J Pankration, Boxing and Wrestling: 3 Combat Sports From Ancient Greece, Black Belt Magazine, March 23, 2011

[100]Miller, C, Submission Fighting and the Rules of Ancient Greek Wrestling, Judo Information, May, 2004, http://JudoInfo.com

[101]Miller, C, Submission Fighting and the Rules of Ancient Greek Wrestling, Judo Information, May, 2004, http://JudoInfo.com

[102]Miller, C, Submission Fighting and the Rules of Ancient Greek Wrestling, Judo Information, May, 2004, http://JudoInfo.com

[103]Arvanitis, J Pankration, Boxing and Wrestling: 3 Combat Sports From Ancient Greece, Black Belt Magazine, March 23, 2011

[104]Olympics MU, Ancient Olympic Wrestling, Olympics.

muhttp://www.olympics.mu/ancient-olympic-wrestling.html

[105]Miller, C, Submission Fighting and the Rules of Ancient Greek Wrestling, Judo Information, May, 2004, http://JudoInfo.com

[106]FILA, Roots and history of Olympic wrestling, Filla-official.com

http://www.fila-official.com/index.php?option=com_content&view=article&id=14&Itemid=100246&lang=en

[107]Dellinger, B, The Oldest Sport, National Wrestling Hall of Fame

http://nwhof.org/stillwater/resources-library/history/the-oldest-sport/

[108]Arvanitis, J Pankration, Boxing and Wrestling: 3 Combat Sports From Ancient Greece, Black Belt Magazine, March 23, 2011

[109]Arvanitis, J Pankration, Boxing and Wrestling: 3 Combat Sports From Ancient Greece, Black Belt Magazine, March 23, 2011

[110]Miller, C, Submission Fighting and the Rules of Ancient Greek Wrestling, Judo Information, May, 2004, http://JudoInfo.com

[111]Miller, C, Submission Fighting and the Rules of Ancient Greek Wrestling, Judo Information, May, 2004, http://JudoInfo.com

[112]Miller, C, Submission Fighting and the Rules of Ancient Greek Wrestling, Judo Information, May, 2004, http://JudoInfo.com

[113]Miller, C, Submission Fighting and the Rules of Ancient Greek Wrestling, Judo Information, May, 2004, http://JudoInfo.com

[114]FILA, Roots and history of Olympic wrestling, Filla-official.com http://www.fila-official.com/index.php?option=com_content&view=article&id=14&Itemid=100246&lang=en

[115]Perseus.Tufts, Milo of Kroton, Athletes' Stories http://www.perseus.tufts.edu/Olympics/milo.html

[116]Theodoros II, 10 Greatest Ancient Athletes, Listverse, APRIL 14, 2013 http://listverse.com/2013/04/14/10-greatest-ancient-athletes/

[117]Muscle Old School, Milo of Croton: Father Of Progressive Resistance, Muscle Old School http://muscleoldschool.com/milo-of-croton-father-of-progressive-resistance/

[118]Theodoros II, 10 Greatest Ancient Athletes, Listverse, APRIL 14, 2013 http://listverse.com/2013/04/14/10-greatest-ancient-athletes/

[119]Smallwood, K Ass-Kicking Athletes of Antiquity: Theagenes, Man Cave Daily, September 27, 2013 http://mancave.cbslocal.com/2013/09/27/ass-kicking-athletes-of-antiquity-theagenes/

[120]Jones, T, The Pugilist at Rest: Stories, Little, Brown and Company, 1994

[121]Holloway, A Newly deciphered papyrus reveals ancient Greek wrestling matches were fixed, Ancient Origins, 17 APRIL, 2014 http://www.ancient-origins.net/news-history-archaeology/newly-deciphered-papyrus-reveals-ancient-greek-wrestling-matches-0998877

[122]FILA, Roots and history of Olympic wrestling, Filla-official.com

http://www.fila-
official.com/index.php?option=com_content&view=article&id=14&Itemid
=100246&lang=en

[123]UAE Wrestling, From Brawling to Wrestling, History, uaewjif.com

http://www.uaewjjf.com/index.php/wrestling/wrestling-history.html

[124]Sparta Club, The history of the Greco-Roman wrestling,

http://sparta-club.org/eng_about_history.shtml

[125]FILA, Roots and history of Olympic wrestling, Filla-official.com

http://www.fila-
official.com/index.php?option=com_content&view=article&id=14&Itemid
=100246&lang=en

[126] Dervenis, K, Functional Analysis of Ancient Greek Pankration, April
1996 and April 2004, http://historical-Pankration.com/

[128] Dervenis, K, Functional Analysis of Ancient Greek Pankration, April
1996 and April 2004, http://historical-Pankration.com/

[129] International Federation of Pankration (IFPA), historical background,

http://www.Pankration.gr/history.htm

[130] International Federation of Pankration (IFPA), historical background,

http://www.Pankration.gr/history.htm

[131] International Federation of Pankration (IFPA), historical background,

http://www.Pankration.gr/history.htm

[132] Renner, J, Pankration Greek martial arts, Classical Wisdom, October
1, 2013

http://classicalwisdom.com/Pankration-greek-martial-arts

[133] International Federation of Pankration (IFPA), historical background,

http://www.Pankration.gr/history.htm

[134] Dervenis, K, Functional Analysis of Ancient Greek Pankration, April
1996 and April 2004, http://historical-Pankration.com/

[135] Grant, T, MMA Origins: Exploring Fight Sport's Ancient Roots, Bloody Elbows, December 1, 2011,

http://www.bloodyelbow.com/2011/12/1/2601718/mma-origins-ancient-roots-ufc-history

[136] Pankration Academy, history, Pankration Canada

http://www.Pankrationcanada.com/HISTORY.html

[137] Pankration Academy, history, Pankration Canada

http://www.Pankrationcanada.com/HISTORY.html

[138] Semaan, J Ancient Greek Pankration: the Origins of MMA, Part One, The Bleacher Report, Jun 9, 2008

http://bleacherreport.com/articles/28473-ancient-greek-Pankration-the-origins-of-mma-part-one

[139] Semaan, J Ancient Greek Pankration: the Origins of MMA, Part One, The Bleacher Report, Jun 9, 2008,

http://bleacherreport.com/articles/28473-ancient-greek-Pankration-the-origins-of-mma-part-one

[140] Professor Dai Guo Bing, Head of the Wushu Department of Shanghai University of Sport, Interview, June, 2016

[141] Sophia, F, Pankration, An Ancient Martial Art, News Finder, JUNE 16, 2002
http://www.newsfinder.org/site/more/Pankration_an_ancient_martial_art/

[142] Sophia, F, Pankration, An Ancient Martial Art, News Finder, JUNE 16, 2002
http://www.newsfinder.org/site/more/Pankration_an_ancient_martial_art/

[143] ATHLETICS AND EDUCATION
https://erenow.com/ancient/athletics-in-the-ancient-world/6.php

[144] Nurse , M, Pankration: Martial Art of Classical Greece, Fight Times,
http://www.fightingarts.com/reading/article.php?id=164

[145] Sophia, F, Pankration, An Ancient Martial Art, News Finder, JUNE 16, 2002
http://www.newsfinder.org/site/more/Pankration_an_ancient_martial_art/

[146] Grant, T, MMA Origins: Exploring Fight Sport's Ancient Roots, Bloody Elbows, December 1, 2011,
http://www.bloodyelbow.com/2011/12/1/2601718/mma-origins-ancient-roots-ufc-history

[147] International Federation of Pankration (IFPA), historical background, http://www.Pankration.gr/history.htm

[148] Nurse , M, Pankration: Martial Art of Classical Greece, Fight Times, http://www.fightingarts.com/reading/article.php?id=164

[149] Semaan, J Ancient Greek Pankration: the Origins of MMA, Part One, The Bleacher Report, Jun 9, 2008,
http://bleacherreport.com/articles/28473-ancient-greek-Pankration-the-origins-of-mma-part-one

[150] Sophia, F, Pankration, An Ancient Martial Art, News Finder, JUNE 16, 2002
http://www.newsfinder.org/site/more/Pankration_an_ancient_martial_art/

[151] Dervenis, K, Functional Analysis of Ancient Greek Pankration, April 1996 and April 2004, http://historical-Pankration.com/

[152] Stella Nenova , Pankration – the Ancient MMA , November 5, 2015
http://www.ancientworldalive.com/single-post/2015/11/05/Pankration-the-Ancient-MMA

[153] Pankration Academy, history, Pankration Canada
http://www.Pankrationcanada.com/HISTORY.html

[154] Pankration Academy, history, Pankration Canada
http://www.Pankrationcanada.com/HISTORY.html

[155] Nurse , M, Pankration: Martial Art of Classical Greece, Fight Times, http://www.fightingarts.com/reading/article.php?id=164

[156] Dervenis, K, Functional Analysis of Ancient Greek Pankration, April 1996 and April 2004, http://historical-Pankration.com/

[157] Forum Romana, History, http://www.forumromanum.org/history/

[158] Instone, S, The Olympics: Ancient versus Modern, BBC History, Feb. 17, 2011
http://www.bbc.co.uk/history/ancient/greeks/greek_olympics_01.shtml

[159] Grant, T, MMA Origins: Exploring Fight Sport's Ancient Roots, Bloody Elbows, December 1, 2011,
http://www.bloodyelbow.com/2011/12/1/2601718/mma-origins-ancient-roots-ufc-history

[160] UShistory.org, (2014). Gladiators, Chariots, and the Roman Games [ushistory.org]. [online] Available at: http://www.ushistory.org/civ/6e.asp [Accessed 28 Oct. 2014].

[161] UShistory.org, (2014). Gladiators, Chariots, and the Roman Games [ushistory.org]. [online] Available at: http://www.ushistory.org/civ/6e.asp [Accessed 28 Oct. 2014].

[162] Wilcox, B. (2014). Stanford classics professor debunks image of the 'noble' ancient athlete. [online] Stanford University.
http://news.stanford.edu/news/2013/february/ancient-athletes-myth-020113.html

[163] Wilcox, B. (2014). Stanford classics professor debunks image of the 'noble' ancient athlete. [online] Stanford University.
http://news.stanford.edu/news/2013/february/ancient-athletes-myth-020113.html

[164] Ancientolympics.arts.kuleuven.be, (2014). The Romans and Greek sport. [online] Available at:
http://ancientolympics.arts.kuleuven.be/eng/TB023EN.html [Accessed 29 Oct. 2014].

[165] Sewell, B. (2012). Gouging, biting, disembowelling, strangling – those were the good old days of wrestling.
[online] The Evening Standard.
http://www.standard.co.uk/olympics/olympic-news/gouging-biting-disembowelling-strangling – those-were-the-good-old-days-of-wrestling-8004816.html

[166] Sewell, B. (2012). Gouging, biting, disembowelling, strangling – those were the good old days of wrestling.
[online] The Evening Standard.
http://www.standard.co.uk/olympics/olympic-news/gouging-biting-disembowelling-strangling – those-were-the-good-old-days-of-wrestling-8004816.html

[167] Ancientolympics.arts.kuleuven.be, (2014). The Romans and Greek sport.
[online] Available at:
http://ancientolympics.arts.kuleuven.be/eng/TB023EN.html [Accessed 29 Oct. 2014].

[168] Fife, S. (2014). Athletics, Leisure, and Entertainment in Ancient Rome. [online] Ancient History, http://www.ancient.eu/article/98/

[169] UShistory.org, (2014). Gladiators, Chariots, and the Roman Games [ushistory.org]. [online] Available at: http://www.ushistory.org/civ/6e.asp [Accessed 28 Oct. 2014].

[170] Semaan, J. (2008). Roman Gladiator Games: the Origins of MMA, Part Two. Bleacher Report.
http://bleacherreport.com/articles/30004-roman-gladiator-games-the-origins-of-mma-part-two

[171] UShistory.org, (2014). Gladiators, Chariots, and the Roman Games, ushistory.org, http://www.ushistory.org/civ/6e.asp

[172] Ancientolympics.arts.kuleuven.be, (2014). The Romans and Greek sport. [online] Available at:
http://ancientolympics.arts.kuleuven.be/eng/TB023EN.html
[Accessed 29 Oct. 2014].

[173] Grimes, W. (2014). The Pride and Terror of Those Who Fought to the Death – New York Times.
http://www.nytimes.com/2005/12/09/books/09book.html?_r=0

[174] Grimes, W. (2014). The Pride and Terror of Those Who Fought to the Death – New York Times.
http://www.nytimes.com/2005/12/09/books/09book.html?_r=0

[175] Grimes, W. (2014). The Pride and Terror of Those Who Fought to the Death – New York Times.
http://www.nytimes.com/2005/12/09/books/09book.html?_r=0

[176] Concannon, C, Gladiators, Athletes, and Early Christian Bodies, Journal of Biblical Literature 133, no. 1, Duke University, Durham(2014): 193–214, p. 195

[177] Tataki, A. (2009). Nemeseis, and the Gladiatorial Games at Smyrna. Mnemosyne, 62(4), pp.639-648.

[178] Tataki, A. (2009). Nemeseis, and the Gladiatorial Games at Smyrna. Mnemosyne, 62(4), pp.639-648.

[179] Tribunesandtriumphs.org, (2014). Spartacus Timeline, http://www.tribunesandtriumphs.org/gladiators/spartacus-timeline.htm

[180] Tribunesandtriumphs.org, (2014). Spartacus Timeline, http://www.tribunesandtriumphs.org/gladiators/spartacus-timeline.htm

[181] Tribunesandtriumphs.org, (2014). Spartacus Timeline, http://www.tribunesandtriumphs.org/gladiators/spartacus-timeline.htm

[182] Tribunesandtriumphs.org, (2014). Spartacus Timeline, http://www.tribunesandtriumphs.org/gladiators/spartacus-timeline.htm

[183] Steiger, B, The Roman Emperor Who Claimed To Be The World's Greatest Athlete, April 23, 2008, http://www.rense.com/general81/great.htm

[184] Steiger, B, The Roman Emperor Who Claimed To Be The World's Greatest Athlete, April 23, 2008, http://www.rense.com/general81/great.htm

[185] Bbc.co.uk, (2014). BBC – History – The Coliseum: Emblem of Rome. http://www.bbc.co.uk/history/ancient/romans/colosseum_01.shtml

[186] UShistory.org, (2014). Gladiators, Chariots, and the Roman Games [ushistory.org]. http://www.ushistory.org/civ/6e.asp

[187] Hopkins, K. (2014). Murderous Games: Gladiatorial Contests in Ancient Rome, Historytoday.com, http://www.historytoday.com/keith-hopkins/murderous-games-gladiatorial-contests-ancient-rome

[188] Pbs.org, (2014). The Roman Empire: in the First Century. The Roman Empire. Life In Roman Times. Gladiators, PBS, http://www.pbs.org/empires/romans/empire/gladiators.html

[189] Tribunesandtriumphs.org, (2014). Spartacus Timeline,
http://www.tribunesandtriumphs.org/gladiators/spartacus-timeline.htm

[190] King, C. (2014). The Romans: Gladiators. [online] ITALY Magazine.
http://www.italymagazine.com/featured-story/romans-gladiators

[191] Semaan, J. (2008). Roman Gladiator Games: the Origins of MMA,
Part Two. Bleacher Report.
http://bleacherreport.com/articles/30004-roman-gladiator-games-the-
origins-of-mma-part-two

[192] Pbs.org, (2014). The Roman Empire: in the First Century. The Roman
Empire. Life In Roman Times. Gladiators, PBS,
http://www.pbs.org/empires/romans/empire/gladiators.html

[193] Coliseum: A Gladiator's Story. (2014). [DVD] UK: BBC.
https://www.youtube.com/watch?v=l0fRqc_pChY

[194] Historyonthenet.com, (2014). The Romans – Gladiators,
http://www.historyonthenet.com/Romans/gladiators.htm

[195] Coleman, K. (2014). BBC – History – Ancient History in depth:
Gladiators: Heroes of the Roman Amphitheatre. [online] Bbc.co.uk.
Available   at:
http://www.bbc.co.uk/history/ancient/romans/gladiators_01.shtml

[196] Pbs.org, (2014). The Roman Empire: in the First Century. The Roman
Empire. Life In Roman Times. Gladiators, PBS,
http://www.pbs.org/empires/romans/empire/gladiators.html

[197] Meijer cited in Grimes, W. (2014). The Pride and Terror of Those
Who Fought to the Death – New York Times.
http://www.nytimes.com/2005/12/09/books/09book.html?_r=0

[198] King, C. (2014). The Romans: Gladiators. [online] ITALY Magazine.
http://www.italymagazine.com/featured-story/romans-gladiators

[199] Semaan, J. (2008). Roman Gladiator Games: the Origins of MMA,
Part Two. Bleacher Report.
http://bleacherreport.com/articles/30004-roman-gladiator-games-the-
origins-of-mma-part-two

[200] Semaan, J. (2008). Roman Gladiator Games: the Origins of MMA, Part Two. Bleacher Report.
http://bleacherreport.com/articles/30004-roman-gladiator-games-the-origins-of-mma-part-two

[201] Historyonthenet.com, (2014). The Romans – Gladiators,
http://www.historyonthenet.com/Romans/gladiators.htm

[202] Coliseum: A Gladiator's Story. (2014). [DVD] UK: BBC.
https://www.youtube.com/watch?v=l0fRqc_pChY

[203] King, C. (2014). The Romans: Gladiators. [online] ITALY Magazine.
http://www.italymagazine.com/featured-story/romans-gladiators

[204] Coliseum: A Gladiator's Story. (2014). [DVD] UK: BBC.
https://www.youtube.com/watch?v=l0fRqc_pChY

[205] Unrv.com, (2014). Gladiator,
http://www.unrv.com/culture/gladiator.php

[206] Coliseum: A Gladiator's Story. (2014). [DVD] UK: BBC.
https://www.youtube.com/watch?v=l0fRqc_pChY

[207] UShistory.org, (2014). Gladiators, Chariots, and the Roman Games, UShistory.org, http://www.ushistory.org/civ/6e.asp

[208] Jewell, R., Moti, A. and Coates, D. (2012). A Brief History of Violence and Aggression in Spectator Sports. Springer, pp.11–26.

[209] UShistory.org, (2014). Gladiators, Chariots, and the Roman Games, UShistory.org, http://www.ushistory.org/civ/6e.asp

[210] King, C. (2014). The Romans: Gladiators. [online] ITALY Magazine.
http://www.italymagazine.com/featured-story/romans-gladiators

[211] Coleman, K. (2014). BBC – History – Ancient History in depth: Gladiators: Heroes of the Roman Amphitheatre. [online] Bbc.co.uk.
Available at:
http://www.bbc.co.uk/history/ancient/romans/gladiators_01.shtml

[212] Jewell, R., Moti, A. and Coates, D. (2012). A Brief History of Violence and Aggression in Spectator Sports. Springer, pp.11–26.

213 Worldanimalprotection.ca, (2014). Blood sports.
http://www.worldanimalprotection.ca/ourwork/bloodsports/

214   Usatoday30.usatoday.com,   (2008).   MMA   timeline   –
USATODAY.com.
http://usatoday30.usatoday.com/sports/2008-05-29-mma-
timeline_n.htm

215 Jewell, R., Moti, A. and Coates, D. (2012). A Brief History of Violence
and Aggression in Spectator Sports. Springer, pp.11–26.

216 Jewell, R., Moti, A. and Coates, D. (2012). A Brief History of Violence
and Aggression in Spectator Sports. Springer, pp.11–26.

217 Jewell, R., Moti, A. and Coates, D. (2012). A Brief History of Violence
and Aggression in Spectator Sports. Springer, pp.11–26.

218 Jewell, R., Moti, A. and Coates, D. (2012). A Brief History of Violence
and Aggression in Spectator Sports. Springer, pp.11–26.

219 Jewell, R., Moti, A. and Coates, D. (2012). A Brief History of Violence
and Aggression in Spectator Sports. Springer, pp.11–26.

220 Jewell, R., Moti, A. and Coates, D. (2012). A Brief History of Violence
and Aggression in Spectator Sports. Springer, pp.11–26.

221 Jewell, R., Moti, A. and Coates, D. (2012). A Brief History of Violence
and Aggression in Spectator Sports. Springer, pp.11–26.

222 Concannon, C, Gladiators, Athletes, and Early Christian Bodies, Journal
of Biblical Literature 133, no. 1, Duke University, Durham(2014): 193–214

223 Concannon, C, Gladiators, Athletes, and Early Christian Bodies,
Journal of Biblical Literature 133, no. 1, Duke University, Durham(2014):
193–214

224 Coleman, K. (2014). BBC – History – Ancient History in depth:
Gladiators: Heroes of the Roman Amphitheatre. [online] Bbc.co.uk.
Available at:
http://www.bbc.co.uk/history/ancient/romans/gladiators_01.shtml

225 Epictetus (2.18.22)1 cited in Concannon, C, Gladiators, Athletes, and
Early Christian Bodies, Journal of Biblical Literature 133, no. 1, Duke
University, Durham(2014): 193–214

226 Concannon, C, Gladiators, Athletes, and Early Christian Bodies, Journal
of Biblical Literature 133, no. 1, Duke University, Durham(2014): 193–214

[227] Concannon, C, Gladiators, Athletes, and Early Christian Bodies, Journal of Biblical Literature 133, no. 1, Duke University, Durham(2014): 193–214

[228] Concannon, C, Gladiators, Athletes, and Early Christian Bodies, Journal of Biblical Literature 133, no. 1, Duke University, Durham(2014): 193–214

[229] Concannon, C, Gladiators, Athletes, and Early Christian Bodies, Journal of Biblical Literature 133, no. 1, Duke University, Durham(2014): 193–214

[230] Hopkins, K. (2014). Murderous Games: Gladiatorial Contests in Ancient Rome, Historytoday.com, http://www.historytoday.com/keith-hopkins/murderous-games-gladiatorial-contests-ancient-rome

[231] Hopkins, K. (2014). Murderous Games: Gladiatorial Contests in Ancient Rome, Historytoday.com, http://www.historytoday.com/keith-hopkins/murderous-games-gladiatorial-contests-ancient-rome

[232] Wilcox, B. (2014). Stanford classics professor debunks image of the 'noble' ancient athlete. [online] Stanford University.

http://news.stanford.edu/news/2013/february/ancient-athletes-myth-020113.html

[233] Jewell, R., Moti, A. and Coates, D. (2012). A Brief History of Violence and Aggression in Spectator Sports. Springer, pp.11–26.

[234] UShistory.org, (2014). Gladiators, Chariots, and the Roman Games, ushistory.org, http://www.ushistory.org/civ/6e.asp

[235] Hopkins, K. (2014). Murderous Games: Gladiatorial Contests in Ancient Rome, Historytoday.com, http://www.historytoday.com/keith-hopkins/murderous-games-gladiatorial-contests-ancient-rome

[236] Fitzgerald, A. (2014). 10 Famous Gladiators From Ancient Rome – Listverse.
http://listverse.com/2013/04/02/10-famous-gladiators-from-ancient-rome/

[237] Grimes, W. (2014). The Pride and Terror of Those Who Fought to the Death – New York Times.
http://www.nytimes.com/2005/12/09/books/09book.html?_r=0

[238] Hopkins, K. (2014). Murderous Games: Gladiatorial Contests in Ancient Rome, Historytoday.com, http://www.historytoday.com/keith-hopkins/murderous-games-gladiatorial-contests-ancient-rome

[239] Concannon, C, Gladiators, Athletes, and Early Christian Bodies, Journal of Biblical Literature 133, no. 1, Duke University, Durham(2014): 193–214

[240] Concannon, C, Gladiators, Athletes, and Early Christian Bodies, Journal of Biblical Literature 133, no. 1, Duke University, Durham(2014): 193–214

[241] Hopkins, K. (2014). Murderous Games: Gladiatorial Contests in Ancient Rome, Historytoday.com, http://www.historytoday.com/keith-hopkins/murderous-games-gladiatorial-contests-ancient-rome

[242] Grimes, W. (2014). The Pride and Terror of Those Who Fought to the Death – New York Times.
http://www.nytimes.com/2005/12/09/books/09book.html?_r=0

[243] Grimes, W. (2014). The Pride and Terror of Those Who Fought to the Death – New York Times.
http://www.nytimes.com/2005/12/09/books/09book.html?_r=0

[244] Grimes, W. (2014). The Pride and Terror of Those Who Fought to the Death – New York Times.
http://www.nytimes.com/2005/12/09/books/09book.html?_r=0

[245] Wilcox, B. (2014). Stanford classics professor debunks image of the 'noble' ancient athlete, Stanford University.
http://news.stanford.edu/news/2013/february/ancient-athletes-myth-020113.html

[246] Semaan, J. (2008). Roman Gladiator Games: the Origins of MMA, Part Two, Bleacher Report.
http://bleacherreport.com/articles/30004-roman-gladiator-games-the-origins-of-mma-part-two

[247] Hopkins, K. (2014). Murderous Games: Gladiatorial Contests in Ancient Rome, Historytoday.com, http://www.historytoday.com/keith-hopkins/murderous-games-gladiatorial-contests-ancient-rome

[248] Hopkins, K. (2014). Murderous Games: Gladiatorial Contests in Ancient Rome, Historytoday.com, http://www.historytoday.com/keith-hopkins/murderous-games-gladiatorial-contests-ancient-rome

[249] King, C. (2014). The Romans: Gladiators. [online] ITALY Magazine.
http://www.italymagazine.com/featured-story/romans-gladiators

[250] Coliseum: A Gladiator's Story. (2014). [DVD] UK: BBC.
https://www.youtube.com/watch?v=I0fRqc_pChY

[251] Coliseum: A Gladiator's Story. (2014). [DVD] UK: BBC.
https://www.youtube.com/watch?v=I0fRqc_pChY

[252] Coleman, K. (2014). BBC – History – Ancient History in depth:
Gladiators: Heroes of the Roman Amphitheatre. [online] Bbc.co.uk.
Available at:
http://www.bbc.co.uk/history/ancient/romans/gladiators_01.shtml

[253] Unrv.com, (2014). Gladiator,
http://www.unrv.com/culture/gladiator.php

[254]Morgan, J. (2014). Roman 'gladiator school' recreated. [online] BBC
News.
http://www.bbc.com/news/science-environment-26359012

[255] Morgan, J. (2014). Roman 'gladiator school' recreated. [online] BBC
News.
http://www.bbc.com/news/science-environment-26359012

[256] Tataki, A. (2009). Nemeseis, and the Gladiatorial Games at Smyrna.
Mnemosyne, 62(4), pp.639-648.

[257] Bbc.co.uk, (2014). BBC – History – The Coliseum: Emblem of Rome.
http://www.bbc.co.uk/history/ancient/romans/colosseum_01.shtml

[258] UShistory.org, (2014). Gladiators, Chariots, and the Roman Games,
ushistory.org, http://www.ushistory.org/civ/6e.asp

[259] Coliseum: A Gladiator's Story. (2014). [DVD] UK: BBC.
https://www.youtube.com/watch?v=I0fRqc_pChY

[260] Tribunesandtriumphs.org, (2014). Spartacus Timeline,
http://www.tribunesandtriumphs.org/gladiators/spartacus-
timeline.htm

[261] Unrv.com, (2014). Gladiator,
http://www.unrv.com/culture/gladiator.php

[262]Coliseum: A Gladiator's Story. (2014). [DVD] UK: BBC.
https://www.youtube.com/watch?v=I0fRqc_pChY

[263] Tribunesandtriumphs.org, (2014). Spartacus Timeline, http://www.tribunesandtriumphs.org/gladiators/spartacus-timeline.htm

[264] Fitzgerald, A. (2014). 10 Famous Gladiators From Ancient Rome – Listverse. http://listverse.com/2013/04/02/10-famous-gladiators-from-ancient-rome/

[265] Grimes, W. (2014). The Pride and Terror of Those Who Fought to the Death – New York Times. http://www.nytimes.com/2005/12/09/books/09book.html?_r=0

[266] Quinn, D. (2014). Roman Emperors – DIR commodus. [online] Luc.edu. Available at: http://www.luc.edu/roman-emperors/commod.htm

[267] Neelin, D. (2014). Gladiator: The Real Story. [online] Exovedate.com, http://www.exovedate.com/the_real_gladiator_one.html

[268] Neelin, D. (2014). Gladiator: The Real Story. [online] Exovedate.com, http://www.exovedate.com/the_real_gladiator_one.html

[269] Fitzgerald, A. (2014). 10 Famous Gladiators From Ancient Rome – Listverse. http://listverse.com/2013/04/02/10-famous-gladiators-from-ancient-rome/

[270] Hopkins, K. (2014). Murderous Games: Gladiatorial Contests in Ancient Rome, Historytoday.com, http://www.historytoday.com/keith-hopkins/murderous-games-gladiatorial-contests-ancient-rome

[271] Fitzgerald, A. (2014). 10 Famous Gladiators From Ancient Rome – Listverse. http://listverse.com/2013/04/02/10-famous-gladiators-from-ancient-rome/

[272] Neelin, D. (2014). Gladiator: The Real Story. [online] Exovedate.com, http://www.exovedate.com/the_real_gladiator_one.html

[273] Hopkins, K. (2014). Murderous Games: Gladiatorial Contests in Ancient Rome, Historytoday.com, http://www.historytoday.com/keith-hopkins/murderous-games-gladiatorial-contests-ancient-rome

[274] Jarus, O. (2012). Fighting champ was recruiter for ancient Roman army. [online] msnbc.com.

http://www.nbcnews.com/id/46905163/ns/technology_and_science-science/t/fighting-champ-was-recruiter-ancient-roman-army/

[275] Jarus, O. (2012). Fighting champ was recruiter for ancient Roman army. [online] msnbc.com.

http://www.nbcnews.com/id/46905163/ns/technology_and_science-science/t/fighting-champ-was-recruiter-ancient-roman-army/

[276] Fitzgerald, A. (2014). 10 Famous Gladiators From Ancient Rome – Listverse.

http://listverse.com/2013/04/02/10-famous-gladiators-from-ancient-rome/

[277] Fitzgerald, A. (2014). 10 Famous Gladiators From Ancient Rome – Listverse.

http://listverse.com/2013/04/02/10-famous-gladiators-from-ancient-rome/

[278] Fitzgerald, A. (2014). 10 Famous Gladiators From Ancient Rome – Listverse.

http://listverse.com/2013/04/02/10-famous-gladiators-from-ancient-rome/

[279] Tribunesandtriumphs.org, (2014). Spartacus Timeline,

http://www.tribunesandtriumphs.org/gladiators/spartacus-timeline.htm

[280] Coliseum: A Gladiator's Story. (2014). [DVD] UK: BBC.

https://www.youtube.com/watch?v=I0fRqc_pChY

[281] Fitzgerald, A. (2014). 10 Famous Gladiators From Ancient Rome – Listverse.

http://listverse.com/2013/04/02/10-famous-gladiators-from-ancient-rome/

[282] Forsythe, G. and Guisepi, R. (2014). Rome, Spartacus. [online] History-world.org. http://history-world.org/spartacus.htm

[283] Tribunesandtriumphs.org, (2014). Spartacus Timeline,

http://www.tribunesandtriumphs.org/gladiators/spartacus-timeline.htm

[284] Libcom.org, (2010). 'As many enemies as there are slaves': Spartacus and the politics of servile rebellion in the late republic. http://libcom.org/history/many-enemies-there-are-slaves%E2%80%99-spartacus-politics-servile-rebellion-late-republic

[285] Jarus, O. (2014). Spartacus: History of Gladiator Revolt Leader. [online] LiveScience.com.

Available at: http://www.livescience.com/39730-spartacus.html

[286] Jarus, O. (2014). Spartacus: History of Gladiator Revolt Leader. [online] LiveScience.com.

Available at: http://www.livescience.com/39730-spartacus.html

[287] Fitzgerald, A. (2014). 10 Famous Gladiators From Ancient Rome – Listverse. http://listverse.com/2013/04/02/10-famous-gladiators-from-ancient-rome/

[288] Jarus, O. (2014). Spartacus: History of Gladiator Revolt Leader. [online] LiveScience.com.

Available at: http://www.livescience.com/39730-spartacus.html

[289] Jarus, O. (2014). Spartacus: History of Gladiator Revolt Leader. [online] LiveScience.com.

Available at: http://www.livescience.com/39730-spartacus.html

[290] Owen Jarus, Spartacus: History of Gladiator Revolt Leader, September 17, 2013, Live Science Contributor, https://www.livescience.com/39730-spartacus.html

[291] Jarus, O. (2014). Spartacus: History of Gladiator Revolt Leader. [online] LiveScience.com.

Available at: http://www.livescience.com/39730-spartacus.html

[292] Forsythe, G. and Guisepi, R. (2014). Rome, Spartacus. [online] History-world.org. http://history-world.org/spartacus.htm

[293] Jarus, O. (2014). Spartacus: History of Gladiator Revolt Leader. [online] LiveScience.com.

Available at: http://www.livescience.com/39730-spartacus.html

[294] Tribunesandtriumphs.org, (2014). Spartacus Timeline, http://www.tribunesandtriumphs.org/gladiators/spartacus-timeline.htm

[295] Tribunesandtriumphs.org, (2014). Spartacus Timeline, http://www.tribunesandtriumphs.org/gladiators/spartacus-timeline.htm

[296] Forsythe, G. and Guisepi, R. (2014). Rome, Spartacus. [online] History-world.org. http://history-world.org/spartacus.htm

[297] Forsythe, G. and Guisepi, R. (2014). Rome, Spartacus. [online] History-world.org. http://history-world.org/spartacus.htm

[298] Gill, N. (2014). How Spartacus Led a Slave Revolt and Defied Rome. [online] About. http://ancienthistory.about.com/cs/slavesandslavery/a/spartacus.htm

[299] Tribunesandtriumphs.org, (2014). Spartacus Timeline, http://www.tribunesandtriumphs.org/gladiators/spartacus-timeline.htm

[300] Forsythe, G. and Guisepi, R. (2014). Rome, Spartacus. [online] History-world.org. http://history-world.org/spartacus.htm

[301] Sophia, F. (2014). Pankration, An Ancient Martial Art presented in Non Famous section. [online] Newsfinder.org. http://www.newsfinder.org/site/more/Pankration_an_ancient_martial_art/

[302] Wilcox, B. (2014). Stanford classics professor debunks image of the 'noble' ancient athlete. [online] Stanford University. http://news.stanford.edu/news/2013/february/ancient-athletes-myth-020113.html

[303] Kreit, A, Professional Wrestling and its Fans: A Sociological Study of the Sport of Pro wrestling, solie.org, Jump City Productions, 1998, http://www.solie.org/articles/pwandfans.html

[304] Crigger, K. Catch As Catch Can, FIGHT! Magazine, February 2010 https://www.fightmagazine.com/mma-magazine/catch-as-catch-can-624/ search

[305] Crigger, K. Catch As Catch Can, FIGHT! Magazine, February 2010 https://www.fightmagazine.com/mma-magazine/catch-as-catch-can-624/ search

[306] Crigger, K. Catch As Catch Can, FIGHT! Magazine, February 2010 https://www.fightmagazine.com/mma-magazine/catch-as-catch-can-624/ search

[307] Kreit, A, Professional Wrestling and its Fans: A Sociological Study of the Sport of Pro wrestling, solie.org, Jump City Productions, 1998, http://www.solie.org/articles/pwandfans.html

[308] Nash, J, Wrestling with the Past: The Man of a Thousand Holds, CAGESIDE SEATS, Oct 17 2012, 7:00p 40

[309] Kreit, A, Professional Wrestling and its Fans: A Sociological Study of the Sport of Pro wrestling, solie.org, Jump City Productions, 1998, http://www.solie.org/articles/pwandfans.html

[310] Kreit, A, Professional Wrestling and its Fans: A Sociological Study of the Sport of Pro wrestling, solie.org, Jump City Productions, 1998, http://www.solie.org/articles/pwandfans.html

[311] Kreit, A, Professional Wrestling and its Fans: A Sociological Study of the Sport of Pro wrestling, solie.org, Jump City Productions, 1998, http://www.solie.org/articles/pwandfans.html

[312] Snake Pit USA, Catch Wrestling Association, year in review, 2013, January 9, 2014

[313] Crigger, K. Catch As Catch Can, FIGHT! Magazine, February 2010 https://www.fightmagazine.com/mma-magazine/catch-as-catch-can-624/ search

[314] Crigger, K. Catch As Catch Can, FIGHT! Magazine, February 2010 https://www.fightmagazine.com/mma-magazine/catch-as-catch-can-624/ search

[315] Nash, J, The Martial Chronicles: The Forgotten Olympic History of Catch-As-Catch-Can Wrestling, Bloody Elbow, August 13 2012

http://www.bloodyelbow.com/2012/8/13/3238285/martial-chronicles-olympics-history-catch-wrestling

[316] Nash, J, The Martial Chronicles: The Forgotten Olympic History of Catch-As-Catch-Can Wrestling, Bloody Elbow, August 13 2012

http://www.bloodyelbow.com/2012/8/13/3238285/martial-chronicles-olympics-history-catch-wrestling

[317] Snake Pit USA, Catch Wrestling Association, year in review, 2013, January 9, 2014

[318] Kris Iatskevich, Modern Catch As Catch Can, Damagecontrolmma, August 9, 2009, http://damagecontrolmma.com/2009/08/modern-catch-as-catch-can-written-by-kris-iatskevich/

[319] Kris Iatskevich, Modern Catch As Catch Can, Damagecontrolmma, August 9, 2009, http://damagecontrolmma.com/2009/08/modern-catch-as-catch-can-written-by-kris-iatskevich/

[320] Crigger, K. Catch As Catch Can, FIGHT! Magazine, February 2010

https://www.fightmagazine.com/mma-magazine/catch-as-catch-can-624/ search

[321] Nash, J, Wrestling with the Past: The Man of a Thousand Holds, CAGESIDE SEATS, Oct 17 2012, 7:00p 40

[322] Nash, J, The Martial Chronicles: The Forgotten Olympic History of Catch-As-Catch-Can Wrestling, Bloody Elbow, August 13 2012
http://www.bloodyelbow.com/2012/8/13/3238285/martial-chronicles-olympics-history-catch-wrestling

[323] Nash, J, Wrestling with the Past: The Man of a Thousand Holds, CAGESIDE SEATS, Oct 17 2012, 7:00p 40

[324] Nash, J, The Martial Chronicles: The Forgotten Olympic History of Catch-As-Catch-Can Wrestling, Bloody Elbow, August 13 2012
http://www.bloodyelbow.com/2012/8/13/3238285/martial-chronicles-olympics-history-catch-wrestling

[325] Nash, J, The Martial Chronicles: The Forgotten Olympic History of Catch-As-Catch-Can Wrestling, Bloody Elbow, August 13 2012
http://www.bloodyelbow.com/2012/8/13/3238285/martial-chronicles-olympics-history-catch-wrestling

[326] Nash, J, The Martial Chronicles: The Forgotten Olympic History of Catch-As-Catch-Can Wrestling, Bloody Elbow, August 13 2012
http://www.bloodyelbow.com/2012/8/13/3238285/martial-chronicles-olympics-history-catch-wrestling

[327] Squared Circle of Wrestling, 10 Great Early Professional Wrestlers, Squared Circle of Wrestling, September 13, 2012,
http://www.squaredcircleofwrestling.com/2012/09/13/10-great-early-professional-wrestlers/

[328] Squared Circle of Wrestling, 10 Great Early Professional Wrestlers, Squared Circle of Wrestling, September 13, 2012,
http://www.squaredcircleofwrestling.com/2012/09/13/10-great-early-professional-wrestlers/

[329] Squared Circle of Wrestling, 10 Great Early Professional Wrestlers, Squared Circle of Wrestling, September 13, 2012,
http://www.squaredcircleofwrestling.com/2012/09/13/10-great-early-professional-wrestlers/

[330] Squared Circle of Wrestling, 10 Great Early Professional Wrestlers, Squared Circle of Wrestling, September 13, 2012,
http://www.squaredcircleofwrestling.com/2012/09/13/10-great-early-professional-wrestlers/

[331] Squared Circle of Wrestling, 10 Great Early Professional Wrestlers, Squared Circle of Wrestling, September 13, 2012,
http://www.squaredcircleofwrestling.com/2012/09/13/10-great-early-professional-wrestlers/

[332] Squared Circle of Wrestling, 10 Great Early Professional Wrestlers, Squared Circle of Wrestling, September 13, 2012,
http://www.squaredcircleofwrestling.com/2012/09/13/10-great-early-professional-wrestlers/

[333] IBB, The Great Gama, Indian Body Building, n.d.
https://www.indianbodybuilding.co.in/bodybuilders/the-great-gama/

[334] IBB, The Great Gama, Indian Body Building, n.d.
https://www.indianbodybuilding.co.in/bodybuilders/the-great-gama/

[335] IBB, The Great Gama, Indian Body Building, n.d.
https://www.indianbodybuilding.co.in/bodybuilders/the-great-gama/

[336] Squared Circle of Wrestling, 10 Great Early Professional Wrestlers, Squared Circle of Wrestling, September 13, 2012,
http://www.squaredcircleofwrestling.com/2012/09/13/10-great-early-professional-wrestlers/

[337] Sussman,G, The Most Popular Soap Opera in the World: Professional Wrestling, Sport History Blog, 2008

[338] Professional Wrestling Hall of Fame, William Muldoon, Copyright 2009 http://www.pwhf.org/halloffamers/bios/muldoon.asp

[339] Welsh, J William Muldoon A Veteran of the Civil War, Wrestling Revue, June, 1975
http://www.wrestling-titles.com/personalities/muldoon_william/veteran.html

[340] Welsh, J William Muldoon A Veteran of the Civil War, Wrestling Revue, June, 1975
http://www.wrestling-titles.com/personalities/muldoon_william/veteran.html

[341] Welsh, J William Muldoon A Veteran of the Civil War, Wrestling Revue, June, 1975
http://www.wrestling-titles.com/personalities/muldoon_william/veteran.html

[342] Professional Wrestling Hall of Fame, William Muldoon, Copyright 2009 http://www.pwhf.org/halloffamers/bios/muldoon.asp

[343] Professional Wrestling Hall of Fame, William Muldoon, Copyright 2009 http://www.pwhf.org/halloffamers/bios/muldoon.asp

[344] Welsh, J William Muldoon A Veteran of the Civil War, Wrestling Revue, June, 1975
http://www.wrestling-titles.com/personalities/muldoon_william/veteran.html

[345] Robert Lipsyte and Peter Levine, Idols of the Game: A Sporting History of the American Century, Hardcover, October 1, 1995, p. 24

[346] Welsh, J William Muldoon A Veteran of the Civil War, Wrestling Revue, June, 1975
http://www.wrestling-titles.com/personalities/muldoon_william/veteran.html

[347] Robert Lipsyte and Peter Levine, Idols of the Game: A Sporting History of the American Century, Hardcover, October 1, 1995, p. 28,29

[348] Welsh, J William Muldoon A Veteran of the Civil War, Wrestling Revue, June, 1975
http://www.wrestling-titles.com/personalities/muldoon_william/veteran.html

[349] Squared Circle of Wrestling, 10 Great Early Professional Wrestlers, Squared Circle of Wrestling, September 13, 2012,
http://www.squaredcircleofwrestling.com/2012/09/13/10-great-early-professional-wrestlers/

[350] The MSW productions, Frank Gotch Wrestler, Documentary film
https://www.youtube.com/watch?v=spaWVTFFf0E

[351] The MSW productions, Frank Gotch Wrestler, Documentary film
https://www.youtube.com/watch?v=spaWVTFFf0E

[352] The MSW productions, Frank Gotch Wrestler, Documentary film
https://www.youtube.com/watch?v=spaWVTFFf0E

[353] The MSW productions, Frank Gotch Wrestler, Documentary film
https://www.youtube.com/watch?v=spaWVTFFf0E

[354] Squared Circle of Wrestling, 10 Great Early Professional Wrestlers, Squared Circle of Wrestling, September 13, 2012,
http://www.squaredcircleofwrestling.com/2012/09/13/10-great-early-professional-wrestlers/

[355] The MSW productions, Frank Gotch Wrestler, Documentary film
https://www.youtube.com/watch?v=spaWVTFFf0E

[356] The MSW productions, Frank Gotch Wrestler, Documentary film
https://www.youtube.com/watch?v=spaWVTFFf0E

[357] Nat Fleischer, From Milo to Londos: The Story of Wrestling Through the Ages, The Ring Athletic Library; 1st edition (1936)

[358] Nat Fleischer, From Milo to Londos: The Story of Wrestling Through the Ages, The Ring Athletic Library; 1st edition (1936)

[359] The MSW productions, Frank Gotch Wrestler, Documentary film
https://www.youtube.com/watch?v=spaWVTFFf0E

[360] The MSW productions, Frank Gotch Wrestler, Documentary film
https://www.youtube.com/watch?v=spaWVTFFf0E

[361] The MSW productions, Frank Gotch Wrestler, Documentary film
https://www.youtube.com/watch?v=spaWVTFFf0E

[362] The MSW productions, Frank Gotch Wrestler, Documentary film
https://www.youtube.com/watch?v=spaWVTFFf0E

[363] The MSW productions, Frank Gotch Wrestler, Documentary film https://www.youtube.com/watch?v=spaWVTFFf0E

[364] The MSW productions, Frank Gotch Wrestler, Documentary film https://www.youtube.com/watch?v=spaWVTFFf0E

[365] Mac Davis, 100 greatest sports heroes, 1954, Grosset & Dunlap

[366] Mac Davis, 100 greatest sports heroes, 1954, Grosset & Dunlap

[367] Kevin Sherrington, Iowa Owes Its Passion For Wrestling To Gotch, Dallas Morning News, March 01, 1998
http://articles.chicagotribune.com/1998-03-01/sports/9803010232_1_iowa-state-wrestling-gotch

[368] The MSW productions, Frank Gotch Wrestler, Documentary film https://www.youtube.com/watch?v=spaWVTFFf0E

[369] Nash, J, Wrestling with the Past: The Man of a Thousand Holds, CAGESIDE SEATS, Oct 17 2012, 7:00p 40

[370] Nash, J, Wrestling with the Past: The Man of a Thousand Holds, CAGESIDE SEATS, Oct 17 2012, 7:00p 40

[371] Nash, J, Wrestling with the Past: The Man of a Thousand Holds, CAGESIDE SEATS, Oct 17 2012, 7:00p 40

[372] Nash, J, Wrestling with the Past: The Man of a Thousand Holds, CAGESIDE SEATS, Oct 17 2012, 7:00p 40

[373] Nash, J, Wrestling with the Past: The Man of a Thousand Holds, CAGESIDE SEATS, Oct 17 2012, 7:00p 40

[374] Nash, J, Wrestling with the Past: The Man of a Thousand Holds, CAGESIDE SEATS, Oct 17 2012, 7:00p 40

[375] Nash, J, Wrestling with the Past: The Man of a Thousand Holds, CAGESIDE SEATS, Oct 17 2012, 7:00p 40

[376] Nash, J, Wrestling with the Past: The Man of a Thousand Holds, CAGESIDE SEATS, Oct 17 2012, 7:00p 40

[377] Nash, J, Wrestling with the Past: The Man of a Thousand Holds, CAGESIDE SEATS, Oct 17 2012, 7:00p 40

[378] Nash, J, Wrestling with the Past: The Man of a Thousand Holds, CAGESIDE SEATS, Oct 17 2012, 7:00p 40

[379] Nash, J, Wrestling with the Past: The Man of a Thousand Holds, CAGESIDE SEATS, Oct 17 2012, 7:00p 40

[380] Nash, J, Wrestling with the Past: The Man of a Thousand Holds, CAGESIDE SEATS, Oct 17 2012, 7:00p 40

[381] Snake Pit USA, Catch Wrestling Association, year in review, 2013, January 9, 2014

[382] Snake Pit USA, Catch Wrestling Association, year in review, 2013, January 9, 2014

[383] Snake Pit USA, Catch Wrestling Association, year in review, 2013, January 9, 2014

[384] Crigger, K. Catch As Catch Can, FIGHT! Magazine, February 2010
https://www.fightmagazine.com/mma-magazine/catch-as-catch-can-624/ search

[385] Phantom of the Ring, Karl Gotch: The Godfather of Mixed Marshal Arts, Pro Wrestling Digest, June 28th, 2008

http://www.prowrestlingdigest.com/2008/06/28/phantom-karl-gotch-the-godfather-of-mixed-marshal-arts/

[386] Phantom of the Ring, Karl Gotch: The Godfather of Mixed Marshal Arts, Pro Wrestling Digest, June 28th, 2008

http://www.prowrestlingdigest.com/2008/06/28/phantom-karl-gotch-the-godfather-of-mixed-marshal-arts/

[387] Phantom of the Ring, Karl Gotch: The Godfather of Mixed Marshal Arts, Pro Wrestling Digest, June 28th, 2008
http://www.prowrestlingdigest.com/2008/06/28/phantom-karl-gotch-the-godfather-of-mixed-marshal-arts/

[388] T.P. Grant, MMA Origins: Birth of Japanese MMA, Bloody Elbows, Feb 20, 2012,
https://www.bloodyelbow.com/2012/2/20/2808780/UFC-144-Japan-mma-history

[389] Andy Bull , The forgotten story of Muhammad Ali v Antonio Inoki, The Guardian, November 11, 2009,
https://www.theguardian.com/sport/blog/2009/nov/11/the-forgotten-story-of-ali-inoki

[390] Andy Bull, The forgotten story of Muhammad Ali v Antonio Inoki, The Guardian, November 11, 2009,
https://www.theguardian.com/sport/blog/2009/nov/11/the-forgotten-story-of-ali-inoki

[391] Phantom of the Ring, Karl Gotch: The Godfather of Mixed Marshal Arts, Pro Wrestling Digest, June 28th, 2008
http://www.prowrestlingdigest.com/2008/06/28/phantom-karl-gotch-the-godfather-of-mixed-marshal-arts/

[392] Mike AKA the Professor, Edouard Carpentier Passes Away: A Pro Wrestling Legend Is Gone, Bleacher Report, Nov 2, 2010
http://bleacherreport.com/articles/508008-a-pro wrestling-legend-is-gone-edouard-carpentier

[393] Mike AKA the Professor, Edouard Carpentier Passes Away: A Pro Wrestling Legend Is Gone, Bleacher Report, Nov 2, 2010
http://bleacherreport.com/articles/508008-a-pro wrestling-legend-is-gone-edouard-carpentier

[394] Mike AKA the Professor, Edouard Carpentier Passes Away: A Pro Wrestling Legend Is Gone, Bleacher Report, Nov 2, 2010
http://bleacherreport.com/articles/508008-a-pro wrestling-legend-is-gone-edouard-carpentier

[395] Kreit, A, Professional Wrestling and its Fans: A Sociological Study of the Sport of Pro wrestling, solie.org, Jump City Productions, 1998,
http://www.solie.org/articles/pwandfans.html

[396] NWA, National Wrestling Alliance History, Legacy of Wrestling, n.d.
http://www.legacyofwrestling.com/NWA_History.html

[397] Kreit, A, Professional Wrestling and its Fans: A Sociological Study of the Sport of Pro wrestling, solie.org, Jump City Productions, 1998,
http://www.solie.org/articles/pwandfans.html

[398] Kreit, A, Professional Wrestling and its Fans: A Sociological Study of the Sport of Pro wrestling, solie.org, Jump City Productions, 1998,
http://www.solie.org/articles/pwandfans.html

[399] Amhistory.si.edu, (2014). Sports: Breaking Records, Breaking Barriers | The First Modern Olympic Games, Athens, Greece, 1896 |

Smithsonian's National Museum of American History |, http://amhistory.si.edu/sports/exhibit/olympians/first/

400 Baxter, W. (2004). History of Wrestling – 2004 Oceania Wrestling Championships – FOX SPORTS PULSE. [online] SportingPulse.
http://www.foxsportspulse.com/assoc_page.cgi?c=4-2643-0-0-0&sID=24206

401 Baxter, W. (2004). History of Wrestling – 2004 Oceania Wrestling Championships – FOX SPORTS PULSE. [online] SportingPulse.
http://www.foxsportspulse.com/assoc_page.cgi?c=4-2643-0-0-0&sID=24206

402 Baxter, W. (2004). History of Wrestling – 2004 Oceania Wrestling Championships – FOX SPORTS PULSE. [online] SportingPulse.
http://www.foxsportspulse.com/assoc_page.cgi?c=4-2643-0-0-0&sID=24206

403 Miller, C. (2004). Submission Fighting and the Rules of Ancient Greek Wrestling. [online] Judoinfo.com. Available at: http://JudoInfo.com

404 Awakening Fighters, (2014). Greco-Roman Wrestling – Awakening Fighters. [online] Available at:
http://www.awakeningfighters.com/awakepedia/greco-roman-wrestling/

405 Awakening Fighters, (2014). Greco-Roman Wrestling – Awakening Fighters. [online] Available at:
http://www.awakeningfighters.com/awakepedia/greco-roman-wrestling/

406 Gustavfristensky.com, (2014). GUSTAV FRIŠTENSKÝ, The Czech Legend. [online] Available at: http://gustavfristensky.com/greco.html

407 Baxter, W. (2004). History of Wrestling – 2004 Oceania Wrestling Championships – FOX SPORTS PULSE. [online] SportingPulse.
http://www.foxsportspulse.com/assoc_page.cgi?c=4-2643-0-0-0&sID=24206

408 Wrestle.co.uk, (2014). Belgium & Greco-Roman Wrestling Part 1, http://www.wrestle.co.uk/bwc1.htm

409 Wrestle.co.uk, (2014). Belgium & Greco-Roman Wrestling Part 1, http://www.wrestle.co.uk/bwc1.htm

[410] Amhistory.si.edu, (2014). Sports: Breaking Records, Breaking Barriers | The First Modern Olympic Games, Athens, Greece, 1896 | Smithsonian's National Museum of American History |, http://amhistory.si.edu/sports/exhibit/olympians/first/

[411] Sternfeld, J. (2012). The First Modern Olympics | National Endowment for the Humanities. [online] Neh.gov.
http://www.neh.gov/divisions/preservation/featured-project/the-first-modern-olympics

[412] Fila-official.com, (2014). United World Wrestling,
http://www.fila-official.com/index.php?option=com_content&view=article&id=14&Itemid=100246&lang=en

[413] Baxter, W. (2004). History of Wrestling – 2004 Oceania Wrestling Championships – FOX SPORTS PULSE. [online] SportingPulse.

http://www.foxsportspulse.com/assoc_page.cgi?c=4-2643-0-0-0&sID=24206

[414] Sternfeld, J. (2012). The First Modern Olympics | National Endowment for the Humanities. [online] Neh.gov.

http://www.neh.gov/divisions/preservation/featured-project/the-first-modern-olympics

[415] Sternfeld, J. (2012). The First Modern Olympics | National Endowment for the Humanities. [online] Neh.gov.

http://www.neh.gov/divisions/preservation/featured-project/the-first-modern-olympics

[416] Sternfeld, J. (2012). The First Modern Olympics | National Endowment for the Humanities. [online] Neh.gov.

http://www.neh.gov/divisions/preservation/featured-project/the-first-modern-olympics

[417] Sternfeld, J. (2012). The First Modern Olympics | National Endowment for the Humanities. [online] Neh.gov.

http://www.neh.gov/divisions/preservation/featured-project/the-first-modern-olympics

[418] Wrestling.isport.com, (2014). History of Wrestling | iSport.com. [online] Available at: http://wrestling.isport.com/wrestling-guides/history-of-wrestling

[419] Olympics at Sports-Reference.com, (2014). Wrestling at the 1896 Athina Summer Games | Olympics at Sports-Reference.com. [online] Available at: http://www.sports-reference.com/olympics/summer/1896/WRE/

[420] Fila-official.com, (2014). United World Wrestling,

http://www.fila-official.com/index.php?option=com_content&view=article&id=14&Itemid=100246&lang=en

[421] Baxter, W. (2004). History of Wrestling – 2004 Oceania Wrestling Championships – FOX SPORTS PULSE. [online] SportingPulse.

http://www.foxsportspulse.com/assoc_page.cgi?c=4-2643-0-0-0&sID=24206

[422] Olympics at Sports-Reference.com, (2014). Wrestling at the 1896 Athina Summer Games | Olympics at Sports-Reference.com. [online] Available at: http://www.sports-reference.com/olympics/summer/1896/WRE/

[423] Wrestle.co.uk, (2014). Belgium & Greco-Roman Wrestling Part 1, http://www.wrestle.co.uk/bwc1.htm

[424] Wrestle.co.uk, (2014). Belgium & Greco-Roman Wrestling Part 1, http://www.wrestle.co.uk/bwc1.htm

[425] Baxter, W. (2004). History of Wrestling – 2004 Oceania Wrestling Championships – FOX SPORTS PULSE. [online] SportingPulse.

http://www.foxsportspulse.com/assoc_page.cgi?c=4-2643-0-0-0&sID=24206

[426] Fila-official.com, (2014). United World Wrestling,

http://www.fila-official.com/index.php?option=com_content&view=article&id=14&Itemid=100246&lang=en

[427] Wrestle.co.uk, (2014). Belgium & Greco-Roman Wrestling Part 1, http://www.wrestle.co.uk/bwc1.htm

[428] Sewell, B. (2012). Gouging, biting, disembowelling, strangling – those were the good old days of wrestling. [online] The Evening Standard. Available at: http://www.standard.co.uk/olympics/olympic-news/gouging-biting-disembowelling-strangling–those-were-the-good-old-days-of-wrestling-8004816.html

[429] Wrestling.isport.com, (2014). History of Wrestling | iSport.com. [online] Available at: http://wrestling.isport.com/wrestling-guides/history-of-wrestling

[430] Fila-official.com, (2014). United World Wrestling, http://www.fila-official.com/index.php?option=com_content&view=article&id=14&Itemid=100246&lang=en

[431] Nash, J. (2012). The Martial Chronicles: The Forgotten Olympic History of Catch-As-Catch-Can Wrestling. [online] Bloody Elbow. Available at: http://www.bloodyelbow.com/2012/8/13/3238285/martial-chronicles-olympics-history-catch-wrestling

[432] Fila-official.com, (2014). United World Wrestling, http://www.fila-official.com/index.php?option=com_content&view=article&id=14&Itemid=100246&lang=en

[433] Baxter, W. (2004). History of Wrestling – 2004 Oceania Wrestling Championships – FOX SPORTS PULSE. [online] SportingPulse. http://www.foxsportspulse.com/assoc_page.cgi?c=4-2643-0-0-0&sID=24206

[434] Chicago Tribune, (2004). Nine Hours On The Mat, 1912. [online] Available at: http://articles.chicagotribune.com/1996-06-15/sports/9606150166_1_finland-greco-roman-silver [Accessed 9 Nov. 2014].

[435] Nash, J. (2012). The Martial Chronicles: The Forgotten Olympic History of Catch-As-Catch-Can Wrestling. [online] Bloody Elbow. Available at: http://www.bloodyelbow.com/2012/8/13/3238285/martial-

chronicles-olympics-history-catch-wrestling

[436] Nash, J. (2012). The Martial Chronicles: The Forgotten Olympic History of Catch-As-Catch-Can Wrestling. [online] Bloody Elbow.
Available at:
http://www.bloodyelbow.com/2012/8/13/3238285/martial-chronicles-olympics-history-catch-wrestling

[437] Nash, J. (2012). The Martial Chronicles: The Forgotten Olympic History of Catch-As-Catch-Can Wrestling. [online] Bloody Elbow.
Available at:
http://www.bloodyelbow.com/2012/8/13/3238285/martial-chronicles-olympics-history-catch-wrestling

[438] Sparta-club.org, (2014). Sparta, The history of the Greco-Roman wrestling. [online]
Available at:
http://sparta-club.org/eng_about_history.shtml [Accessed 14 Nov. 2014].

[439] Nash, J. (2012). The Martial Chronicles: The Forgotten Olympic History of Catch-As-Catch-Can Wrestling. [online] Bloody Elbow.
Available at:
http://www.bloodyelbow.com/2012/8/13/3238285/martial-chronicles-olympics-history-catch-wrestling

[440] Nash, J. (2012). The Martial Chronicles: The Forgotten Olympic History of Catch-As-Catch-Can Wrestling. [online] Bloody Elbow.
Available at:
http://www.bloodyelbow.com/2012/8/13/3238285/martial-chronicles-olympics-history-catch-wrestling

[441] Fila-official.com, (2014). United World Wrestling,
http://www.fila-official.com/index.php?option=com_content&view=article&id=14&Itemid=100246&lang=en

[442] Sparta-club.org, (2014). Sparta, The history of the Greco-Roman wrestling. [online] Available at:
http://sparta-club.org/eng_about_history.shtml [Accessed 14 Nov. 2014].

[443] Loomischaffee.org, (2014). Origins of Wrestling. [online]
Available at:
https://www.loomischaffee.org/uploaded/Athletics_photos/athletics_

downloads/Origins_of_Wrestling_revised.pdf

[444] BBC Sport, (2013). *How to get into Wrestling.* [online]
Available at: http://www.bbc.com/sport/0/get-inspired/23169983

[445] Baxter, W. (2004). History of Wrestling – 2004 Oceania Wrestling Championships – FOX SPORTS PULSE. [online] SportingPulse.
http://www.foxsportspulse.com/assoc_page.cgi?c=4-2643-0-0-0&sID=24206

[446] Fila-official.com, (2014). United World Wrestling,
http://www.fila-official.com/index.php?option=com_content&view=article&id=14&Itemid=100246&lang=en

[447] Rio 2016, (2012). The Warriors of The Olympic Movement: Wrestling. http://www.rio2016.com/en/news/news/the-warriors-of-the-olympic-movement-wrestling

[448] Amhistory.si.edu, (2014). Sports: Breaking Records, Breaking Barriers | The First Modern Olympic Games, Athens, Greece, 1896 | Smithsonian's National Museum of American History |, http://amhistory.si.edu/sports/exhibit/olympians/first/

[449] Bbc.com, (2014). BBC Sport – London 2012 Olympics – Countries. [online] Available at:
http://www.bbc.com/sport/olympics/2012/countries

[450] Rogers, S. (2012). London 2012 Olympic athletes: the full list. [online] the Guardian.
http://www.theguardian.com/sport/datablog/2012/jul/27/london-olympic-athletes-full-list

[451] Amhistory.si.edu, (2014). Sports: Breaking Records, Breaking Barriers | The First Modern Olympic Games, Athens, Greece, 1896 | Smithsonian's National Museum of American History |, http://amhistory.si.edu/sports/exhibit/olympians/first/

[452] Rogers, S. (2012). London 2012 Olympic athletes: the full list. [online] the Guardian.
http://www.theguardian.com/sport/datablog/2012/jul/27/london-

olympic-athletes-full-list

453 Databaseolympics.com, (2014). All Time Medal Count for Wrestling. [online] Available at:
http://www.databaseolympics.com/sport/sportpage.htm?sp=WRE

454 Rio 2016, (2012). The Warriors of The Olympic Movement: Wrestling. http://www.rio2016.com/en/news/news/the-warriors-of-the-olympic-movement-wrestling

455 Rio 2016, (2012). The Warriors of The Olympic Movement: Wrestling. http://www.rio2016.com/en/news/news/the-warriors-of-the-olympic-movement-wrestling

456 Olympic.org, (2014). Wrestling Greco-Roman Equipment, History and Rules, Olympic.org.
http://www.olympic.org/wrestling-greco-roman-equipment-and-history?tab=history

457 J.P., (2013). What next, get rid of the discus?. [online] The Economist. Available at:
http://www.economist.com/blogs/gametheory/2013/02/wrestling-and-olympics

458 Sowell, J. (2013). Ending What Started in St. Louis. [online] Historyhappenshere.org. Available at:
http://historyhappenshere.org/archives/tag/freestyle-wrestling

459 Paventa, V. (2014). History of Wrestling: From Ancient Times To Today, Theadrenalist.com, http://www.theadrenalist.com/sports/history-of-wrestling-from-ancient-times-to-today

460 J.P., (2013). What next, get rid of the discus?. [online] The Economist. Available at:
http://www.economist.com/blogs/gametheory/2013/02/wrestling-and-olympics

461 Cbsnews.com, (2014). Wrestling reinstated to Olympic Games. [online] Available at:
http://www.cbsnews.com/news/wrestling-reinstated-to-olympic-games/

462 Sternfeld, J. (2012). The First Modern Olympics | National Endowment for the Humanities. [online] Neh.gov.

http://www.neh.gov/divisions/preservation/featured-project/the-first-modern-olympics

463 Whiteside, K. (2012). "Women Outnumber Men on U.S. Olympic Team for London." USATODAY.COM. 10 July 2012.
http://usatoday30.usatoday.com/sports/olympics/london/swimming/story/2012-07-10/us-olympic-team-more-women-than-men-first-time/56134806/1

464 Sternfeld, J. (2012). The First Modern Olympics | National Endowment for the Humanities. [online] Neh.gov.
http://www.neh.gov/divisions/preservation/featured-project/the-first-modern-olympics

465 Fila-official.com, (2014). United World Wrestling,
http://www.fila-official.com/index.php?option=com_content&view=article&id=14&Itemid=100246&lang=en

466 Indianapride, (2014). Indianapride,
http://www.indianaprideacademy.com/#!history-of-wrestling/c1sxl

467 Topendsports.com, (2014). All-Time Olympic Games Medal Tally Analysis. http://www.topendsports.com/events/summer/medal-tally/all-time.htm

468 Databaseolympics.com, (2014). All Time Medal Count for Wrestling. http://www.databaseolympics.com/sport/sportpage.htm?sp=WRE

469 NFHS, (2008), National Federation of State High School Associations, Indianapolis, IN, The 2007–2008 High School Athletics, Participation Survey <http://www.nfhs.org/>.

470 NCAA Public Home Page – NCAA.org, (2013). Gender Equity / Title IX Important Facts. http://www.ncaa.org/about/resources/inclusion/gender-equity/title-ix-important-facts and NCAA, (2013), Tne National Collegiate Athletic Association, Student-Athlete Participation report, October 2012, Report Prepared By: Erin Irick, Assistant Director of Research, P.O. Box 6222, Indianapolis, Indiana 46206-6222, 317/917-6222, www.ncaa.org

471 LIM, L. (2008). Boarding Schools Generate China's Sport Stars. [online] NPR.org.
http://www.npr.org/templates/story/story.php?storyId=92479526

[472] LIM, L. (2008). Boarding Schools Generate China's Sport Stars. [online] NPR.org.
http://www.npr.org/templates/story/story.php?storyId=92479526

[473] NFHS, (2008), National Federation of State High School Associations, Indianapolis, IN, The 2007–2008 High School Athletics, Participation Survey <http://www.nfhs.org/>.

[474] Malina, R. (2014). School Sports – Overview, Role in Student's Social and Emotional Development,Education.stateuniversity.com,
http://education.stateuniversity.com/pages/2443/Sports-School.html

[475] Malina, R. (2014). School Sports – Overview, Role in Student's Social and Emotional Development,Education.stateuniversity.com,
http://education.stateuniversity.com/pages/2443/Sports-School.html

[476] Malina, R. (2014). School Sports – Overview, Role in Student's Social and Emotional Development,Education.stateuniversity.com,
http://education.stateuniversity.com/pages/2443/Sports-School.html

[477] NFHS, (2008), National Federation of State High School Associations, Indianapolis, IN, The 2007–2008 High School Athletics, Participation Survey <http://www.nfhs.org/>.

[478] Indianapride, (2014). Indiana Pride,
http://www.indianaprideacademy.com/#!history-of-wrestling/c1sxl

[479] Macur, J. (2008). In China, Athletes Train for the Olympics, but Not for the Life After, NYTimes.com,
http://www.nytimes.com/2008/06/21/sports/olympics/21athlete.html ?pagewanted=all&_r=0

[480] Macur, J. (2008). In China, Athletes Train for the Olympics, but Not for the Life After, NYTimes.com,
http://www.nytimes.com/2008/06/21/sports/olympics/21athlete.html ?pagewanted=all&_r=0

[481] Iaamsports.com, (2014). 2014-15 IAAM High School Rules and Regulations – IAAM Sports.
http://www.iaamsports.com/information/rules/2011-12/highschool

[482] NCAA Public Home Page – NCAA.org, (2013). Gender Equity / Title IX Important Facts.
http://www.ncaa.org/about/resources/inclusion/gender-equity/title-

ix-important-facts

[483] Clark, K. (2008). How Much Does College Cost? – US News. [online] US News & World Report,
  http://www.usnews.com/education/articles/2008/04/10/how-much-does-college-cost

[484] NCAA Public Home Page – NCAA.org, (2013). Gender Equity / Title IX Important Facts.
  http://www.ncaa.org/about/resources/inclusion/gender-equity/title-ix-important-facts

[485] Total number of female participants in high school athletics in the U.S. from 1992/93 to 2016/17
  https://www.statista.com/statistics/197591/female-participation-in-us-high-school-athletic-programs/

[486] Number of participants in U.S. high school wrestling from 2009/10 to 2016/17
  https://www.statista.com/statistics/268028/participation-in-us-high-school-wrestling/

[487] Bill Poehler, Women's wrestling experiencing exponential growth, May 28, 2016, The Statesman Journal
  http://www.statesmanjournal.com/story/sports/high-school/2016/05/28/womens-wrestling-experiencing-exponential-growth/84501908/

[488] Joshua Needelman, More high school girls are wrestling, but they're still grappling for respect, February 10, The Washington Post,
  https://www.washingtonpost.com/sports/highschools/more-high-school-girls-are-wrestling-but-theyre-still-grappling-for-respect/2017/02/10/de00814a-e7ee-11e6-bf6f-301b6b443624_story.html?utm_term=.9fe7facb60f9

[489] Lewin, T. (2007). More Girls Take Part in High School Wrestling – New York Times, Nytimes.com.
  http://www.nytimes.com/2007/02/17/nyregion/17wrestle.html?_r=1 & [Accessed 27 Nov. 2014].

[490] Lewin, T. (2007). More Girls Take Part in High School Wrestling – New York Times, Nytimes.com.

http://www.nytimes.com/2007/02/17/nyregion/17wrestle.html?_r=1 & [Accessed 27 Nov. 2014].

491 Lewin, T. (2007). More Girls Take Part in High School Wrestling – New York Times, Nytimes.com.
http://www.nytimes.com/2007/02/17/nyregion/17wrestle.html?_r=1 & [Accessed 27 Nov. 2014].

492 Fermino, J. (2014). Girls wrestling takes hold in city high schools. [online] NY Daily News.
http://www.nydailynews.com/new-york/education/girls-wrestling-takes-hold-city-high-schools-article-1.1890040

493 Fermino, J. (2014). Girls wrestling takes hold in city high schools. [online] NY Daily News.
http://www.nydailynews.com/new-york/education/girls-wrestling-takes-hold-city-high-schools-article-1.1890040

494 NCAA, Student-Athlete Participation 1981-82 – 2014-15, The National Collegiate Athletic Association, October 2015

495 Bill Poehler, Women's wrestling experiencing exponential growth, May 28, 2016, The Statesman Journal
http://www.statesmanjournal.com/story/sports/high-school/2016/05/28/womens-wrestling-experiencing-exponential-growth/84501908/

496 Joshua Needelman, More high school girls are wrestling, but they're still grappling for respect, February 10, The Washington Post,
https://www.washingtonpost.com/sports/highschools/more-high-school-girls-are-wrestling-but-theyre-still-grappling-for-respect/2017/02/10/de00814a-e7ee-11e6-bf6f-301b6b443624_story.html?utm_term=.9fe7facb60f9

497 Thewrestlergirl, (2012). Women's College Wrestling Association,
https://thewrestlergirl.wordpress.com/opportunities/womens-college-wrestling-association/

498 Thewrestlergirl, (2012). Women's College Wrestling Association,
https://thewrestlergirl.wordpress.com/opportunities/womens-college-wrestling-association/

[499] Joshua Needelman, More high school girls are wrestling, but they're still grappling for respect, February 10, The Washington Post,
https://www.washingtonpost.com/sports/highschools/more-high-school-girls-are-wrestling-but-theyre-still-grappling-for-respect/2017/02/10/de00814a-e7ee-11e6-bf6f-301b6b443624_story.html?utm_term=.9fe7facb60f9

[500] David Owen, Exclusive: Women's Greco-Roman wrestling could make 2024 Olympic programme, September 6, 2015, Inside the Games,
https://www.insidethegames.biz/articles/1029859/exclusive-womens-greco-roman-wrestling-could-make-2024-olympic-programme

[501] Lancaster, M. (2014). Title IX And Its Effect On College Athletic Programs. Athleticscholarships.net.
http://www.athleticscholarships.net/title-ix-college-athletics.htm

[502] Lancaster, M. (2014). Title IX And Its Effect On College Athletic Programs. Athleticscholarships.net.
http://www.athleticscholarships.net/title-ix-college-athletics.htm

[503] College Sports Council cited in Lancaster, M. (2014). Title IX And Its Effect On College Athletic Programs. Athleticscholarships.net.
http://www.athleticscholarships.net/title-ix-college-athletics.htm

[504] Cook cited in Lancaster, M. (2014). Title IX And Its Effect On College Athletic Programs. Athleticscholarships.net.
http://www.athleticscholarships.net/title-ix-college-athletics.htm

[505] Nash, J. (2012). The Martial Chronicles: The Forgotten Olympic History of Catch-As-Catch-Can Wrestling. [online] Bloody Elbow.
Available at:
http://www.bloodyelbow.com/2012/8/13/3238285/martial-chronicles-olympics-history-catch-wrestling

[506] Nash, J. (2012). The Martial Chronicles: The Forgotten Olympic History of Catch-As-Catch-Can Wrestling. [online] Bloody Elbow.
Available at:
http://www.bloodyelbow.com/2012/8/13/3238285/martial-chronicles-olympics-history-catch-wrestling

[507] Indianapride, (2014). Indiana Pride,
http://www.indianaprideacademy.com/#!history-of-wrestling/c1sxl

[508] Indianapride, (2014). Indiana Pride,
http://www.indianaprideacademy.com/#!history-of-wrestling/c1sxl

[509] Indianapride, (2014). Indiana Pride,
http://www.indianaprideacademy.com/#!history-of-wrestling/c1sxl

[510] Dellinger, B. (2011). The Oldest Sport | National Wrestling Hall of Fame. [online] Nwhof.org. Available at:
http://nwhof.org/stillwater/resources-library/history/the-oldest-sport/

[511] Indianapride, (2014). Indiana Pride,
http://www.indianaprideacademy.com/#!history-of-wrestling/c1sxl

[512] Dellinger, B. (2011). The Oldest Sport | National Wrestling Hall of Fame. [online] Nwhof.org. Available at:
http://nwhof.org/stillwater/resources-library/history/the-oldest-sport/

[513] Dellinger, B. (2011). The Oldest Sport | National Wrestling Hall of Fame. [online] Nwhof.org. Available at:
http://nwhof.org/stillwater/resources-library/history/the-oldest-sport/

[514] Gaines, C. (2012). These 20 Programs Are The Biggest Money Makers In College Sports.

http://www.businessinsider.com/these-20-college-sports-programs-are-the-biggest-moneymakers-2012-1

[515] ESPN.com, (2008). College Athletics Revenues and Expenses – ESPN. [online] Available at: http://espn.go.com/ncaa/revenue

[516] Gaines, C. (2012). These 20 Programs Are The Biggest Money Makers In College Sports.

http://www.businessinsider.com/these-20-college-sports-programs-are-the-biggest-moneymakers-2012-1

[517] USATODAY.COM, (2014). NCAA college athletics department finances database.
http://usatoday30.usatoday.com/sports/college/story/2012-05-14/ncaa-college-athletics-finances-database/54955804/1

[518] USATODAY.COM, (2014). NCAA college athletics department finances database.

http://usatoday30.usatoday.com/sports/college/story/2012-05-14/ncaa-college-athletics-finances-database/54955804/1

[519] Kahn, 2007; Zimbalist, 2003, cited in Cooper, C. (2011). The motivational preferences of consumers attending multiple NCAA wrestling events. Thefreelibrary.com.

http://www.thefreelibrary.com/The+motivational+preferences+of+consumers+attending+multiple+NCAA...-a0323258618

[520] Ridpath, Yiamouyiannis, Lawrence, &Galles, 2008 cited in Cooper, C. (2011). The motivational preferences of consumers attending multiple NCAA wrestling events. Thefreelibrary.com.

http://www.thefreelibrary.com/The+motivational+preferences+of+consumers+attending+multiple+NCAA...-a0323258618

[521] National Collegiate Athletic Association, 2008, cited in Cooper, C. (2011). The motivational preferences of consumers attending multiple NCAA wrestling events. Thefreelibrary.com.

http://www.thefreelibrary.com/The+motivational+preferences+of+consumers+attending+multiple+NCAA...-a0323258618

[522] Kristi Dosh , The Future of Collegiate Wrestling Isn't At Division I Level, March 17, 2016, Forbes,

https://www.forbes.com/sites/kristidosh/2016/03/17/the-future-of-collegiate-wrestling-isnt-at-division-i-level/#72f1db52fcc0

[523] Macur, J. (2008). In China, Athletes Train for the Olympics, but Not for the Life After, NYTimes.com,

http://www.nytimes.com/2008/06/21/sports/olympics/21athlete.html?pagewanted=all&_r=0

[524] Loomischaffee.org, (2014). Origins of Wrestling. [online] Available at:

https://www.loomischaffee.org/uploaded/Athletics_photos/athletics_downloads/Origins_of_Wrestling_revised.pdf

[525] Manfred, T. (2012). Here Are The Odds That Your Kid Becomes A Professional Athlete (Hint: They're Small). [online] Business Insider http://www.businessinsider.com/odds-college-athletes-become-professionals-2012-2

[526] NCAA Public Home Page – NCAA.org, (2013). Gender Equity / Title IX Important Facts. http://www.ncaa.org/about/resources/inclusion/gender-equity/title-ix-important-facts, NCAA, (2013), Tne National Collegiate Athletic Association, Student-Athlete Participation report, October 2012, Report Prepared By: Erin Irick, Assistant Director of Research, P.O. Box 6222, Indianapolis, Indiana 46206-6222, 317/917-6222, www.ncaa.org

[527] Irish Times, Paralympics to test Chinese attitudes to disability, September 6, 2008,
https://www.irishtimes.com/news/paralympics-to-test-chinese-attitudes-to-disability-1.936738

[528] Irish Times, Paralympics to test Chinese attitudes to disability, September 6, 2008,
https://www.irishtimes.com/news/paralympics-to-test-chinese-attitudes-to-disability-1.936738

[529] Clifford Coonan, How the Beijing Paralympics brought China's disabled population in from the cold, Independent, August 24, 2012
http://www.independent.co.uk/sport/olympics/paralympics/how-the-beijing-paralympics-brought-china-s-disabled-population-in-from-the-cold-8079314.html

[530] Alex Linder, China dominates the 2016 Paralympic Games with 107 golds, but athletes don't get much coverage, September 2016, Shanghaiist,
http://shanghaiist.com/2016/09/19/2016_paralympic_games.php

[531] Duncan, A. (2013). We Must Provide Equal Opportunity in Sports to Students with Disabilities, ED.gov Blog. [online] Ed.gov. Available at:
http://www.ed.gov/blog/2013/01/we-must-provide-equal-opportunity-in-sports-to-students-with-disabilities/

[532] Deaflympics.com, (2014). Sports · International Committee of Sports for the Deaf. [online] Available at:
http://www.deaflympics.com/sports.asp

[533] Usaba.org, (2014). The United States Association of Blind Athletes. [online] Available at:
http://usaba.org/index.php/sports/sports-adaptations/#Wrestling

[534] Usaba.org, (2014). The United States Association of Blind Athletes. [online] Available at:

http://usaba.org/index.php/sports/sports-adaptations/#Wrestling

[535] Warsinskey, T. (2014). NCAA Division III Wrestling Championships: Baldwin Wallace's Jesse Gunter had to prove he was blind, then prove himself. [online] cleveland.com. Available at:

http://www.cleveland.com/sports/college/index.ssf/2014/03/ncaa_div ision_iii_wrestling_ch.html

[536] Keown, T. (2013). Keown: Blind high school wrestler Anthony Ferraro. [online] ESPN.com. Available at:

http://espn.go.com/espn/story/_/id/9032132/blind-high-school-wrestler-anthony-ferraro

[537] Warsinskey, T. (2014). NCAA Division III Wrestling Championships: Baldwin Wallace's Jesse Gunter had to prove he was blind, then prove himself. [online] cleveland.com. Available at:

http://www.cleveland.com/sports/college/index.ssf/2014/03/ncaa_div ision_iii_wrestling_ch.html

[538] Warsinskey, T. (2014). NCAA Division III Wrestling Championships: Baldwin Wallace's Jesse Gunter had to prove he was blind, then prove himself. [online] cleveland.com. Available at:

http://www.cleveland.com/sports/college/index.ssf/2014/03/ncaa_div ision_iii_wrestling_ch.html

[539] Palmer, M. (2011). InterMat Rewind: Opportunity For All. [online] InterMat. Available at: http://www.intermatwrestle.com/articles/8826

[540] Cbn.com, (2014). Disabled Wrestling Champ Unstoppable with God. [online] Available at:
http://www.cbn.com/700club/guests/bios/Anthony_Robles_100812.aspx

[541] Cbn.com, (2014). Disabled Wrestling Champ Unstoppable with God. [online] Available at:
http://www.cbn.com/700club/guests/bios/Anthony_Robles_100812.aspx

[542] Cbn.com, (2014). Disabled Wrestling Champ Unstoppable with God. [online] Available at:
http://www.cbn.com/700club/guests/bios/Anthony_Robles_100812.aspx

[543] Cbn.com, (2014). Disabled Wrestling Champ Unstoppable with God. [online] Available at: http://www.cbn.com/700club/guests/bios/Anthony_Robles_100812.aspx

[544] Palmer, M. (2011). InterMat Rewind: Opportunity For All. [online] InterMat. Available at: http://www.intermatwrestle.com/articles/8826

[545] Palmer, M. (2011). InterMat Rewind: Opportunity For All. [online] InterMat. Available at: http://www.intermatwrestle.com/articles/8826

[546] Cbn.com, (2014). Disabled Wrestling Champ Unstoppable with God. [online] Available at: http://www.cbn.com/700club/guests/bios/Anthony_Robles_100812.aspx

[547] Disability in Action. (2013). The amazing wrestler with no limbs Dustin Carter | Disability in action – Disabled & Disability. [online] Disabilityinaction.com.

http://www.disabilityinaction.com/the-amazing-wrestler-with-no-limbs-dustin-carter.html

[548] Disability in Action. (2013). The amazing wrestler with no limbs Dustin Carter | Disability in action – Disabled & Disability. [online] Disabilityinaction.com.

http://www.disabilityinaction.com/the-amazing-wrestler-with-no-limbs-dustin-carter.html

[549] No Arms, No Legs, All Heart-Dustin Carter Documentary Teaser-(2008)

http://www.youtube.com/watch?v=qmicID3JwsE

[550] Green-Miner, B. and Rhineer, J. (2013). Disabled Jordan High wrestler an inspiration to teammates. [online] fox13now.com. Available at: http://fox13now.com/2013/01/16/disabled-jordan-high-wrestler-an-inspiration-to-teammates/

[551] Green-Miner, B. and Rhineer, J. (2013). Disabled Jordan High wrestler an inspiration to teammates. [online] fox13now.com. Available at: http://fox13now.com/2013/01/16/disabled-jordan-high-wrestler-an-inspiration-to-teammates/

[552] Green-Miner, B. and Rhineer, J. (2013). Disabled Jordan High wrestler an inspiration to teammates. [online] fox13now.com. Available at: http://fox13now.com/2013/01/16/disabled-jordan-high-wrestler-an-inspiration-to-teammates/

[553] Green-Miner, B. and Rhineer, J. (2013). Disabled Jordan High wrestler an inspiration to teammates. [online] fox13now.com. Available at: http://fox13now.com/2013/01/16/disabled-jordan-high-wrestler-an-inspiration-to-teammates/

[554] Green-Miner, B. and Rhineer, J. (2013). Disabled Jordan High wrestler an inspiration to teammates. [online] fox13now.com. Available at: http://fox13now.com/2013/01/16/disabled-jordan-high-wrestler-an-inspiration-to-teammates/

[555] Kindelan, K. (2012). Middle Schoolers' Act of Sportsmanship Goes Viral. [online] ABC News Blogs. Available at: http://abcnews.go.com/blogs/lifestyle/2012/12/middle-schoolers-act-of-sportsmanship-goes-viral/

[556] Kindelan, K. (2012). Middle Schoolers' Act of Sportsmanship Goes Viral. [online] ABC News Blogs. Available at: http://abcnews.go.com/blogs/lifestyle/2012/12/middle-schoolers-act-of-sportsmanship-goes-viral/

[557] Kindelan, K. (2012). Middle Schoolers' Act of Sportsmanship Goes Viral. [online] ABC News Blogs. Available at: http://abcnews.go.com/blogs/lifestyle/2012/12/middle-schoolers-act-of-sportsmanship-goes-viral/

[558] Kindelan, K. (2012). Middle Schoolers' Act of Sportsmanship Goes Viral. [online] ABC News Blogs. Available at: http://abcnews.go.com/blogs/lifestyle/2012/12/middle-schoolers-act-of-sportsmanship-goes-viral/

[559] Kindelan, K. (2012). Middle Schoolers' Act of Sportsmanship Goes Viral. [online] ABC News Blogs. Available at: http://abcnews.go.com/blogs/lifestyle/2012/12/middle-schoolers-act-of-sportsmanship-goes-viral/

[560] Kindelan, K. (2012). Middle Schoolers' Act of Sportsmanship Goes Viral. [online] ABC News Blogs. Available at: http://abcnews.go.com/blogs/lifestyle/2012/12/middle-schoolers-act-of-sportsmanship-goes-viral/

[561] Mowl, A. (n.d.). Inside the Cage With Matt Hamill. [online] DeafNation. Available at: http://deafnation.com/nobarriers/inside-the-cage-with-matt-hamill/

[562] Whittaker, G. (2009). The Franchise Exclusive Interview: Matt Hamill. [online] Bleacher Report. Available at:

http://bleacherreport.com/articles/122378-the-franchise-exclusive-interview-matt-hamill

[563] Brakob, A. (2013). Matt Hamill: Fighting in Silence. [online] AthletesLiveHere.com. http://www.athleteslivehere.com/blog/2013/03/matt-hamill-fighting-in-silence/

[564] Mindenhall, C. (2011). Hamill an inspiration for deaf community. [online] ESPN.com. Available at: http://sports.espn.go.com/extra/mma/news/story?id=6586926

[565] The Hammer. (2011). [DVD] USA: Film Harvest, Fifth Year Productions, TapouT Films.

[566] The Hammer. (2011). [DVD] USA: Film Harvest, Fifth Year Productions, TapouT Films.

[567] TUF, The Ultimate Fighter, Season 3. (2006). [DVD] USA: Pilgrim Films & Television.

[568] The Hammer. (2011). [DVD] USA: Film Harvest, Fifth Year Productions, TapouT Films.

[569] The Hammer. (2011). [DVD] USA: Film Harvest, Fifth Year Productions, TapouT Films.

[570] Deafyouvideo.blogspot.com, (n.d.). Deaf YouVideo: ZVRS: Exclusive Interview With Matt Hamill. [online] Available at:

http://deafyouvideo.blogspot.com/2012/09/zvrs-exclusive-interview-with-matt.html

[571] Deafyouvideo.blogspot.com, (n.d.). Deaf YouVideo: ZVRS: Exclusive Interview With Matt Hamill. [online] Available at:

http://deafyouvideo.blogspot.com/2012/09/zvrs-exclusive-interview-with-matt.html

[572] Brakob, A. (2013). Matt Hamill: Fighting in Silence. [online] AthletesLiveHere.com.
http://www.athleteslivehere.com/blog/2013/03/matt-hamill-fighting-in-silence/

[573] Whittaker, G. (2009). The Franchise Exclusive Interview: Matt Hamill. [online] Bleacher Report. Available at:

http://bleacherreport.com/articles/122378-the-franchise-exclusive-interview-matt-hamill

[574] Deaffriendly.com, (2012). Hammer 2.0: Matt Hamill Coming Out of Retirement at UFC 152. [online] Available at:

http://deaffriendly.com/articles/hammer-20-matt-hamill-coming-out-of-retirement-at-ufc-152/

[575] Whittaker, G. (2009). The Franchise Exclusive Interview: Matt Hamill. [online] Bleacher Report. Available at:

http://bleacherreport.com/articles/122378-the-franchise-exclusive-interview-matt-hamill

[576] Deaffriendly.com, (2012). Hammer 2.0: Matt Hamill Coming Out of Retirement at UFC 152. [online] Available at:

http://deaffriendly.com/articles/hammer-20-matt-hamill-coming-out-of-retirement-at-ufc-152/

[577] Rinaldi, T. (2009). High school teammates carry on. [online] ESPN.com. Available at:
http://sports.espn.go.com/espn/otl/news/story?id=4371874

[578] Rinaldi, T. (2009). High school teammates carry on. [online] ESPN.com. Available at:
http://sports.espn.go.com/espn/otl/news/story?id=4371874

[579] Rinaldi, T. (2009). High school teammates carry on. [online] ESPN.com. Available at:
http://sports.espn.go.com/espn/otl/news/story?id=4371874

[580] Rinaldi, T. (2009). High school teammates carry on. [online] ESPN.com. Available at: http://sports.espn.go.com/espn/otl/news/story?id=4371874

[581] Rinaldi, T. (2009). High school teammates carry on. [online] ESPN.com. Available at: http://sports.espn.go.com/espn/otl/news/story?id=4371874

[582] Rinaldi, T. (2009). High school teammates carry on. [online] ESPN.com. Available at: http://sports.espn.go.com/espn/otl/news/story?id=4371874

[583] Rinaldi, T. (2009). High school teammates carry on. [online] ESPN.com. Available at: http://sports.espn.go.com/espn/otl/news/story?id=4371874

[584] Rinaldi, T. (2009). High school teammates carry on. [online] ESPN.com. Available at: http://sports.espn.go.com/espn/otl/news/story?id=4371874

[585] Rinaldi, T. (2009). High school teammates carry on. [online] ESPN.com. Available at: http://sports.espn.go.com/espn/otl/news/story?id=4371874

[586] Rinaldi, T. (2009). High school teammates carry on. [online] ESPN.com. Available at: http://sports.espn.go.com/espn/otl/news/story?id=4371874

[587] Life Achievement Services Life Achievement Services (2009), Two Cleveland wrestlers successful struggle, https://www.youtube.com/watch?v=GlKjRdTCKwc

[588] Carry On: The Story of Lisa Fenn, Dartanyon Crockett, and Leroy Sutton 11.7.13, Published on Nov 11, 2013, The City Club of Cleveland, https://www.youtube.com/watch?v=SAVCGBTMz3c

[589] Carry On Trust for Education, n.d. http://www.carryontrust.org/meet-leroy/

[590] Carry On Trust for Education, n.d. http://www.carryontrust.org/meet-leroy/

[591] Team USA, Wrestler Dartanyon Crockett wins second Paralympic judo medal, taking 90 kg bronze in Rio, USA Judo and USA Wrestling, September 11, 2016,

https://www.teamusa.org/USA-Wrestling/Features/2016/September/11/Wrestler-Dartanyon-Crockett-wins-second-Paralympic-judo-bronze-medal

[592] Sussman,G, The Most Popular Soap Opera in the World: Professional Wrestling, Sport History Blog, 2008

[593] Sussman,G, The Most Popular Soap Opera in the World: Professional Wrestling, Sport History Blog, 2008

[594] Lindman 2000 cited in Sussman,G, The Most Popular Soap Opera in the World: Professional Wrestling, Sport History Blog, 2008

[595] Lindman 2000 cited in Sussman,G, The Most Popular Soap Opera in the World: Professional Wrestling, Sport History Blog, 2008

[596] Rineman, J, The History of Pro Wrestling, Life123.com, 2014 http://www.life123.com/sports/martial-arts/wrestling/history-of-pro wrestling.shtml

[597] Malice, Professional Wrestling in the United States of America, The Wrestling Game http://www.thewrestlinggame.com/wrestling/articles/the_history_of_ professional_wrestling_part_1.asp

[598] Hester , M, The History Pro Wrestling in the US, Bleacher Report, Aug 15, 2010

[599] Slagle 2000 cited in Miss Cellania, The Legend of Gorgeous George, June 27, 2011, http://www.neatorama.com/2011/06/27/the-legend-of-gorgeous-george/

[600] Sussman,G, The Most Popular Soap Opera in the World: Professional Wrestling, Sport History Blog, 2008

[601] Morton, G. and O'Brien, G. (1985). Wrestling to rasslin. Bowling Green, Ohio: Bowling Green State University Popular Press.

[602] Cellania, The Legend of Gorgeous George, Neatorama, June 27, 2011

[603] Cellania, The Legend of Gorgeous George, Neatorama, June 27, 2011

604Cellania, The Legend of Gorgeous George, Neatorama, June 27, 2011

605Hester , M, The History Pro Wrestling in the US, Bleacher Report, Aug 15, 2010

606Cellania, The Legend of Gorgeous George, Neatorama, June 27, 2011

607Cellania, The Legend of Gorgeous George, Neatorama, June 27, 2011

608Cellania, The Legend of Gorgeous George, Neatorama, June 27, 2011

609Cellania, The Legend of Gorgeous George, Neatorama, June 27, 2011

610Cellania, The Legend of Gorgeous George, Neatorama, June 27, 2011

611Hester , M, The History Pro Wrestling in the US, Bleacher Report, Aug 15, 2010

612Cellania, The Legend of Gorgeous George, Neatorama, June 27, 2011

613Biography, Hulk Hogan, The Biography.com website, 2014, http://www.biography.com/people/hulk-hogan-9542305.

614Biography, Hulk Hogan, The Biography.com website, 2014, http://www.biography.com/people/hulk-hogan-9542305.

615Cellania, The Legend of Gorgeous George, Neatorama, June 27, 2011

616Kreit, A, Professional Wrestling and its Fans: A Sociological Study of the Sport of Pro wrestling, solie.org, http://www.solie.org/articles/pwandfans.html

617Kreit, A, Professional Wrestling and its Fans: A Sociological Study of the Sport of Pro wrestling, solie.org, http://www.solie.org/articles/pwandfans.html

618Kreit, A, Professional Wrestling and its Fans: A Sociological Study of the Sport of Pro wrestling, solie.org, http://www.solie.org/articles/pwandfans.html

619Richard English, The Greatest Drunk on Earth: Andre the Giant, n.d. http://www.drunkard.com/10_06_andre_giant/

620Richard English, The Greatest Drunk on Earth: Andre the Giant, n.d. http://www.drunkard.com/10_06_andre_giant/

[621]The Masked Man, Dead Wrestler Of The Week: André The Giant, 3/23/10
http://deadspin.com/5500057/dead-wrestler-of-the-week-andre-the-giant

[622]Richard English, The Greatest Drunk on Earth: Andre the Giant, n.d.
http://www.drunkard.com/10_06_andre_giant/

[623]WWF: Andre the Giant - Larger Than Life, Documentary, 1999
https://www.youtube.com/watch?v=LZbmR8rnJvk

[624]WWF: Andre the Giant - Larger Than Life, Documentary, 1999
https://www.youtube.com/watch?v=LZbmR8rnJvk

[625]Richard English, The Greatest Drunk on Earth: Andre the Giant, n.d.
http://www.drunkard.com/10_06_andre_giant/

[626]Richard English, The Greatest Drunk on Earth: Andre the Giant, n.d.
http://www.drunkard.com/10_06_andre_giant/

[627]Richard English, The Greatest Drunk on Earth: Andre the Giant, n.d.
http://www.drunkard.com/10_06_andre_giant/

[628]Biography, Hulk Hogan, The Biography.com website, 2014,
http://www.biography.com/people/hulk-hogan-9542305.

[629]Biography, Hulk Hogan, The Biography.com website, 2014,
http://www.biography.com/people/hulk-hogan-9542305.

[630]Raskin, E, 'Real Rocky' Wepner finally getting due, ESPN.com, October 25, 2011
http://espn.go.com/boxing/story/_/page/IamChuckWepner/chuck-wepner-recognized-rocky-fame

[631]WWF: Andre the Giant - Larger Than Life, Documentary, 1999
https://www.youtube.com/watch?v=LZbmR8rnJvk

[632]Richard English, The Greatest Drunk on Earth: Andre the Giant, n.d.
http://www.drunkard.com/10_06_andre_giant/

[633]WWF: Andre the Giant - Larger Than Life, Documentary, 1999
https://www.youtube.com/watch?v=LZbmR8rnJvk

[634]Richard English, The Greatest Drunk on Earth: Andre the Giant, n.d.
http://www.drunkard.com/10_06_andre_giant/

[635]Richard English, The Greatest Drunk on Earth: Andre the Giant, n.d.
http://www.drunkard.com/10_06_andre_giant/

[636]WWF: Andre the Giant - Larger Than Life, Documentary, 1999
https://www.youtube.com/watch?v=LZbmR8rnJvk

[637]WWF: Andre the Giant - Larger Than Life, Documentary, 1999
https://www.youtube.com/watch?v=LZbmR8rnJvk

[638]WWF: Andre the Giant - Larger Than Life, Documentary, 1999
https://www.youtube.com/watch?v=LZbmR8rnJvk

[639]Richard English, The Greatest Drunk on Earth: Andre the Giant, n.d.
http://www.drunkard.com/10_06_andre_giant/

[640]Kreit, A, Professional Wrestling and its Fans: A Sociological Study of
the Sport of Pro wrestling, solie.org,
http://www.solie.org/articles/pwandfans.html

[641]Kreit, A, Professional Wrestling and its Fans: A Sociological Study of
the Sport of Pro wrestling, solie.org,
http://www.solie.org/articles/pwandfans.html

[642]Kreit, A, Professional Wrestling and its Fans: A Sociological Study of
the Sport of Pro wrestling, solie.org,
http://www.solie.org/articles/pwandfans.html

[643]Biography, Hulk Hogan, The Biography.com website, 2014,
http://www.biography.com/people/hulk-hogan-9542305.

[644]Biography, Hulk Hogan, The Biography.com website, 2014,
http://www.biography.com/people/hulk-hogan-9542305.

[645]Hester , M, The History Pro Wrestling in the US, Bleacher Report,
Aug 15, 2010

[646]Hester , M, The History Pro Wrestling in the US, Bleacher Report,
Aug 15, 2010

[647]American Experience, The Iranian Hostage Crisis, American
Experience, PBS
http://www.pbs.org/wgbh/americanexperience/features/general-
article/carter-hostage-crisis/

[648]Biography, Hulk Hogan, The Biography.com website, 2014,
http://www.biography.com/people/hulk-hogan-9542305.

[649]Biography, Hulk Hogan, The Biography.com website, 2014, http://www.biography.com/people/hulk-hogan-9542305.

[650]Biography, Hulk Hogan, The Biography.com website, 2014, http://www.biography.com/people/hulk-hogan-9542305.

[651]Biography, Hulk Hogan, The Biography.com website, 2014, http://www.biography.com/people/hulk-hogan-9542305.

[652]Biography, Hulk Hogan, The Biography.com website, 2014, http://www.biography.com/people/hulk-hogan-9542305.

[653]Biography, Hulk Hogan, The Biography.com website, 2014, http://www.biography.com/people/hulk-hogan-9542305.

[654]Biography, Hulk Hogan, The Biography.com website, 2014, http://www.biography.com/people/hulk-hogan-9542305.

[655]Hester , M, The History Pro Wrestling in the US, Bleacher Report, Aug 15, 2010

[656]Grabianowski, E How Pro Wrestling Works, How Stuff Works,

[657]Grabianowski, E How Pro Wrestling Works, How Stuff Works,

[658]Martin, G, Inside the secret world of pro wrestling: The media's complicated relationship with a controversial sport, Salon.com, MAY 14, 2014

[659]Martin, G, Inside the secret world of pro wrestling: The media's complicated relationship with a controversial sport, Salon.com, MAY 14, 2014

[660]Kreit, A, Professional Wrestling and its Fans: A Sociological Study of the Sport of Pro wrestling, solie.org,
http://www.solie.org/articles/pwandfans.html

[661]Gerry, J, The Top 5 "Eras" in Professional Wrestling, hubpages, February 15, 2012

[662]Grabianowski, E How Pro Wrestling Works, How Stuff Works,

[663]Grabianowski, E How Pro Wrestling Works, How Stuff Works,

[664]Grabianowski, E How Pro Wrestling Works, How Stuff Works,

[665]Grabianowski, E How Pro Wrestling Works, How Stuff Works,

[666]Grabianowski, E How Pro Wrestling Works, How Stuff Works,

[667]Grabianowski, E How Pro Wrestling Works, How Stuff Works,

[668]Grabianowski, E How Pro Wrestling Works, How Stuff Works,

[669]Finding Hulk Hogan (2010), TV Movie-Documentary, Production Co: Bischoff/Hervey Entertainment, 17 November 2010 (USA)
https://www.youtube.com/watch?v=oUAF6n7Wg5M

[670]Finding Hulk Hogan (2010), TV Movie-Documentary, Production Co: Bischoff/Hervey Entertainment, 17 November 2010 (USA)
https://www.youtube.com/watch?v=oUAF6n7Wg5M

[671]Biography, Hulk Hogan, The Biography.com website, 2014,
http://www.biography.com/people/hulk-hogan-9542305.

[672]One on One with Hulk Hogan, The Fight Network, 2010
https://www.youtube.com/watch?v=Guh-0Jt55JQ

[673] U.S. Inflation Rate, 1911-2015 ($100)
http://www.in2013dollars.com/1911-dollars-in-2015

[674]George A. Barton, "Saw Frank Gotch As The Superlative", December 1968,
Ring Wrestling,
http://www.wrestling-titles.com/personalities/gotch_frank/superlative.html

[675] Geoff Williams, A Glimpse at Your Expenses 100 Years Ago
Everything costs much less – but, of course, you also earned a lot less, January 2, 2015,
https://money.usnews.com/money/personal-finance/articles/2015/01/02/a-glimpse-at-your-expenses-100-years-ago

[676]Kreit, A, Professional Wrestling and its Fans: A Sociological Study of the Sport of Pro wrestling, solie.org,
http://www.solie.org/articles/pwandfans.html

[677]Kreit, A, Professional Wrestling and its Fans: A Sociological Study of the Sport of Pro wrestling, solie.org,
http://www.solie.org/articles/pwandfans.html

[678]Glenday, D Professional wrestling as culturally embedded spectacles in five core countries, Revue de rechercheencivilisationaméricaine, 2013

274

[679] 2011,WWE annual Report, pg 4 cited in Glenday, D Professional wrestling as culturally embedded spectacles in five core countries, Revue de rechercheencivilisationaméricaine, 2013

[680] 2011,WWE annual Report, pg 4 cited in Glenday, D Professional wrestling as culturally embedded spectacles in five core countries, Revue de rechercheencivilisationaméricaine, 2013

[681] Sussman,G, The Most Popular Soap Opera in the World: Professional Wrestling, Sport History Blog, 2008

[682] Rock 'n' Wrestling , Internet Movie Database, n.d. http://www.imdb.com/title/tt0203265/

[683] Sussman,G, The Most Popular Soap Opera in the World: Professional Wrestling, Sport History Blog, 2008

[684] Crave, The Ten Best Wrestlers Turned Actors, Crave online, July 13th, 2011 http://www.craveonline.com/film/articles/170917-the-ten-best-wrestlers-turned-actors

[685] USA TODAY, From entertainment to fighting: 9 pro wrestlers who impacted MMA, USA TODAY, Jul 14, 2009 http://usatoday30.usatoday.com/sports/mma/post/2009/07/68494433/1

[686] Dana Canedy, Sentence of Life Without Parole For Boy, 14, in Murder of Girl, 6 March 10, 2001, The New York Times, www.nytimes.com/.../sentence-of-life-without-parole-for-boy-14-in-murder-of-girl-6....

[687] Hunter, M, Despite warnings from professional wrestlers, imitation sometimes has deadly consequences, NOLA.com, The Times-Picayune, June 18, 2013

[688] Hunter, M, Despite warnings from professional wrestlers, imitation sometimes has deadly consequences, NOLA.com, The Times-Picayune, June 18, 2013

[689] ABC News, Pro Wrestling Under Fire After Child's Death, July 25, 2014 http://abcnews.go.com/US/story?id=92804

[690]Hunter, M, Despite warnings from professional wrestlers, imitation sometimes has deadly consequences, NOLA.com, The Times-Picayune, June 18, 2013

[691]WWE, Warning, Youtube
https://www.youtube.com/watch?v=E6bJO3T8R1Q

[692]Montgomery, J, Chair Shots and Ladder Matches: The Role of Violence in Pro Wrestling, Bleacher Report, 2008
http://bleacherreport.com/articles/69983-chair-shots-and-ladder-matches-the-role-of-violence-in-pro wrestling

[693]Tamborini 2 cited in Montgomery, J, Chair Shots and Ladder Matches: The Role of Violence in Pro Wrestling, Bleacher Report, 2008
http://bleacherreport.com/articles/69983-chair-shots-and-ladder-matches-the-role-of-violence-in-pro wrestling.

[694]Grabianowski, E How Pro Wrestling Works, How Stuff Works,

[695]Grabianowski, E How Pro Wrestling Works, How Stuff Works,

[696] Ufc.com, (2014). Rules and Regulations - Unified Rules and Other MMA Regulations. [online] Available at:

http://www.ufc.com/discover/sport/rules-and-regulations

[697] Meltzer, D. (2014). Former NCAA champ starting professional amateur wrestling group. [online] MMA Fighting. Available at: http://www.mmafighting.com/2014/11/21/7258663/former-ncaa-champ-starting-professional-amateur-wrestling-group

[698] Semaan, J. (2008). Ancient Greek Pankration: the Origins of MMA, Part One, Bleacher Report,

http://bleacherreport.com/articles/28473-ancient-greek-pankration-the-origins-of-mma-part-one

[699] Nash, J. (2011). The Forgotten Golden Age of Mixed Martial Arts – Part IV: Ultimate Fighting of the Belle Époque. [online] Bloody Elbow. Available at: http://www.bloodyelbow.com/2011/10/31/2521315/the-forgotten-golden-age-of-mixed-martial-arts-part-iv-ultimate

[700] Althoff, E. (2011). What Do MMA, Pro Wrestling and Traditional Martial Arts Have in Common? – - Black Belt. [online] Blackbeltmag.com,

http://www.blackbeltmag.com/daily/mixed-martial-arts-training/boxing/what-do-mma-pro wrestling-and-traditional-martial-arts-have-in-common/

[701] Nash, J. (2011). The Forgotten Golden Age of Mixed Martial Arts – Part IV: Ultimate Fighting of the Belle Époque. [online] Bloody Elbow. Available at: http://www.bloodyelbow.com/2011/10/31/2521315/the-forgotten-golden-age-of-mixed-martial-arts-part-iv-ultimate

[702] Nash, J. (2011). The Forgotten Golden Age of Mixed Martial Arts – Part IV: Ultimate Fighting of the Belle Époque. [online] Bloody Elbow. Available at: http://www.bloodyelbow.com/2011/10/31/2521315/the-forgotten-golden-age-of-mixed-martial-arts-part-iv-ultimate

[703] Althoff, E. (2011). What Do MMA, Pro Wrestling and Traditional Martial Arts Have in Common? – - Black Belt. [online] Blackbeltmag.com,

http://www.blackbeltmag.com/daily/mixed-martial-arts-training/boxing/what-do-mma-pro wrestling-and-traditional-martial-arts-have-in-common/

[704] Nash, J. (2011). The Forgotten Golden Age of Mixed Martial Arts – Part IV: Ultimate Fighting of the Belle Époque. [online] Bloody Elbow. Available at: http://www.bloodyelbow.com/2011/10/31/2521315/the-forgotten-golden-age-of-mixed-martial-arts-part-iv-ultimate

[705] Crigger, K. (2010). <%=ogTitle%>. [online] FIGHT! Magazine. Available at: https://www.fightmagazine.com/mma-magazine/catch-as-catch-can-624/

[706] Nash, J. (2011). The Forgotten Golden Age of Mixed Martial Arts – Part IV: Ultimate Fighting of the Belle Époque. [online] Bloody Elbow. Available at: http://www.bloodyelbow.com/2011/10/31/2521315/the-forgotten-golden-age-of-mixed-martial-arts-part-iv-ultimate

[707] Nash, J. (2011). The Forgotten Golden Age of Mixed Martial Arts – Part IV: Ultimate Fighting of the Belle Époque. [online] Bloody Elbow. Available at: http://www.bloodyelbow.com/2011/10/31/2521315/the-forgotten-golden-age-of-mixed-martial-arts-part-iv-ultimate

[708] Nash, J. (2011). The Forgotten Golden Age of Mixed Martial Arts – Part IV: Ultimate Fighting of the Belle Époque. [online] Bloody Elbow. Available at: http://www.bloodyelbow.com/2011/10/31/2521315/the-forgotten-golden-age-of-mixed-martial-arts-part-iv-ultimate

[709] Snowden, J. (2013). New Gloves Could Dumb Down MMA. [online] Bleacher Report, http://bleacherreport.com/articles/1634155-new-ufc-gloves-could-lead-to-a-dumbing-down-of-mixed-martial-arts

[710] McKay, B. and McKay, K. (2009). Bartitsu: The Martial Art of Gentlemen, The Art of Manliness.

http://www.artofmanliness.com/2009/01/05/bartitsu-gentlemen/

[711] Brett & Kate McKay, Bartitsu: The Martial Art of Gentlemen, The Art of manliness, January 5, 2009,

https://www.artofmanliness.com/2009/01/05/bartitsu-gentlemen/

[712] Nash, J. (2011). The Forgotten Golden Age of Mixed Martial Arts – Part IV: Ultimate Fighting of the Belle Époque. [online] Bloody Elbow. Available at: http://www.bloodyelbow.com/2011/10/31/2521315/the-forgotten-golden-age-of-mixed-martial-arts-part-iv-ultimate

[713] Nash, J. (2011). The Forgotten Golden Age of Mixed Martial Arts – Part IV: Ultimate Fighting of the Belle Époque. [online] Bloody Elbow. Available at: http://www.bloodyelbow.com/2011/10/31/2521315/the-forgotten-golden-age-of-mixed-martial-arts-part-iv-ultimate

[714] Nash, J. (2011). The Forgotten Golden Age of Mixed Martial Arts – Part IV: Ultimate Fighting of the Belle Époque. [online] Bloody Elbow. Available at: http://www.bloodyelbow.com/2011/10/31/2521315/the-forgotten-golden-age-of-mixed-martial-arts-part-iv-ultimate

[715] Nash, J. (2011). The Forgotten Golden Age of Mixed Martial Arts – Part IV: Ultimate Fighting of the Belle Époque. [online] Bloody Elbow. Available at: http://www.bloodyelbow.com/2011/10/31/2521315/the-forgotten-golden-age-of-mixed-martial-arts-part-iv-ultimate

[716] Sarah Kurchak, The Strenuous Life: Theodore Roosevelt's Mixed Martial Arts, n.d. Fightland Blog,

http://fightland.vice.com/blog/the-strenuous-life-theodore-roosevelts-mixed-martial-arts

[717] Joseph R. Svinth, Professor Yamashita Goes to Washington, October 2000, Journal of Combative Sport,
http://ejmas.com/jcs/jcsart_svinth1_1000.htm

[718] Joseph R. Svinth, Professor Yamashita Goes to Washington, October 2000, Journal of Combative Sport,
http://ejmas.com/jcs/jcsart_svinth1_1000.htm

[719] Joseph R. Svinth, Professor Yamashita Goes to Washington, October 2000, Journal of Combative Sport,
http://ejmas.com/jcs/jcsart_svinth1_1000.htm

[720] Joseph R. Svinth, Professor Yamashita Goes to Washington, October 2000, Journal of Combative Sport,
http://ejmas.com/jcs/jcsart_svinth1_1000.htm

[721] Joseph R. Svinth, Professor Yamashita Goes to Washington, October 2000, Journal of Combative Sport,
http://ejmas.com/jcs/jcsart_svinth1_1000.htm

[722] Nash, J. (2011). The Forgotten Golden Age of Mixed Martial Arts – Part IV: Ultimate Fighting of the Belle Époque. [online] Bloody Elbow. Available at: http://www.bloodyelbow.com/2011/10/31/2521315/the-forgotten-golden-age-of-mixed-martial-arts-part-iv-ultimate

[723] Nash, J. (2011). The Forgotten Golden Age of Mixed Martial Arts – Part IV: Ultimate Fighting of the Belle Époque. [online] Bloody Elbow. Available at: http://www.bloodyelbow.com/2011/10/31/2521315/the-forgotten-golden-age-of-mixed-martial-arts-part-iv-ultimate

[724] Nash, J. (2011). The Forgotten Golden Age of Mixed Martial Arts – Part IV: Ultimate Fighting of the Belle Époque. [online] Bloody Elbow. Available at: http://www.bloodyelbow.com/2011/10/31/2521315/the-forgotten-golden-age-of-mixed-martial-arts-part-iv-ultimate

[725] Cagepotato.com, (2011). On This Day in MMA History: The Godfather of North American MMA, 'Judo' Gene LeBell Was Born in 1932 | Cagepotato.

[726] Gene LeBell and Ronda Rousey's gold lineage, n.d. Fox Sports, https://www.foxsports.com/ufc/story/gene-lebell-and-ronda-rousey-s-gold-lineage-021914

[727] Young, R. (2014). "Judo" Gene LeBell vs. Boxer Milo Savage: America's First MMA Fight – Black Belt. [online] Blackbeltmag.com.
Available at: http://www.blackbeltmag.com/daily/mixed-martial-arts-training/boxing/judo-gene-lebell-vs-boxer-milo-savage-americas-first-mma-fight/

[728] IMDB, Gene LeBell, n.d. Internet Movie Database, http://m.imdb.com/name/nm0494061/trivia

[729] Gene LeBell and Ronda Rousey's gold lineage, n.d. Fox Sports, https://www.foxsports.com/ufc/story/gene-lebell-and-ronda-rousey-s-gold-lineage-021914

[730] Gene LeBell and Ronda Rousey's gold lineage, n.d. Fox Sports, https://www.foxsports.com/ufc/story/gene-lebell-and-ronda-rousey-s-gold-lineage-021914

[731] Young, R. (2014). "Judo" Gene LeBell vs. Boxer Milo Savage: America's First MMA Fight – - Black Belt. [online] Blackbeltmag.com. Available at: http://www.blackbeltmag.com/daily/mixed-martial-arts-training/boxing/judo-gene-lebell-vs-boxer-milo-savage-americas-first-mma-fight/

[732] Althoff, E. (2011). What Do MMA, Pro Wrestling and Traditional Martial Arts Have in Common? – - Black Belt. [online] Blackbeltmag.com, http://www.blackbeltmag.com/daily/mixed-martial-arts-training/boxing/what-do-mma-pro wrestling-and-traditional-martial-arts-have-in-common/

[733] House of Lee, Inside Bruce Lee's Personal Library, n.d. http://houseofbrucelee.blogspot.co.id/2012/08/books.html

[734] Bull, A. (2009). The forgotten story of ... Muhammad Ali v Antonio Inoki | Andy Bull. [online] the Guardian. Available at: http://www.theguardian.com/sport/blog/2009/nov/11/the-forgotten-story-of-ali-inoki

[735] Bull, A. (2009). The forgotten story of ... Muhammad Ali v Antonio Inoki | Andy Bull. [online] the Guardian. Available at: http://www.theguardian.com/sport/blog/2009/nov/11/the-forgotten-story-of-ali-inoki

[736] Bull, A. (2009). The forgotten story of ... Muhammad Ali v Antonio Inoki | Andy Bull. [online] the Guardian. Available at:
http://www.theguardian.com/sport/blog/2009/nov/11/the-forgotten-story-of-ali-inoki

[737] Bull, A. (2009). The forgotten story of ... Muhammad Ali v Antonio Inoki | Andy Bull. [online] the Guardian. Available at:
http://www.theguardian.com/sport/blog/2009/nov/11/the-forgotten-story-of-ali-inoki

[738] Bull, A. (2009). The forgotten story of ... Muhammad Ali v Antonio Inoki | Andy Bull. [online] the Guardian. Available at:
http://www.theguardian.com/sport/blog/2009/nov/11/the-forgotten-story-of-ali-inoki

[739] Althoff, E. (2011). What Do MMA, Pro Wrestling and Traditional Martial Arts Have in Common? - - Black Belt. [online] Blackbeltmag.com,
http://www.blackbeltmag.com/daily/mixed-martial-arts-training/boxing/what-do-mma-pro wrestling-and-traditional-martial-arts-have-in-common/

[740] Raj Giri, Judo Gene LeBell On What Roddy Piper Said Days Before He Passed, Ronda Rousey In Pro Wrestling, October 31, 2015, Wrestling Inc.
http://www.wrestlinginc.com/wi/news/2015/1031/603310/judo-gene-lebell-on-what-roddy-piper-said-days-before-he-passed/

[741] Gracieacademy.com, (2014). Gracie History. [online] Available at: http://www.gracieacademy.com/history.asp

[742] Polly, M. (2011). Tapped out. New York: Gotham Books.

[743] Alonso, M. (2013). *Vale tudo*: A Rich, Storied & Complex Past - Conde Koma and the Gracies. [online] Sherdog. Available at:
http://www.sherdog.com/news/articles/1/Vale-Tudo-A-Rich-Storied-Complex-Past-59571

[744] Gracieacademy.com, (2014). Gracie History. [online] Available at: http://www.gracieacademy.com/history.asp

745 Grant, T. (2012). MMA Origins: Brazilian *Vale tudo* Evolves As Chute Boxe Emerges. [online] Bloody Elbow. And, Grant, T. (2012). MMA Origins: The First King of Pancrase. [online] Bloody Elbow. Available at:

http://www.bloodyelbow.com/2012/5/2/2979275/mma-origins-king-of-pancrase-mma-history-bas-rutten-shamrock and Grant, T. (2012). MMA Origins: *Vale tudo* and The Original MMA Rivalry. [online] Bloody Elbow. Available at:

http://www.bloodyelbow.com/2012/1/1/2663021/mma-origins-vale-tudo-and-the-original-mma-rivalry

746 Gracieacademy.com, (2014). Gracie History. [online] Available at: http://www.gracieacademy.com/history.asp

747 Alonso, M. (2013). *Vale tudo*: A Rich, Storied & Complex Past - Conde Koma and the Gracies. [online] Sherdog. Available at:

http://www.sherdog.com/news/articles/1/Vale-Tudo-A-Rich-Storied-Complex-Past-59571

748 Fightland Staff, Waldemar Santana: A Challenger to the Gracie Throne, Fightland Blog, November 5, 2014,

http://fightland.vice.com/blog/waldemar-santana-a-challenger-to-the-gracie-throne

749 BJJ Heroes, Royler Gracie Jiu Jitsu, n.d.
https://www.bjjheroes.com/bjj-fighters/royler-gracie-facts-and-bio

750 Grant, T. (2012). MMA Origins: Brazilian *Vale tudo* Evolves As Chute Boxe Emerges. [online] Bloody Elbow. Available at:

http://www.bloodyelbow.com/2012/6/25/3097737/mma-origins-UFC-History-UFC-147-Wanderlei-Silva-Anderson-Silva-Chute-Boxe

751 Grant, T. (2012). MMA Origins: Brazilian *Vale tudo* Evolves As Chute Boxe Emerges. [online] Bloody Elbow. Available at:

http://www.bloodyelbow.com/2012/6/25/3097737/mma-origins-UFC-History-UFC-147-Wanderlei-Silva-Anderson-Silva-Chute-Boxe, And, Grant, T. (2012). MMA Origins: The First King of Pancrase. [online] Bloody Elbow. Available at:

http://www.bloodyelbow.com/2012/5/2/2979275/mma-origins-king-of-pancrase-mma-history-bas-rutten-shamrock and Grant, T. (2012). MMA Origins: *Vale tudo* and The Original MMA Rivalry. [online] Bloody Elbow. Available at: http://www.bloodyelbow.com/2012/1/1/2663021/mma-origins-vale-tudo-and-the-original-mma-rivalry

[752] Grant, T. (2012). MMA Origins: Brazilian *Vale tudo* Evolves As Chute Boxe Emerges. [online] Bloody Elbow. Available at:

http://www.bloodyelbow.com/2012/6/25/3097737/mma-origins-UFC-History-UFC-147-Wanderlei-Silva-Anderson-Silva-Chute-Boxe, And, Grant, T. (2012). MMA Origins: The First King of Pancrase. [online] Bloody Elbow. Available at:

http://www.bloodyelbow.com/2012/5/2/2979275/mma-origins-king-of-pancrase-mma-history-bas-rutten-shamrock and Grant, T. (2012). MMA Origins: *Vale tudo* and The Original MMA Rivalry. [online] Bloody Elbow. Available at: http://www.bloodyelbow.com/2012/1/1/2663021/mma-origins-vale-tudo-and-the-original-mma-rivalry

[753] Sunshine, A. (2010). Recipe for success: Becoming well rounded in mixed martial arts (Part Three). [online] MMAmania.com. Available at: http://www.mmamania.com/2010/11/24/1834403/recipe-for-success-becoming-well-rounded-in-mixed-martial-arts-part

[754] Harty, C. (2014). The 10 Best Jiu-Jitsu Practitioners in MMA. [online] TheRichest.

http://www.therichest.com/sports/mma-sports/the-10-best-jiu-jitsu-practitioners-in-mma/

[755] Crigger, K. (2010). <%=ogTitle%>. [online] FIGHT! Magazine. Available at: https://www.fightmagazine.com/mma-magazine/catch-as-catch-can-624/

[756] Jacobs, M. (2013). Wrestling: Gene LeBell and Bart Vale on the Ancestor of Jiu-jitsu, Sambo and Judo – - Black Belt. [online] Blackbeltmag.com. Available at:

http://www.blackbeltmag.com/daily/mixed-martial-arts-training/wrestling/wrestling-gene-lebell-and-bart-vale-on-the-ancestor-of-jiu-jitsu-sambo-and-judo/

[757] Crigger, K. (2010). <%=ogTitle%>. [online] FIGHT! Magazine. Available at: https://www.fightmagazine.com/mma-magazine/catch-as-catch-can-624/

[758] Crigger, K. (2010). <%=ogTitle%>. [online] FIGHT! Magazine. Available at: https://www.fightmagazine.com/mma-magazine/catch-as-catch-can-624/

759 Crigger, K. (2010). <%=ogTitle%>. [online] FIGHT! Magazine. Available at: https://www.fightmagazine.com/mma-magazine/catch-as-catch-can-624/

760 Sherdog, Josh Barnett, Viewed on December 1, 2017, http://www.sherdog.com/fighter/Josh-Barnett-272

761 Crigger, K. (2010). <%=ogTitle%>. [online] FIGHT! Magazine. Available at: https://www.fightmagazine.com/mma-magazine/catch-as-catch-can-624/

762 Crigger, K. (2010). <%=ogTitle%>. [online] FIGHT! Magazine. Available at: https://www.fightmagazine.com/mma-magazine/catch-as-catch-can-624/

763 Grant, T. (2013). MMA Fan's Guide to Grappling: American Folk Style/Freestyle Wrestling. [online] Bloody Elbow. Available at: http://www.bloodyelbow.com/2013/7/10/4489896/ufc-mma-fan-guide-to-grappling-american-folk-ncaa-style-freestyle-wrestling-highlights-video/in/4287243

764 Grant, T. (2013). MMA Fan's Guide to Grappling: American Folk Style/Freestyle Wrestling. [online] Bloody Elbow. Available at: http://www.bloodyelbow.com/2013/7/10/4489896/ufc-mma-fan-guide-to-grappling-american-folk-ncaa-style-freestyle-wrestling-highlights-video/in/4287243

765 Grant, T. (2012). MMA Origins: Brazilian *Vale tudo* Evolves As Chute Boxe Emerges. [online] Bloody Elbow. Available at: http://www.bloodyelbow.com/2012/6/25/3097737/mma-origins-UFC-History-UFC-147-Wanderlei-Silva-Anderson-Silva-Chute-Boxe

766 Grant, T. (2012). MMA Origins: Brazilian *Vale tudo* Evolves As Chute Boxe Emerges. [online] Bloody Elbow. Available at: http://www.bloodyelbow.com/2012/6/25/3097737/mma-origins-UFC-History-UFC-147-Wanderlei-Silva-Anderson-Silva-Chute-Boxe

767 Grant, T. (2013). MMA Fan's Guide to Grappling: American Folk Style/Freestyle Wrestling. [online] Bloody Elbow. Available at: http://www.bloodyelbow.com/2013/7/10/4489896/ufc-mma-fan-guide-to-grappling-american-folk-ncaa-style-freestyle-wrestling-highlights-video/in/4287243

[768] Grant, T. (2013). MMA Fan's Guide to Grappling: American Folk Style/Freestyle Wrestling. [online] Bloody Elbow. Available at:
http://www.bloodyelbow.com/2013/7/10/4489896/ufc-mma-fan-guide-to-grappling-american-folk-ncaa-style-freestyle-wrestling-highlights-video/in/4287243

[769] Polly, M. (2011). Tapped out. New York: Gotham Books.

[770] Jonathan Snowden, Sex, Drugs, Gangsters and MMA: Remembering Pride, UFC's Wild Predecessor, July 6, 2017, Bleacher Report,
http://bleacherreport.com/articles/2718986-sex-drugs-gangsters-and-mma-remembering-pride-ufcs-wild-predecessor

[771] Gregory & Osborne, 2009 cited in Martin, T. (2012). Nixed Martial Arts (MMA) And the Media: Using the Content Analytic Method to Examine the Print Communication Coverage Devoted to an Emerging Sport. Doctor of Philosophy. Indiana University.

[772] Guilherme Cruz, Rorion Gracie and the day he created the UFC, November 12, 2013, MMA Fighting,
https://www.mmafighting.com/2013/11/12/5043630/rorion-gracie-and-the-day-he-created-the-ufc

[773] Guilherme Cruz, Rorion Gracie and the day he created the UFC, November 12, 2013, MMA Fighting,
https://www.mmafighting.com/2013/11/12/5043630/rorion-gracie-and-the-day-he-created-the-ufc

[774] Nash, J. (2011). The Forgotten Golden Age of Mixed Martial Arts – Part IV: Ultimate Fighting of the Belle Époque. [online] Bloody Elbow. Available at: http://www.bloodyelbow.com/2011/10/31/2521315/the-forgotten-golden-age-of-mixed-martial-arts-part-iv-ultimate

[775] Shaer, M. (2012). How science is transforming the sport of MMA fighting. Popular Science, pp.48-84.

[776] Hill, A. (2013). The Evolution of UFC Rules. [online] Bleacher Report. Available at:http://bleacherreport.com/articles/1614213-a-timeline-of-ufc-rules-from-no-holds-barred-to-highly-regulated

[777] Polly, M. (2011). Tapped out. New York: Gotham Books.

[778] Guilherme Cruz, Rorion Gracie and the day he created the UFC, November 12, 2013, MMA Fighting,

https://www.mmafighting.com/2013/11/12/5043630/rorion-gracie-and-the-day-he-created-the-ufc

[780] Robert J. Szczerba, Mixed Martial Arts and the Evolution of John McCain, April 3, 2014, Forbes, https://www.forbes.com/sites/robertszczerba/2014/04/03/mixed-martial-arts-and-the-evolution-of-john-mccain/

[781] Usatoday30.usatoday.com, (2008). MMA timeline - USATODAY.com. [online] Available at: http://usatoday30.usatoday.com/sports/2008-05-29-mma-timeline_n.htm

[782] Hill, A. (2013). The Evolution of UFC Rules. [online] Bleacher Report. Available at:http://bleacherreport.com/articles/1614213-a-timeline-of-ufc-rules-from-no-holds-barred-to-highly-regulated

[783] Polly, M. (2011). Tapped out. New York: Gotham Books.

[784] Polly, M. (2011). Tapped out. New York: Gotham Books.

[785] Hill, A. (2013). The Evolution of UFC Rules. [online] Bleacher Report. Available at:http://bleacherreport.com/articles/1614213-a-timeline-of-ufc-rules-from-no-holds-barred-to-highly-regulated

[786] Hill, A. (2013). The Evolution of UFC Rules. [online] Bleacher Report. Available at:http://bleacherreport.com/articles/1614213-a-timeline-of-ufc-rules-from-no-holds-barred-to-highly-regulated

[787] Hill, A. (2013). The Evolution of UFC Rules. [online] Bleacher Report. Available at:http://bleacherreport.com/articles/1614213-a-timeline-of-ufc-rules-from-no-holds-barred-to-highly-regulated

[788] Polly, M. (2011). Tapped out. New York: Gotham Books.

[789] Polly, M. (2011). Tapped out. New York: Gotham Books.

[790] Usatoday30.usatoday.com, (2008). MMA timeline - USATODAY.com. [online] Available at: http://usatoday30.usatoday.com/sports/2008-05-29-mma-timeline_n.htm

[791] Nason, J. (2009). The History of The Ultimate Fighter. [online] FIGHT! Magazine. Available at:

http://www.fightmagazine.com/mma-magazine/the-history-of-the-ultimate-fighter-529/

[792] Hill, A. (2013). The Evolution of UFC Rules. [online] Bleacher Report. Available at:http://bleacherreport.com/articles/1614213-a-timeline-of-ufc-rules-from-no-holds-barred-to-highly-regulated

[793] Hill, A. (2013). The Evolution of UFC Rules. [online] Bleacher Report. Available at:http://bleacherreport.com/articles/1614213-a-timeline-of-ufc-rules-from-no-holds-barred-to-highly-regulated

[794] Boggan, 2009, cited in Martin, T. (2012). Mixed Martial Arts (MMA) And the Media: Using the Content Analytic Method to Examine the Print Communication Coverage Devoted to an Emerging Sport. Doctor of Philosophy. Indiana University

[795] Borchardt, 2014, cited in Martin, T. (2012). Mixed Martial Arts (MMA) And the Media: Using the Content Analytic Method to Examine the Print Communication Coverage Devoted to an Emerging Sport. Doctor of Philosophy. Indiana University

[796] Jhabvala, 2008, cited in Martin, T. (2012). Mixed Martial Arts (MMA) And the Media: Using the Content Analytic Method to Examine the Print Communication Coverage Devoted to an Emerging Sport. Doctor of Philosophy. Indiana University

[797] Miller, 2008, cited in Martin, T. (2012). Mixed Martial Arts (MMA) And the Media: Using the Content Analytic Method to Examine the Print Communication Coverage Devoted to an Emerging Sport. Doctor of Philosophy. Indiana University

[798] Hill, A. (2013). The Evolution of UFC Rules. [online] Bleacher Report. Available at:http://bleacherreport.com/articles/1614213-a-timeline-of-ufc-rules-from-no-holds-barred-to-highly-regulated

[799] Bryan Armen Graham, New York ends ban and becomes 50th state to legalize mixed martial arts, The Guardian, March 22, 2016

https://www.theguardian.com/sport/2016/mar/22/new-york-legalizes-mma-ufc

[800] Robby Kalland, UFC sells for $4 billion to WME-IMG group, Dana White remains president, July 11, 2016, CBS Sports, https://www.cbssports.com/mma/news/reports-ufc-sells-for-4-billion-to-wme-img-dana-white-remains-president/

[823] Snowden, J. (2009). Mark Kerr: The Smashing Machine Returns. [online] Inside Pulse, http://insidepulse.com/2009/08/28/mark-kerr-the-smashing-machine-returns/

[824] Snowden, J. (2009). Mark Kerr: The Smashing Machine Returns. [online] Inside Pulse, http://insidepulse.com/2009/08/28/mark-kerr-the-smashing-machine-returns/

[825] Teal, B. (2010). WHATEVER HAPPENED TO... "The Smashing Machine" Mark Kerr. [online] Mmatorch.com. http://www.mmatorch.com/artman2/publish/specialists/article_4195.shtml#.VIZhmjHF-So

[826] Teal, B. (2010). WHATEVER HAPPENED TO... "The Smashing Machine" Mark Kerr. [online] Mmatorch.com. http://www.mmatorch.com/artman2/publish/specialists/article_4195.shtml#.VIZhmjHF-So

[827] Teal, B. (2010). WHATEVER HAPPENED TO... "The Smashing Machine" Mark Kerr. [online] Mmatorch.com. http://www.mmatorch.com/artman2/publish/specialists/article_4195.shtml#.VIZhmjHF-So

[828] Teal, B. (2010). WHATEVER HAPPENED TO... "The Smashing Machine" Mark Kerr. [online] Mmatorch.com. http://www.mmatorch.com/artman2/publish/specialists/article_4195.shtml#.VIZhmjHF-So

[829] Chan, J. (2014). Top 10 Wrestlers In MMA 2014 | MMA Verse. [online] Mmaverse.com. http://www.mmaverse.com/top-10-wrestlers-in-mma-2014/

[830] Clifford, R. (2013). Mat Men – The 7 Best World-Class Wrestlers in MMA. [online] FIGHT! Magazine. Available at: https://www.fightmagazine.com/mma-magazine/mat-men-mmas-top-7-world-class-wrestlers-6333/

[831] Jenkins, B. (2014). Wrestling 101: Wrestling in Mixed Martial Arts.

[online] Breaking Muscle. Available at:
http://breakingmuscle.com/martial-arts/wrestling-101-wrestling-in-mixed-martial-arts

[832] Sherdog, Dan Henderson, Viewed on ovember 29, 2017

http://www.sherdog.com/fighter/Dan-Henderson-195

[833] UFC, (2014). Randy Couture. [online] Available at:
http://www.ufc.com/fighter/Randy-Couture

[834] Sherdog, (2014). Randy Couture. [online] Available at:
http://www.sherdog.com/fighter/Randy-Couture-166

[835] UFC, (2014). Randy Couture. [online] Available at:
http://www.ufc.com/fighter/Randy-Couture

[836] Couture, R. and Hunt, L. (2008). Becoming the natural. New York:
Simon Spotlight Entertainment. P. 36

[837] Couture, R. and Hunt, L. (2008). Becoming the natural. New York:
Simon Spotlight Entertainment. P. 70

[838] Couture, R. and Hunt, L. (2008). Becoming the natural. New York:
Simon Spotlight Entertainment. P. 45

[839] Chan, J. (2014). Top 10 Wrestlers In MMA 2014 | MMA Verse.
[online] Mmaverse.com. http://www.mmaverse.com/top-10-wrestlers-in-mma-2014/

[840] Sherdog, Daniel Cormier, Viewed on November 29, 2017
http://www.sherdog.com/fighter/Daniel-Cormier-52311

[841] Chan, J. (2014). Top 10 Wrestlers In MMA 2014 | MMA Verse.
[online] Mmaverse.com.
http://www.mmaverse.com/top-10-wrestlers-in-mma-2014/

[842] Critchfield, T. (2014). Daniel Cormier: UFC 182 Bout vs. Jon Jones
'Feels Bigger' Than Competing at Olympics. [online] Sherdog. Available at:
http://www.sherdog.com/news/news/Daniel-Cormier-UFC-182-Bout-vs-Jon-Jones-Feels-Bigger-Than-Competing-at-Olympics-78961

[843] The MSW productions, Frank Gotch Wrestler, Documentary film
https://www.youtube.com/watch?v=spaWVTFFf0E

[844] Furey, M. (2014). Martin "Farmer" Burns - The Grandmaster of American Catch Wrestling. Farmer-burns.com, http://www.farmer-burns.com/aboutfarmerburns.html

[845] Crigger, K. (2010). <%=ogTitle%>. [online] FIGHT! Magazine. Available at: https://www.fightmagazine.com/mma-magazine/catch-as-catch-can-624/

[846] Crigger, K. (2010). <%=ogTitle%>. [online] FIGHT! Magazine. Available at: https://www.fightmagazine.com/mma-magazine/catch-as-catch-can-624/

[847] Jacobs, M. (2013). Wrestling: Gene LeBell and Bart Vale on the Ancestor of Jiu-jitsu, Sambo and Judo – - Black Belt. [online] Blackbeltmag.com. Available at:
http://www.blackbeltmag.com/daily/mixed-martial-arts-training/wrestling/wrestling-gene-lebell-and-bart-vale-on-the-ancestor-of-jiu-jitsu-sambo-and-judo/

[848] weheartmma.com/, (2014). 5 Reasons Why Wrestling is the Best MMA Base. [online]
Available at: http://weheartmma.com/post/841109708/5-reasons-why-wrestling-is-the-best-mma-base

[849] Mixedmartialarts.com, (2014). 2013: Year of the All American wrestler - Mixed Martial Arts News. [online] Available at:
http://www.mixedmartialarts.com/news/440651/2013-Year-of-the-All-American-wrestler/

[850] Sunshine, A. (2010). Recipe for success: Becoming well rounded in mixed martial arts (Part Three). [online] MMAmania.com. Available at: http://www.mmamania.com/2010/11/24/1834403/recipe-for-success-becoming-well-rounded-in-mixed-martial-arts-part

[851] Hresko, M. (2013). Fightland Talks To: An MMA Wrestling Coach, Fightland,
http://fightland.vice.com/blog/fightland-talks-to-an-mma-wrestling-coach

[852] Sunshine, A. (2010). Recipe for success: Becoming well rounded in mixed martial arts (Part Three). [online] MMAmania.com. Available at: http://www.mmamania.com/2010/11/24/1834403/recipe-for-success-becoming-well-rounded-in-mixed-martial-arts-part

853 Grant, T. (2013). MMA Fan's Guide to Grappling: American Folk Style/Freestyle Wrestling. [online] Bloody Elbow. Available at:
http://www.bloodyelbow.com/2013/7/10/4489896/ufc-mma-fan-guide-to-grappling-american-folk-ncaa-style-freestyle-wrestling-highlights-video/in/4287243

854 Rousseau, R. (2014). The Top Wrestling Styles of MMA Fighters. [online] Extremeprosports.com. Available at:
http://www.extremeprosports.com/MMA/wrestling_styles.html

855 Awakening Fighters, (2014). Greco-Roman Wrestling - Awakening Fighters. http://www.awakeningfighters.com/awakepedia/greco-roman-wrestling

856 Jacobs, M. (2013). Wrestling: Gene LeBell and Bart Vale on the Ancestor of Jiu-jitsu, Sambo and Judo – - Black Belt. [online] Blackbeltmag.com. Available at:
http://www.blackbeltmag.com/daily/mixed-martial-arts-training/wrestling/wrestling-gene-lebell-and-bart-vale-on-the-ancestor-of-jiu-jitsu-sambo-and-judo/

857 Griffin, F. and Krauss, E. (2010). Got Fight?: The 50 Zen Principles of Hand-to-Face Combat. USA: William Morrow Paperbacks, pp.19-68.

858 Hresko, M. (2013). Fightland Talks To: An MMA Wrestling Coach, Fightland, http://fightland.vice.com/blog/fightland-talks-to-an-mma-wrestling-coach

859 Polly, M. (2011). Tapped out. New York: Gotham Books.

860 Zavoral, N. (2007). A season on the mat. New York, NY: Simon & Schuster.

861 Gambordella, T. (2009). 10 reasons wrestlers make the best MMA fighters. [online] Examiner.com. Available at:
http://www.examiner.com/article/10-reasons-wrestlers-make-the-best-mma-fighters

862 Couture, R. and Hunt, L. (2008). Becoming the natural. New York: Simon Spotlight Entertainment. P. 34

863 Couture, R. and Hunt, L. (2008). Becoming the natural. New York: Simon Spotlight Entertainment. P. 49

[864] Grant, T. (2013). MMA Fan's Guide to Grappling: American Folk Style/Freestyle Wrestling. [online] Bloody Elbow. Available at:
http://www.bloodyelbow.com/2013/7/10/4489896/ufc-mma-fan-guide-to-grappling-american-folk-ncaa-style-freestyle-wrestling-highlights-video/in/4287243

[865] Grant, T. (2013). MMA Fan's Guide to Grappling: American Folk Style/Freestyle Wrestling. [online] Bloody Elbow. Available at:
http://www.bloodyelbow.com/2013/7/10/4489896/ufc-mma-fan-guide-to-grappling-american-folk-ncaa-style-freestyle-wrestling-highlights-video/in/4287243

[866] Grant, T. (2013). MMA Fan's Guide to Grappling: American Folk Style/Freestyle Wrestling. [online] Bloody Elbow. Available at:
http://www.bloodyelbow.com/2013/7/10/4489896/ufc-mma-fan-guide-to-grappling-american-folk-ncaa-style-freestyle-wrestling-highlights-video/in/4287243

[867] Grant, T. (2013). MMA Fan's Guide to Grappling: American Folk Style/Freestyle Wrestling. [online] Bloody Elbow. Available at:
http://www.bloodyelbow.com/2013/7/10/4489896/ufc-mma-fan-guide-to-grappling-american-folk-ncaa-style-freestyle-wrestling-highlights-video/in/4287243

[868] Grant, T. (2013). MMA Fan's Guide to Grappling: American Folk Style/Freestyle Wrestling. [online] Bloody Elbow. Available at:
http://www.bloodyelbow.com/2013/7/10/4489896/ufc-mma-fan-guide-to-grappling-american-folk-ncaa-style-freestyle-wrestling-highlights-video/in/4287243

[869] Grant, T. (2013). MMA Fan's Guide to Grappling: American Folk Style/Freestyle Wrestling. [online] Bloody Elbow. Available at:
http://www.bloodyelbow.com/2013/7/10/4489896/ufc-mma-fan-guide-to-grappling-american-folk-ncaa-style-freestyle-wrestling-highlights-video/in/4287243

[870] Golokhov, D. (2014). Top 10: Signature Moves At UFC 129. [online] AskMen. Available

[871] Greg Bishop, U.S. Wrestlers Given Incentive to Bypass Mixed Martial Arts, June 4, 2009, the New York Times,
http://www.nytimes.com/2009/06/05/sports/05wrestling.html

872 Snowden, J. (2012). Greatest Pro Wrestlers Turned MMA Fighters. [online] Bleacher Report, http://bleacherreport.com/articles/1148159-wwe-brock-lesnar-and-the-greatest-pro-wrestlers-turned-mma-fighters

873 Falvo, S. (2014). MMA Fighters Transitioning to Pro wrestling: The Good, The Bad, And The Ugly | Cagepotato. [online] Cagepotato.com. Available at: http://www.cagepotato.com/mma-fighters-transitioning-to-pro wrestling-the-good-the-bad-and-the-ugly

874 Sherdog, (2014). Brock Lesnar MMA Stats, Pictures, News, Videos, Biography - Sherdog.com. [online] Available at:
   http://www.sherdog.com/fighter/Brock-Lesnar-17522

875 McElroy, J. (2014). Lesnar Was Circus Act That Went Right. [online] Bleacher Report, http://bleacherreport.com/articles/2014606-the-rock-what-brock-lesnar-did-in-mma-was-epic-and-historic

876 Althoff, E. (2011). What Do MMA, Pro Wrestling and Traditional Martial Arts Have in Common? - - Black Belt. [online] Blackbeltmag.com,
   http://www.blackbeltmag.com/daily/mixed-martial-arts-training/boxing/what-do-mma-pro wrestling-and-traditional-martial-arts-have-in-common/

877 Barr, J. and Gross, J. (2012). OTL: UFC's low pay. [online] ESPN.com. Available at: http://espn.go.com/espn/otl/story/_/page/UFCpay/ufc-fighters-say-low-pay-most-painful-hit-all

878 Scott Harris, For Love, Not Money: How Low Fighter Pay Is Undermining MMA, January 11, 2017, The Bleacher Report,
   http://bleacherreport.com/articles/2685605-for-love-not-money-how-low-fighter-pay-is-undermining-mma

879 Scott Harris, For Love, Not Money: How Low Fighter Pay Is Undermining MMA, January 11, 2017, The Bleacher Report,
   http://bleacherreport.com/articles/2685605-for-love-not-money-how-low-fighter-pay-is-undermining-mma

880 Herbert, G. (2014). WWE: 10 Wrestlers With Salaries You Won't Believe. [online] WhatCulture.com.
   Available at: http://whatculture.com/wwe/wwe-10-wrestlers-salaries-wont-believe.php

881 Fox, J. (2014). UFC Career Fighter Earnings. [online] Mma-manifesto.com. http://mma-manifesto.com/ufc-fighter-salary-database/salary-main/ufc-career-fighter-earnings.html

882 佟忠义, 1935, 中国摔跤法, 国术馆精品】中国摔角法 , Tong Zhongyi, The Method of Chinese Wrestling, translated by Tim Cartmell, 2005, Blue Snake Books, California, Original text written in about 1935, (2005)

883 中国摔跤文化的历史解读:

云南省教育厅基金资助项目(项目编号:07Y40973)

(作者单位:玉溪师范学院) , Zhao Min Li and Jinlong Li, Sports Culture Guide Historical Interpretation of Chinese Wrestling Culture: Fund Project of Yunnan Provincial Department of Education (Project No. 07Y40973) Cuixia Yuxi Teachers College) 200816

884 中国摔跤文化的历史解读:

云南省教育厅基金资助项目(项目编号:07Y40973)

(作者单位:玉溪师范学院) , Zhao Min Li and Jinlong Li, Sports Culture Guide Historical Interpretation of Chinese Wrestling Culture: Fund Project of Yunnan Provincial Department of Education (Project No. 07Y40973) Cuixia Yuxi Teachers College) 200816

885 中国摔跤文化的历史解读:

云南省教育厅基金资助项目(项目编号:07Y40973)

(作者单位:玉溪师范学院) , Zhao Min Li and Jinlong Li, Sports Culture Guide Historical Interpretation of Chinese Wrestling Culture: Fund Project of Yunnan Provincial Department of Education (Project No. 07Y40973) Cuixia Yuxi Teachers College) 200816

886 Xinhua, Ethnic style wrestling amazes wrestlers from Taiwan, September 14, 2011

http://www.chinadaily.com.cn/sports/2011-09/14/content_13686487.htm

[887] 中国摔跤文化的**历史解读**:

云南省教育厅基金资助项目(项目编号:07Y40973)

(作者单位:玉溪师范学院) , Zhao Min Li and Jinlong Li, Sports Culture Guide Historical Interpretation of Chinese Wrestling Culture: Fund Project of Yunnan Provincial Department of Education (Project No. 07Y40973) Cuixia Yuxi Teachers College) 200816, and Interview with 孟师傅Meng Shifu, Chinese traditional wrestling master in Beijing, interview by phone from Shanghai University of Sport, June, 2016

[888] (新华网　　新华网江苏泰州, Xinhua Xinhuanet Jiangsu Taizhou)

[889] 中国摔跤文化的**历史解读**:

云南省教育厅基金资助项目(项目编号:07Y40973)

(作者单位:玉溪师范学院) Historical Interpretation of Chinese Wrestling Culture: Fund Project of Yunnan Provincial Department of Education (Project No. 07Y40973)

(Author: Yuxi Teachers College) 200816 Sports Culture Guide Historical interpretation of the Chinese wrestling culture Zhao Min Li Jinlong Li Cuixia Abstract:

[890]　　中国摔跤文化的**历史解读**:　　云南省教育厅基金资助项目(项目编号:07Y40973)

(作者单位:玉溪师范学院) Historical Interpretation of Chinese Wrestling Culture: Fund Project of Yunnan Provincial Department of Education (Project No. 07Y40973)

(Author: Yuxi Teachers College) 200816 Sports Culture Guide Historical interpretation of the Chinese wrestling culture Zhao Min Li Jinlong Li Cuixia Abstract:

[891]　　中国式摔跤跤绊技术对比分析与研究*收稿日期:2008-06-11;修回日期:2008-08-02, Luo Li, 2008, Comparative Analysis and Research on Chinese-style Wrestling Trip Technology * Received: 2008-06-11; Revised: 2008-08-02

[892] 王文永, 中国掼跤名人录, 北京:华龄出版社, 2006: Wang Wenyong, China Wrestling Celebrity Record, Beijing: Hua Ling Publishing House, 2006:p. 101

[893] Interview with 孟师傅Meng Shifu, Chinese traditional wrestling master in Beijing, interview by phone from Shanghai University of Sport, June, 2016

[894] Interview with 孟师傅Meng Shifu, Chinese traditional wrestling master in Beijing, interview by phone from Shanghai University of Sport, June, 2016

[895] Interview with 孟师傅Meng Shifu, Chinese traditional wrestling master in Beijing, interview by phone from Shanghai University of Sport, June, 2016

[896] He Yanzhong (何彦忠) is a 60 year-old wrestling master of the same lineage as Meng Shifu, teaching Kung Fu wrestling in Beijing.

[897] He Yanzhong (何彦忠) is a 60 year-old wrestling master of the same lineage as Meng Shifu, teaching Kung Fu wrestling in Beijing.

[898] He Yanzhong (何彦忠) is a 60 year-old wrestling master of the same lineage as Meng Shifu, teaching Kung Fu wrestling in Beijing.

[899] He Yanzhong (何彦忠) is a 60 year-old wrestling master of the same lineage as Meng Shifu, teaching Kung Fu wrestling in Beijing.

[900] He Yanzhong (何彦忠) is a 60 year-old wrestling master of the same lineage as Meng Shifu, teaching Kung Fu wrestling in Beijing.

[901] He Yanzhong (何彦忠) is a 60 year-old wrestling master of the same lineage as Meng Shifu, teaching Kung Fu wrestling in Beijing.

[902] Liang, S. and Ngo, T. (1997). Chinese Fast Wrestling for Fighting, The Art of San Shou Kuai jiao. Wolfenboror, NH, USA: YMAA Publication Center, p. 1

296

[903] 释德扬, 少林擒拿术32技/释德扬编著.–成都：成都时 代出版社, 2012.1

Shì dé yáng, Shaolin Qin Na, 32 technology / interpretation Deyang .– Chengdu: Chengdu Times Press, 2012.1

[904] 佟忠义, 1935, 中国摔跤法, 国术馆精品】中国摔角法 , Tong Zhongyi, The Method of Chinese Wrestling, translated by Tim Cartmell, 2005, Blue Snake Books, California, Original, p. 7

[906] Interviews with professor Dai Guobing 戴国斌, Dean of the *Wushu* Institute of Shanghai University of Sport, June 2016

[907] Interview with Luo Yuanzhou (罗源周) Master's degree in *Wushu* student at Shanghai University of Sport, whose graduate advisor was Gai Guobing, Dean of *Wushu*, June 2016

[908] Interviews with professor Dai Guobing 戴国斌, Dean of the *Wushu* Institute of Shanghai University of Sport, June 2016

[909] Interview with Luo Yuanzhou (罗源周) Master's degree in *Wushu* student at Shanghai University of Sport, whose graduate advisor was Gai Guobing, Dean of *Wushu*, June 2016

[910] Interview with Luo Yuanzhou (罗源周) Master's degree in *Wushu* student at Shanghai University of Sport, whose graduate advisor was Gai Guobing, Dean of *Wushu*, June 2016

[911] Interview with Luo Yuanzhou (罗源周) Master's degree in *Wushu* student at Shanghai University of Sport, whose graduate advisor was Gai Guobing, Dean of *Wushu*, June 2016

[912] Interviews with professor Dai Guobing 戴国斌, Dean of the *Wushu* Institute of Shanghai University of Sport, June 2016

[913] On the whole wrestling team there was only one wrestler who came from a Chinese traditional wrestling background. Interview with Zhengtong (郑通), wrestling major, Shanghai University of Sport, June 2016

914 Xinhua, China takes 1st wrestling medal in Rio, Xinhua, http://news.xinhuanet.com/english/2016-08/18/c_135609631.htm

915 Xinhua, China takes 1st wrestling medal in Rio, Xinhua, http://news.xinhuanet.com/english/2016-08/18/c_135609631.htm

916 National Bureau of Statistics of China. http://data.stats.gov.cn/

917 National Bureau of Statistics of China. http://data.stats.gov.cn/

918 National Bureau of Statistics of China. http://data.stats.gov.cn/

919 高考志愿填报参考系统. http://gkcx.eol.cn/

920

《2017年体育类专业报考指南》. 中国高等教育学生信息网（学信网）http://www.chsi.com.cn/. 2017.

921 Interviews with Hong Fangyuan (洪方园), Shanghai University of Sport wrestling major, and Liuxing (刘行), Shanghai University of Sport *Sanda* major, June 2016

922

《2017年普通高等学校运动训练、武术与民族传统体育专业招生管理办法. 中国高等教育学生信息网（学信网）http://www.chsi.com.cn/. 2017.

923 戴国斌，《我国民族传统体育学博士招生20年记》，2017年11月

924 Interview with Lukai 吕凯, Judo major, Shanghai University of Sports, June, 2016

925 Interview with Zhengtong (郑通), wrestling major, Shanghai University of Sport, June 2016

926 Interview with Zhengtong (郑通), wrestling major, Shanghai University of Sport, June 2016

927 Interview with Yang Wenbin (杨文斌) wrestling major, Shanghai University of Sport.

[928] Interview with Yang Wenbin (杨文斌) wrestling major, Shanghai University of Sport.

[929] Interview with Yang Wenbin (杨文斌) wrestling major, Shanghai University of Sport.

[930] Interview with Yang Wenbin (杨文斌) wrestling major, Shanghai University of Sport.

[931] Ma Chi, Xi pushes sports development to achieve Chinese dream, september 8, 2017, The Teleghraph,
http://www.telegraph.co.uk/news/world/china-watch/sport/sport-in-china/

[932] Ma Chi, Xi pushes sports development to achieve Chinese dream, september 8, 2017, The Teleghraph,
http://www.telegraph.co.uk/news/world/china-watch/sport/sport-in-china/

[933] UFC. 百度指数.
http://index.baidu.com/?tpl=trend&type=0&area=0&time=13&word=ufc

[934] WWE Investor Press Release, WrestleMania® Available Live in China for the First Time, March 27, 2017
http://corporate.wwe.com/investors/news/press-releases/2017/03-27-2017-143004929

[935] Kurt Badenhausen, WrestleMania 33: By The Numbers, April 2, 2017, Forbes Magazine,
https://www.forbes.com/sites/kurtbadenhausen/2017/04/02/wrestlemania-33-by-the-numbers/#19ea0ed20bc5

[936] Zach Brendzasep, WWE Signs 7 Chinese Wrestlers, September 10, 2017, Fightful, https://www.fightful.com/wwe-signs-7-chinese-wrestlers

[937] Neil Gough, 'Suplex' in Chinese? Professional Wrestling Tries a Big New Market, New York Times, December 25, 2016,
https://www.nytimes.com/2016/12/25/business/media/professional-wrestling-china-media.html

[938] BBC, Dangal: India's wrestling blockbuster delights China, May 18, 2017, *BBC Monitoring and Beijing Bureau,*
http://www.bbc.com/news/world-asia-39958041

[939] Vaughn Anderson, Interview, May, 2016

[940] Tabuena, A. (2013). Bellator's Vaughn Anderson on Chinese MMA: 'The UFC is not as tempting for fighters here'. [online] Bloody Elbow. Available at:
http://www.bloodyelbow.com/2013/8/25/4656242/ufc-china-vaughn-anderson-mma-bellator-100-interview

[941] Tabuena, A. (2013). Bellator's Vaughn Anderson on Chinese MMA: 'The UFC is not as tempting for fighters here'. [online] Bloody Elbow. Available at:
http://www.bloodyelbow.com/2013/8/25/4656242/ufc-china-vaughn-anderson-mma-bellator-100-interview

[942] Jumabieke Tuerxun Sherdog, Viewed on December 7, 2017,
http://www.sherdog.com/fighter/Jumabieke-Tuerxun-83505

[943] Tiequan Zhang, Non Stop UFC Wiki
http://nonstopufc.wikia.com/wiki/Tiequan_Zhang

[944] Tiequan Zhang, Non Stop UFC Wiki
http://nonstopufc.wikia.com/wiki/Tiequan_Zhang

[945] Tiequan "The Wolf" Zhang sherdog, Sherdog, Viewed on November 4, 2017
http://www.sherdog.com/fighter/Tiequan-Zhang-16984

[946] Sherdog Staff, Cung Le Frustrated with 'TUF: China' But Also Feels Chinese Fighters Showed Promise, March 11, 2014, Sherdog,
http://www.sherdog.com/news/news/Cung-Le-Frustrated-with-TUF-China-But-Also-Feels-Chinese-Fighters-Showed-Promise-64953

[947] Dan Shapiro, As MMA turns focus to China, UFC's Li Jingliang brings advice home to country's fighters, July 16, 2016, MMA Junkie, http://mmajunkie.com/2016/07/as-mma-turns-focus-to-china-ufcs-li-jingliang-brings-advice-home-to-countrys-fighters

[948] Mandy Zuo, Nobody is kung fu fighting: Chinese martial artists ordered to stop organising their own bouts, November, 11, 2017, http://www.scmp.com/news/china/society/article/2119375/nobody-kung-fu-fighting-chinese-martial-artists-ordered-stop

[949] Anton Tabuena, UFC signs first female Chinese fighter, Yan Xiaonan，Sep 9, 2017, Bloody Elbows,

https://www.bloodyelbow.com/2017/9/9/16279862/ufc-signs-first-female-chinese-fighter-yan-xiaonan-mma-china-asia

[950] Trent Reinsmit, Chinese Fighters Have Good Showing At UFC Fight Night 122 In Shanghai November 25, 2017 , Forbes,
https://www.forbes.com/sites/trentreinsmith/2017/11/25/chinese-fighters-have-good-showing-at-ufc-fight-night-122-in-shanghai/#6bea72b5354f

[951] UFC中国赛为何叫好又叫座：观众还是爱看"自家人"打拳，

澎湃新闻记者 陈均

2017-11-26 13:29 来源：澎湃新闻,

http://www.thepaper.cn/newsDetail_forward_1880099

[952] UFC上海赛狂欢后的隐忧 加剧中国搏击焦虑症？2017-11-28 22:11:37 新浪综合,

http://sports.sina.com.cn/others/freefight/2017-11-28/doc-ifyphkhk8405019.shtml

[953] UFC上海赛狂欢后的隐忧 加剧中国搏击焦虑症？2017-11-28 22:11:37 新浪综合,

http://sports.sina.com.cn/others/freefight/2017-11-28/doc-ifyphkhk8405019.shtml

[954] National Olympic Committees, Olympic,org,

https://www.olympic.org/national-olympic-committees

[955] Sean Keeley, UFC's $4 billion sale could mean WWE's value just skyrocketed, July 14, 2016,
http://awfulannouncing.com/2016/ufc-wwe-sale-value-billion.html

Made in the
USA
Monee, IL